The Outsourcer

History of Computing

William Aspray and Thomas J. Misa, editors

The Outsourcer

The Story of India's IT Revolution

Dinesh C. Sharma

The MIT Press
Cambridge, Massachusetts
London, England

© 2015 Massachusetts Institute of Technology

First edition published in India in 2009 by HarperCollins Publishers India as *The Long Revolution: The Birth and Growth of India's IT Industry*.

MIT Press books may be purchased at special quantity discounts for business or sales promotional use. For information, please email special_sales@mitpress.mit.edu.

This book was set in Stone by the MIT Press. Printed and bound in the United States of America.

Library of Congress Cataloging-in-Publication Data

Sharma, Dinesh C.
[Long revolution]
The outsourcer : The story of India's IT revolution / Dinesh C. Sharma.
   pages   cm—(History of computing)
Originally published as: The long revolution.
Includes bibliographical references and index.
ISBN 978-0-262-02875-2 (hardcover : alk. paper) 1. Computer software industry—India—History. 2. Information technology—India—History. I. Title.
HD9696.63.I42S48 2015
338.4'70050954—dc23
2014031500

10 9 8 7 6 5 4 3 2 1

To Ramachandra Guha who ignited my interest in contemporary history and has been a constant source of encouragement, inspiration, and energy

Contents

Preface

Today computers—and other forms of digital technology—are ubiquitous in India. It was not so thirty-five years ago. I became aware of the use of computers in lives of ordinary Indians when I got a computerized mark sheet for my tenth-grade examination in June 1976. A few years later, I was formally introduced to computer science during my undergraduate course in science at Nizam College in the South Indian city of Hyderabad. An introductory course in FORTRAN IV—a computer language released by International Business Machines Corporation (IBM) in 1962—taught students basics of programming, without them seeing or touching a computer. At the end of the course, we were all taken to the College of Engineering at Osmania University to see an IBM mainframe. The computer was placed in a large, air-conditioned hall and we were allowed in small batches to have a peek at the gigantic machine. This brief encounter with an aging computer helped kindle my interest in this technology.

In my first job as a trainee journalist with the Press Trust of India newswire, in early 1984 I was exposed to two generations of data communication technologies—a teleprinter that stored news stories in paper tapes and a computer-based communication network that had just been introduced. It was also the beginning of my interaction with the nascent computer industry as a reporter, an engagement that continued over the next decade and beyond. In the late 1990s, I crossed the fence for a brief while when the dot-com bug bit me. I, along with another journalist friend and budding software engineer, incorporated a dot-com company to run a science and technology news portal. Needless to say, the venture did not last long.

Another opportunity in the dot-com boom followed soon. This time a friend in the United States introduced me to a former investment banker from New York who wished to create a business-to-business portal for Indian software firms. As part-time head of India operations of this company for about eighteen months, I came face to face with several software firms. This venture too fell victim to the dot-com bubble bust. Nevertheless, the experience gave me valuable insights into the inner workings of the industry. While reporting for the U.S. technology news network Cnet.com, I realized that interest in the Indian IT industry was growing in America at the turn of the century and yet there were a lot of misconceptions. This prompted me to pen the story.

When I decided to write on Indian IT, the first thought that came to my mind was the story of IBM and Coca-Cola being "thrown out of India" in 1977. Somehow this dramatic episode had remained ingrained in my mind since my adolescent days. I kept hearing different versions of this story as a news reporter. A book dealing with the story from IBM leaving India in 1977 to IBM's comeback in the early 1990s appeared to be a killer plot to my journalistic mind. Barring IBM's exit and the period of early growth of the industry till 1984, I was a witness as well a recorder of all major events of this period. It was only after I started researching that I realized that the story actually began when early computing machines came to India in the pre-independence days. As a result, I extended the book's plot and the IBM story became one important chapter in it. Much of the research and writing for the Indian edition of this book took place between 2005 and 2007. I made multiple trips to Mumbai, Bangalore, Kolkata, and Hyderabad, besides work done in New Delhi, my place of residence. Subsequently, from 2011 to 2013 I abridged and revised the text for this new edition.

Now it is in your hands. So ends the journey of this book.

Acknowledgments

I would like to thank the New India Foundation, which supported my research with the New India Fellowship in 2006, and the foundation's guiding spirit, Ramachandra Guha, who has been a constant source of inspiration and encouragement. Special thanks are due to Mahesh Rangarajan, director of the Nehru Memorial Museum and Library, for his critical engagement at every stage of writing for the Indian edition of this book. S. P. K. Gupta provided me the transcript of his unpublished interview with A. S. Rao as well as reports of the Electronics Commission. Also generous with their help were Indira Chowdhury, who set up the institutional archive at the Tata Institute of Fundamental Research, Mumbai; Krishna Bhattacharyya of the P. C. Mahalanobis Memorial Museum; and P. K. Upadhyay of the National Informatics Centre (NIC) library.

The work draws primarily from interviews of key players conducted by the author as well as government reports, research papers, and scant archival material available in India. References relating to developments in India can be found in the company archives of IBM, International Computers Limited (ICL), Control Data Corporation (CDC), or personal papers of computer technology veterans who played a role in development of computing in India at some point; however, accessing such documentary sources, all of which are located in the United Kingdom or the United States, would have required more sustained funding. Indian companies are not yet old enough to have developed their own archives or are too busy with their quarter-to-quarter lifecycles. Government records relating to the Electronics Commission (EC) and the Department of Electronics (DoE) have yet to become a part of the National Archives of India and thus are not accessible to researchers. The EC was abolished in 1988 and the DoE has been subsumed in the Ministry of Information Technology. Though limited, the archival material has revealed unknown facts and features about development of computing in India—highlighted for the first time in this book.

I could not have written this book without the insights and experiences shared by many individuals connected with the computer and information technology industry in the past four decades. The same holds true for companies that shared information, old photographs, and newspaper clippings. I express my gratitude to each of them. Prominent among those who granted me extended interviews or provided me with a variety of materials, or both, are R. Narasimhan, N. Seshagiri, Shashi Ullal, Dan Gupta, Ramesh Jhunjhunuwala, and Sharad Marathe. I could not benefit from critical comments on the revised text from Seshagiri, who passed away in middle of 2013.

I sincerely thank Marguerite Avery, senior acquisitions editor, at the MIT Press for having shown great interest and faith in this project, and Katie Persons, assistant acquisitions editor, for helping through the process of submission and editing. Thanks are also due to the editorial team, designers, and members of the marketing team of MIT Press for being enthusiastic about this book. My writing work would not have been fruitful without full support from my wife, Annu Anand, and our children, Maanvi and Kushagr.

Dinesh C. Sharma
New Delhi, India
August 2014

List of Acronyms

ABS	acrylonitrile butadiene styrene
ACC	Associated Cement Companies
ADL	Arthur D. Little
AEC	Atomic Energy Commission
AEE	Atomic Energy Establishment
AES	automatic electronic switch
AFS	Airline Financial Support Services
AIS	Advanced Information Systems
AMCAT	Aspiritng Minds Computer Adaptive Test
APEC	All Purpose Electronic Computer
APPLE	Ariane Passenger PayLoad Experiment
ARCI	Astra Research Centre India
ARPANET	Advanced Research Projects Agency Network
ASEE	American Society for Engineering Education
BA	British Airways
BARC	Bhabha Atomic Research Centre
BASIC	Beginners All Purpose Symbolic Instruction Code
BEL	Bharat Electronics Limited
BPO	business process outsourcing
BSIR	Board of Scientific and Industrial Research
BTM	British Tabulating Machine
CAD	computer-aided design
CAG	Comptroller and Auditor General of India
CAM	Counting and Analytic Machines
CAMP	Comprehensive Apparel Manufacturer's Package
CCEA	Cabinet Committee on Economics Affairs
CCI	Controller of Capital Issues
C-DAC	Centre for Development of Advanced Computing
CDC	Control Data Corporation
C-DOT	Centre for Development of Telematics

CEDT	Centre for Electronics Design and Technology
CERN	European Organization for Nuclear Research
CHILL	CCITT High Level Language
CII	Compagnie Internationale pour Informatique
CIRUS	Canadian-Indian Reactor, U.S.
CIS	Commonwealth of Independent States
CITIL	Citicorp Information Technology Industries Limited
CKD	completely knocked down
CMC	Computer Maintenance Corporation
CMM	Capability Maturity Model for Software
CMOS	complementary metal oxide semiconductor
CMS	Computer Maintenance Services
CN	Canadian National
COMNEX	Computer Networks Experiment
COSL	Citicorp Overseas Software Limited
CRIS	Centre for Railway Information Systems
CSIR	Council of Scientific and Industrial Research
DAE	Department of Atomic Energy
DBC	Data Basics Corporation
DCI	Data Conversion Inc.
DCL	Digital Computer Laboratory
DCM	Delhi Cloth Mills
DCM DP	DCM Data Products
DEC	Digital Equipment Corporation
DGTD	Directorate General of Technology Development
DMAP	Distribution Management Application Package
DoDS	Department of Defence Supplies
DoE	Department of Electronics
DOIS	Directorate of Operations Information System
DOS	Disk Operating System
DoT	Department of Telecommunications
DRDO	Defence Research and Development Organization
DRI	Digital Research Inc.
EC	Electronics Commission
ECIL	Electronics Corporation of India Limited
EDA	electronic design automation
EDP	electronic data processing
EOU	Export Oriented Unit
EPZ	export processing zone
ERNET	Education and Research Network

ESO	engineering services outsourcing
ET&T	Electronics Trade and Technology Development Corporation
FEC	Far Eastern Computers Pte Ltd
FERA	Foreign Exchange Regulation Act
GDA	Gateway Design Automation
GE	General Electric
GECIS	GE Capital International Services
HEC	Hollerith Electronic Computer
HCL	Hindustan Computers Limited
HNS	Hughes Network Systems
HP	Hewlett Packard
HSS	Hughes Software Services
HTL	Hindustan Teleprinters Lmited
IAS	Indian Administrative Service
IBA	Indian Banks Association
ICAT	Indo-American Capital and Technology Corporation
ICC	International Chamber of Commerce
ICIM	International Computers Indian Manufacturing Company Limited
ICL	International Computers Limited
ICT	International Computers and Tabulators Limited
IDM	International Data Management
IEDF	import-export double funneling
IEEE	International Institute of Electrical and Electronics Engineers
IIMs	Indian Institutes of Management
IISc	Indian Institute of Science
IITs	Indian Institutes of Technology
IMD	Indian Meteorological Department
IMSC	Inter-Ministerial Standing Committee
IPO	initial public offering
IR	Indian Railways
ISI	Indian Statistical Institute
ITES	IT-enabled services
ITI	Indian Telephone Industries
JU	Jadavpur University
JFWTC	John F. Welch Technology Centre
KIAP	Kanpur Indo-American Project
KPO	knowledge process outsourcing

KSA	Kurt Salmon Associates
LAN	Local Area Network
LES	Land Earth Station
LEXIS	Legal Exchange Information Service
LPO	legal process outsourcing
LSI	large-scale integration
MAC	multiple access computing
MAX	main automatic exchange
MICO	Motor Industries Company Limited
MIT	Massachusetts Institute of Technology
MNCs	multinational corporations
MOS	metal oxide semiconductor
MRTP	Monopolies and Restrictive Trade Practices
NASSCOM	National Association of Software and Services Companies
NCMRWF	National Centre for Medium Range Weather Forecasting
NCL	National Chemical Laboratory
NCP	new computer policy
NCSDCT	National Centre for Software Development and Computing Techniques
NIC	National Informatics Centre
NPO	New Projects Organization
NPT	Nuclear Proliferation Treaty
NSS	National Sample Survey
OCS	Overseas Communication Service
OEM	original equipment manufacturere
OGL	Open General License
OLDAP	Online Data Processor
OPIC	Overseas Private Investment Corporation
ORDVAC	Ordnance Discrete Variable Automatic Computer
ORG	Operations Research Group
OSDC	offshore software development center
PAC	Public Accounts Committee
PBX	private branch exchange
PCM	pulse code modulation
PCS	Patni Computer Systems
PES	Product Engineering Solutions
PREDA	Philbrick-Rideout Electronic Differential Analyzer
PRL	Physical Research Laboratory
PSI	Processors Systems India

PSP	Personal Software Process
PwC	PricewaterhouseCoopers
R&D	research and development
RAX	rural automatic exchange
RBI	Reserve Bank of India
RCCs	Regional Computer Centres
RISC	Reduced Instruction Set Computing
SDA	significant digit arithmetic
SEEPZ	Santa Cruz Electronics Export Processing Zone
SIPA	Silicon Valley Indian Professionals' Association
SITA	Societe Internationale Telecommunications Aeronautiques
SKD	semi knocked down
STP	Software Technology Park
STPI	Software Technology Parks of India
SWIFT	Society for Worldwide Financial Telecommunications
TAX	trunk automatic exchange
TBDF	transborder dataflow
TBL	Tata Burroughs Limited
TCM	U.S. Technical Cooperation Mission
TCS	Tata Consultancy Services
TDC	Trombay Digital Computer
TI	Texas Instruments
TIE	The Indus Entrepreneurs
TIFAC	Technology Information, Forecasting and Assessment Council
TIFR	Tata Institute of Fundamental Research
TIFRAC	TIFR Automatic Calculator
TISL	Tata Information Systems Limited
TRC	Telecommunications Research Centre
TSP	Team Software Process
TUL	Tata Unisys Limited
UIDAI	Unique Identification Authority of India
UNCTC	United Nations Centre on Transnational Corporations
UNDP	United Nations Development Programme
UNESCO	United Nations Educational, Scientific and Cultural Organization
UNIVAC	Universal Automatic Computer
UNTAA	United Nations Technical Assistance Administration
UNTNC	United Nations Centre on Transnational Corporations

UPTRON	Uttar Pradesh Electronics Corporation Limited
URM	unit record machine
UUNet	Unix-to-Unix Network Technologies
VSNL	Videsh Sanchar Nigam Limited
WITL	Wipro Information Technology Limited
WNS	World Network Services
ZERLINA	Zero Energy Reactor for Lattice Investigations and New Assemblies

Exchange Rate of Indian Rupee vis-à-vis U.S. Dollar (End-of-Year Rates)

1970–1971	7.5020	1988–1989	15.6630
1971–1972	7.2790	1989–1990	17.3248
1972–1973	7.6570	1990–1991	19.6429
1973–1974	7.8370	1991–1992	31.2256
1974–1975	7.7940	1992–1993	31.2354
1975–1976	8.9730	1993–1994	31.3725
1976–1977	8.8040	1994–1995	31.4950
1977–1978	8.4340	1995–1996	34.3500
1978–1979	8.1500	1996–1997	35.9150
1979–1980	8.1930	1997–1998	39.4950
1980–1981	8.1900	1998–1999	42.4350
1981–1982	9.3460	1999–2000	43.6050
1982–1983	9.9700	2000–2001	46.6400
1983–1984	10.7070	2001–2002	48.8000
1984–1985	12.4300	2002–2003	47.5050
1985–1986	12.3061	2003–2004	43.4450
1986–1987	12.8882	2004–2005	43.7550
1987–1988	13.0318	2005–2006	44.6050

Source: Reserve Bank of India.

Introduction

In 1982 an Indian software entrepreneur went to America to participate in a technology trade show, hoping to sign up customers for software applications he had developed. His business meetings would often start with questions about India, because most people he met still regarded his country as some faraway land. One comment that left him dumbfounded was "India does software? We thought people still live on trees there!" The reason for such reactions was obvious. The only India-related news on American television that week was a clip of naked sadhus readying for a dip in the Ganges during a religious congregation called Kumbh in North India. Popular perception of India was still that of the land of Taj Mahal, elephants, and snake charmers.

In 1989, another Indian software entrepreneur had a similar experience when he was trying to convince the chief executive of a software firm in New York to subcontract work in India. The CEO stopped him midway and said, "I am bit confused. What are you trying to say? You want software from us or you are saying you will develop it for us?" When the Indian entrepreneur clarified that it was the latter, the CEO laughed heartily and called all his staff to share the "joke," saying, "This guy is telling me he will do software for us!"

These are not isolated episodes. Leaders of almost every Indian company founded in the 1970s and 1980s has similar tales to share.

Cut to June 2006. Palace Grounds in Bangalore. Some ten thousand software engineers and technicians are gathered for a meeting, while thousands of others in fourteen Indian cities are hooked up via satellite. The event: a briefing for financial analysts from Wall Street and other global markets organized by IBM. Samuel J. Palmisano, chairman and CEO, declares that the event is central to IBM's global business strategy. He minces no words: "If you are not here in India, making the right investments and finding and developing the best employees and business partners, then you won't be able to combine the skills and expertise here with skills and expertise from around the world, in ways that can help our clients be successful." From a land where "people still live on trees" to an importer of technology services, India has transformed itself into a hub central to the business strategies of tech giants such as IBM, within a quarter of a century.

This book tells the story of the Indian information technology (IT) industry. It is a story of great transformation—from being in the backwaters to the frontlines of global technology business; from a land of snake charmers to a land of people with advanced skills and expertise; from a country known for its red tape to a favored destination rolling out the red carpet for foreign investors. It is a story of converting skills and knowledge into capital and wealth. From a meager $30 million of exports in 1981 to $100 billion in 2013, the Indian IT industry's remarkable success story has made the country one of the leading destinations for software and outsourced services. The success of this one industry has given rise to the notion of Brand India or India Inc. among potential investors and international financial institutions.

India has been a land of diversity and contradictions. It is a country that has exploded nuclear bombs, developed long-range missiles, and sent probes to the moon and Mars yet still has millions of people who have no access to drinking water and sanitation. Thousands of children still die of diseases that are vaccine-preventable. Farmers commit suicide due to indebtedness and crop failure despite Indian agriculture scientists boasting of having mastered the best of farm technologies, including genetic engineering. The same kind of contradictions exists in the IT sector as well. India, a country with a very low or no domestic technology penetration in the beginning, was able to penetrate and capture export markets. The glass towers—designed by the best of the architects in the world—in the nation's so-called software enclaves that have facilities such as mini golf courses, malls, and multi-cuisine restaurants have become symbols of growth as well as aspirations—while a large number of Indians remain in poverty, untouched by the fruits of information technology. The lure of export dollars, wealth created by people employed in the IT industry, has fueled rising aspirations among the middle classes and even among the poor.

In popular media and imagery, the rise of India's IT industry is often dubbed a "miracle" of the new millennium or the so-called IT revolution. There are myths and there is hype—"India is an IT superpower." There are claims and counterclaims—on who and what was behind this transformation. Was it a result of the forces of liberalization or a shortage of skilled manpower in the West? Was it chance factors like Y2K that catapulted India to the global arena? This book is a modest effort to chart the course of this industry during the past half a century and to delineate factors that helped India gain its formidable position in the technology sector.

Of late, a number of books on the Indian IT and software industry have hit the stands, dealing with different segments of the story, but most of them have covered the growth of the industry in the past fifteen years or so. Others are company-specific histories or success stories of individuals. The field of information technology and software seems to have fallen in between many schools: it is dealt with by social scientists unfamiliar with technology, Western business schools looking narrowly at outsourcing or firm-level changes, and writers unfamiliar with the interface of markets, ideas, and technology. This book is an attempt to fill this gap in the understanding of the evolution of computing and IT industry in a developing country.

The history of computing and information technology has to be viewed in the larger context of science and technology development in India. The story begins in the years leading to India's freedom in August 1947, when the foundation of the science and technology infrastructure for an independent nation was laid. Leading scientists of the period such as H. J. Bhabha and P. C. Mahalanobis emerge as central characters in this narrative as research institutes established by them became nuclei for the development of computer science and technology. The close links these top scientists had with the political leadership, particularly Nehru, ensured that their projects received necessary support and attention. However, a supporting industry could not develop in electronics and computer technology due to excessive emphasis on import substitution and primacy given to public sector or state enterprises. For high technology, however, IBM and other computer firms were permitted to sell their products and services.

The efforts made by scientists and the institutions they created helped in exposing a large number of Indian scientists and engineers to computer science and technology in the initial period. Program writing skills useful for commercial applications developed through interaction with mainframe and minicomputer makers from the West, mainly the United States. In the hardware sector, restrictions on the import of technology, components, and parts forced Indian firms to develop their own design skills. The growth trajectory started heading north when economic and industrial policies shifted gears—from a socialist and mixed-economy approach to private sector-led liberalization. The state's role gradually changed from being a regulator and player to being a facilitator and champion of private industry.

Chapter Outline

The chapters in the book are organized largely chronologically, but some strong themes have been dealt with in separate chapters.

The early period of computing in India, the role of leading scientists, and founding of key research and academic institutions including the Indian Institutes of Technology (IITs) has been covered in chapter 1, spanning from 1947 to 1970. The first two decades after India's independence saw development of indigenous computers as well as the growth of commercial data processing. Formal education in computer science and technology also began during this period. The planned development of electronics was initiated with the national goal of self-sufficiency and in tune with economic and trade policies that encouraged gradual replacement of import products and technology with domestic production (called import substitution in economic parlance). Given the prevailing political situation after the death of Nehru and pro-socialist tilt in economic policies, scientists opted for a state-controlled and a public sector–led path for the developing computer industry. Chapter 2 elaborates how excessive control and regulation by the Electronics Commission and the Department of Electronics stifled the IT industry's growth. Since IBM was a major player in the 1960s and 1970s, and the new policy regime was in part to contain its growing influence in India, the IBM story has been elaborated separately in chapter 3. The IBM era constitutes an important segment of the historical narrative.

The 1980s was an interesting period in terms of political upheaval and a marked a shift in economic policies of the Nehruvian era. The first chinks in the state-led economic model appeared in the early 1980s and by the end of the decade important steps had been initiated toward the full-scale liberalization that was unleashed only in 1991. The 1980s was a significant period for both the hardware and software sectors. Technology diffusion also got a boost during the regime of Rajiv Gandhi, who wanted India to embrace the computer age. This storyline has been captured in chapter 4. Chapter 5 also covers the 1970s and 1980s, largely focusing on pioneering Indian hardware firms that entered the arena in the post-IBM period.

Chapters 6 and 7 exclusively deal with the birth and growth of software firms in the 1970s and 1980s and reveal how pioneers actually "discovered" the concept of outsourcing. Two major factors—one technological and another policy-related—were critical for the software industry to record exponential growth in the 1990s. The demonstration that satellite communication links can be used for software exports and a government program (Software Technology Parks) that facilitated such links for smaller software firms fueled the growth of exports. The concept of satellite-based data communication links for software exports emerged for the first time in the state's 1984 software policy. It helped the transition from "body shopping" to offshore software work in India. The setting up of state-sponsored duty-free enclaves for software development and export sowed seeds of a robust industry. The decade-long saga of Software Technology Parks has been pieced together for the first time in chapter 7, highlighting turf wars within the government and the changing landscape of India's political economy. Tax incentives, deeper liberalization, guided exploration of key export markets, and the push for quality certification all were critical, in addition to preferential policy treatment of this industry by the state.

The advent of business process outsourcing or IT-enabled services marked another turning point at the beginning of the new millennium. European airlines had begun shifting their backroom operations to India in 1990s, but such outsourcing operations across the spectrum including research and development turned into a tsunami only at the beginning of the new century, as covered in chapter 8.

The long journey has seen the Indian IT industry develop from a small base to a formidable force in the global arena. Several factors—government policies, higher technical education facilities, entrepreneurial spirit, the presence of multinational companies, and skill shortages in Western countries—have contributed to this spectacular growth. In the concluding chapter, some of the oft-asked questions are discussed: What are the factors that led to the growth of the sector? Why did India miss the hardware bus? Is the growth attained so far sustainable? Is it possible for India to retain its competitive edge in this industry? And so on. These issues have been addressed in the final chapter.

The book covers vast ground—beginning in the 1940s to the developments in the early 2000s. Yet a few subjects could not be covered in adequate detail. The development of clusters like Bangalore and Noida, telecom liberalization, the business of semiconductor designing, the dotcom era and the new wave of e-commerce in India, the use of information and communications technology for development, issues relating to engineering education—these are some of the topics that have a great bearing on the Indian IT story but could not be dealt with in this book. Some of these subjects merit dedicated books on each of them.

The names of all the major cities mentioned in the book have changed over a period of time. But in order to retain historical flavor, their old names have been used until the time their new names were adopted. Thus Calcutta, Bombay, Poona, and Madras have been retained until we come to the period when these names changed officially to Kolkata, Mumbai, Pune, and Chennai, respectively. Figures are mentioned mostly in U.S. dollars, and rupee figures have been converted using exchange rate data of that period. A table showing exchange rates for 1970–1971 and 2004–2005 is given for reference.

The selection of software and hardware companies for case studies is entirely the author's choice. The idea was to highlight pioneers in each segment and not to write a strictly chronological history.

1 India's First Computers

In a big country like India, I think there would be a legitimate case of having two computing centers, and getting two computers . . .

—Homi J. Bhabha, August 1961[1]

The emergence of India as an important player in the global technology and outsourcing business is often attributed to economic liberalization policies unveiled in 1991. Liberalization was indeed a turning point in the economic history of the country as it chose to move away from the socialist economic path it had followed since achieving independence in 1947 and embraced market-oriented reforms. The genesis of the information technology industry, however, can be traced back to several decades before this milestone in India's history. The post-freedom economic policies were focused on developing an industrial base to achieve self-reliance in key infrastructure sectors. Jawaharlal Nehru, the first prime minister of India, very well recognized the critical role science would play in national development as well as in the eradication of hunger and poverty.[2] He also initiated certain key science and technology development programs such as atomic energy and defense research early on.

In the decades preceding independence from the United Kingdom, intense interactions among the political, scientific, and industrial elites helped shape science and technology policies that India would pursue after attaining political freedom.[3] Mahatma Gandhi, leader of the Indian National Congress (INC), was opposed to the use of machines to replace humans. In his view, "the abuse of machine" caused "exploitation of the working class."[4] On the one hand, Gandhi saw hand-spun cloth *khadi* and small-scale cottage industry as symbols of economic and political freedom. On the other hand, a new generation of INC leaders, spearheaded by Nehru, was influenced by the emergence of modern science after World War I, and many of them were attracted to experiments on socialism in the Soviet Union. Most such pro-modern science leaders were educated in the West.

Nehru took a position contrasting that of Gandhi when he declared in 1936 that "the only key to the solution of world problems lies in Socialism, and when I use this word I do so not in [a] vague humanitarian way but the scientific, economic sense."[5] A year later at the Indian Science Congress, Nehru professed that "even more than present the future belongs to science and those who make friends with science and seek its help for advancement of humanity."[6] He was thus expressing the faith that science could be a means of development by using the INC as a political platform. Nehru's vision was shared by leading scientists, engineers, and planners who surrounded him. A chance to formulate policies and programs based on this vision came in 1937 when INC was elected to run governments in seven provinces, as a result of provincial autonomy granted under the Government of India Act of 1935.

Revolutionary leader Subhas Chandra Bose, who was the party president then, set up the National Planning Committee (NPC) in 1938 to embark upon the national planning process. Much like Nehru, Bose too was in favor of fast-paced, Soviet-style industrialization. Nehru was called upon to head NPC, which had twenty-nine subcommittees on subjects ranging from electricity to forestation. It was during the deliberations of NPC that Nehru had a chance to interact with several leading scientists and engineers of the period. NPC, historians believe, truly reflected an alliance between the political elite and the scientific elite.[7]

It is not as if there were no voices of disunity in the science-politics alliance. Though all important scientists and technologists sought solutions for the country's problems through application of science, their methods differed.[8] Engineer Mokshgundam Visvesvaraya (1860–1962) wanted rapid industrialization through the use of capital and enterprise, while physicist Meghnad Saha (1893–1956) insisted on "scientific method" in every aspect of national life. Chemist Shanti Swarup Bhatnagar (1894–1955) and physicist Homi Jehangir Bhabha (1909–1966) preferred to build centers of excellence in frontier areas of scientific research. Physicist-turned-statistician Prasanta Chandra Mahalanobis (1893–1972) envisaged statistical method as an important tool in national planning. Regarding economic policies, NPC veered around the idea of democratic socialism with a mixed economy instead of state-led Soviet-style socialism in order to accommodate interests of Indian industrialists.[9] The work related to NPC clearly indicated that the political leadership had decided to modernize India—with heavy input from science and technology—when the country achieved freedom.

In the colonial period, scientific research was largely concentrated in universities and a handful of industrial laboratories that were set up to boost war efforts of the empire. A Board of Scientific and Industrial Research (BSIR) was established under Bhatnagar with a charter similar to that of the British Department of Scientific and Industrial Research (DSIR) in 1939, in the wake of England's involvement in the war. The BISR was elevated to the status of a council in September 1942, and renamed Council of Scientific and Industrial Research (CSIR). The Department of Supplies and Munitions was the client of most of the CSIR projects in its early period.[10] Institutions born out of the nationalist education movement such as the Indian Institute of Science (founded by industrialist Jamsetji Nusserwanji Tata in 1909) in Bangalore and the Banaras Hindu University (founded by INC leader Madan Mohan Malviya in 1916) also served as hubs of academic learning and research.[11]

Most of the equipment needed for research had to be shipped from England and other parts of Europe. Local production and availability of scientific instruments was limited to rudimentary tools such as laboratory glassware, microscopes, mathematical instruments and analytical balances.[12] Early data processing equipment like hand operated calculators and Unit Record Machines (URMs) came to India almost at the same time as anywhere else in the world. Machines from Powers-Samas, Remington Rand, and British Tabulating Company were being imported by users in manufacturing and service sectors. Tata Iron and Steel Company Limited had one of the largest installations of such machines supplied by the British firm, International Computers and Tabulators Limited (ICT), in India. National carrier Air India used such machines for accounting applications in the 1940s.

As India became a free nation in 1947 with Nehru as the first prime minister, the science-politics alliance began translating into formal government projects and programs. Among prominent scientists who enjoyed proximity to Nehru were Mahalanobis and Bhabha, who, while pursuing their respective fields of activity, pioneered the use of modern computers in India. The two scientists also helped shape policies, institutions, and industries for computer hardware and software in the decades following independence. Shanti Swarup Bhatnagar, who headed the CSIR founded under British rule, too was in the inner circle of scientists around Nehru. Critics like Saha were sidelined in the new establishment. Overall organization of science projects and programs in free India was guided to a great extent by advice from Archibald V. Hill, Biological Secretary of the Royal Society, who visited India on an official mission to advise and report on the state of scientific research in 1944. Another prominent British scientist P. M. S.

Blackett too had considerable influence over Nehru in matters of science in India.[13] The general organization of science in India was also discussed at the Empire Scientific Conference hosted by the Royal Society in 1946. Both Hill and Blackett developed and maintained personal rapport with Nehru's scientific advisors including Bhabha, Bhatnagar, and Mahalanobis.

While patronizing scientists close to him and their goals, Nehru was open to foreign technology and capital. He welcomed multinational firms like IBM, which ultimately became a dominant player in the Indian computing industry from 1950 to 1977. The approach was in line with Nehru's mixed economy model, in which the public sector dominated basic and strategic industrial production while private enterprise was allowed to operate in light industries and services. Despite the emphasis on central planning and preference for public enterprises in all important areas, India did not opt for Soviet-style central control over its entire economy. The state had to turn to multinational corporations in key sectors in order to access necessary capital and technology. Both public and private sectors were permitted to import technology and float joint ventures with foreign companies. The overall thrust of economic policies remained on self-reliance and encouraging domestic production to substitute imported products.

Mahalanobis and Bhabha initiated local efforts in computer development as well as application of computers in scientific research programs. The research centers created by the two scientists served as nuclei for the development of early engineering and program writing skills. The government offered fellowships to talented students to pursue higher studies in the United States and the United Kingdom. In addition, initiatives in higher technical and engineering education such as the Indian Institutes of Technology (IITs) helped in generating a skilled workforce. The overall result of all such efforts was the foundation on which a multibillion-dollar industry was built in the decades that followed. The story of computers in India is, thus, closely linked with the development of modern science in India.

Work Begins in Calcutta

Born to a well-established and relatively wealthy businessman in Calcutta (now Kolkata), Mahalanobis studied physics at King's College, Cambridge. He wished to pursue research in physics at the Cavendish Laboratory but ended up studying statistics purely by chance. Exciting work in this area such as development of sampling techniques by Ronald A. Fischer captivated the mind of a young Mahalanobis. Once in Calcutta, he took up a teaching position in the physics department of the Presidency College but kept nurturing his newfound interest in statistics. He did not consider statistics merely as a subject confined to theories of probability or analysis of data but more as a tool in decision making. For his statistical work, Mahalanobis had to make use of mechanical calculating devices. He also deployed a tabulating machine for scientific work.[14] The Indian Statistical Institute (ISI), which he founded in 1932, introduced mechanical desk calculators for the first time in the country. Over the next two decades, ISI helped disseminate use of mechanical, electrical, and electronic calculating machines in India.

The expertise Mahalanobis gained in statistical work was also utilized by the British government. In the postwar years, Bengal—a province of British India with Calcutta as its capital—was hit by an unprecedented famine in 1943 leaving millions of people dead. In order to get a correct estimate of farm output, the provincial government asked Mahalanobis to conduct a survey to assess yields of paddy crops. He needed computing machines to execute this large assignment but importing such machines was difficult for lack of financial resources. This forced Mahalanobis to explore fabrication of such gadgets locally, for which he set up the Indian Calculating Machine and Scientific Instrument Research Society in September 1943. The main goal of this organization was to "manufacture, assemble, repair, purchase, sell or deal in calculating, mathematical and scientific instruments and accessories," besides taking up scientific publishing and other similar activities.[15] ISI already had a workshop for repair and maintenance of calculators.

In 1950, Mahalanobis consolidated all work related to calculating machines under the umbrella of an Electronic Computer Laboratory. The technology had progressed from calculating machines to computers. A long-term plan of the electronic lab was to develop a computer to support statistical work at the institute. In a bid to put together an analog computer from scratch Mahalanobis hired two young graduates—Samarendra Kumar Mitra and Soumyendra Mohan Bose. Mitra, a chemistry graduate, had brief exposure to electronic computers while on a UN-sponsored scholarship in the United States.[16] Engineering a new computer was still a difficult task because components were not available locally and even elementary industrial support for such work was lacking. Importing components needed for the dream machine would have required foreign exchange, which was scarce and involved a tedious bureaucratic process including permission from the central government and the Reserve Bank of India (RBI).

The two technicians were left with no option but to hunt for parts and components from war surplus disposal depots and scrap markets in Calcutta. Along with some components cobbled together at the institute's workshop, they designed and fabricated an analog computer. The machine could solve a system of linear equations with ten variables. A paper describing a new iterative method of solving linear equations using the analog computer was published by ISI engineers in the *Review of Scientific Instruments* in May 1955.[17] The first Indian analytical computing machine "took a long time for solving linear equations, because all operations were manual," Mitra recalled in 1991.[18] Most of the time was taken for setting the 110 potentiometers it had. The development team displayed the computer to the political mentor of their leader, Nehru, at a special event held in December 1953. The analog computer remained functional until 1959.

Meanwhile, ISI continued its hardware fabrication work. However, it could not make much headway, as the quality of locally manufactured desk calculators and punch card sorters was inferior to custom-built sorters marketed in India by IBM and Hollerith India. ISI's electronically controlled sorters could sort up to 675 cards a minute and were supplied to the Army Statistical Organization in 1958.

The indigenous equipment had few standard components and ISI lacked basic facilities such as electroplating. ISI had to use the electroplating workshop of the Gun and Shell Factory—India's oldest ordnance factory located at Cossipore (later Kashipur).[19] Gadgets such as the calculators fabricated at ISI were of poor quality, as noted by a visiting expert from the United Nations Technical Assistance Administration (UNTAA) in the mid-1950s. When the official took apart a calculator prototype, he found that "the parts were badly made, with poor tolerances and sharp edges that made its operation shaky. Also it could overflow in multiplication and there seemed to be a small missing part for which the inter-working parts were prepared and which should have prevented the overflow."[20]

Acutely conscious of such deficiencies, Mahalanobis, while nurturing design and engineering teams at ISI, kept abreast of the latest developments in digital computing. He did so through personal visits to laboratories like the Harvard Mathematical Laboratory and meetings with electronic computing pioneers including John von Neumann and Howard H. Aiken. Mahalanobis figured in the list of potential customers of the UNIVAC (Universal Automatic Computer) the first general data processing machine developed by John Mauchly and J. Presper Eckert long before the unit was delivered by the Eckert–Mauchly Division of Remington Rand to the U.S. Census Bureau in 1951.[21]

In fact, Mahalanobis, a Fellow of the Royal Society, was a highly networked and mobile scientist, maintaining close links with both the socialist and Western worlds. He was respected globally for his contributions to development of statistics as a scientific discipline through new concepts including "Mahalanobis Distance" in multivatate analysis. Under his leadership, ISI blossomed into a multidisciplinary center of learning and research. Biologist J. B. S. Haldane and his wife worked in ISI as regular staff members for about four years, while Norbert Wiener—considered the father of cybernetics—spent six months working with younger members of the staff at the institute. Another significant visitor to the electronics laboratory of ISI in 1959 was C. M. Berners-Lee as a representative of Ferranti Limited of the United Kingdom. The visit was funded through Colombo Plan, an initiative of the Commonwealth. Berners-Lee was stationed at ISI as a data processing expert for six months, and studied problems relating to large-scale data analysis for the National Sample Survey (NSS) and delivered lectures.[22] Mahalanobis regularly hosted visiting scientists, including Nobel laureates, in his capacity as the Foreign Secretary of the Indian Science Congress Association based in Calcutta (figure 1.1). He, along with Bhatnagar, had proposed a program called "Short Visits of Scientists from Abroad" under which eminent scientists were personally invited by Nehru.[23] Mahalanobis believed such visits benefited students who could not go abroad for advanced learning.

Mahalanobis's circle of scientific contacts included John Desmond Bernal (1901–1971), a professor of physics and crystallography at Birkbeck College in London. Bernal had participated in the planning process of CSIR and had personal relations with the Indian scientific elite. At Birkbeck College, Bernal had engaged Andrew Donald Booth, developer of the Automatic Relay Computer and an All Purpose Electronic Computer (APEC), to build a computer for crystallographic purposes in 1945.[24] Booth designed another variant of the electronic computer, APE(X)C, based on which British Tabulating Machine (BTM) evolved its series of commercial machines branded as the Hollerith Electronic Computer (HEC). One such model, HEC4, was renamed ICT 1201 in 1956, and it became a best-selling British computer at the end of the 1950s with a total of nearly one hundred machines installed.

When BTM started marketing Booth's machines, Mahalanobis decided to order one for ISI, even though it was not suitable for data processing jobs being handled by ISI. It was bought more for familiarizing Indian engineers with the functioning of a modern computer so they could develop similar and bigger systems on their own.[25] The machine that BTM custom built for ISI was called HEC-2M. Only a handful of such computers were sold globally, and the one at ISI was Asia's first. ISI engineers were present when the machine was being fabricated and were trained in its operation and maintenance.

Figure 1.1
Prasanta Chandra Mahalanobis, director of the Indian Statistical Institute, Kolkata, showing physicist and Nobel laureate Niels Bohr the URAL electronic computer, which the institute had imported from the USSR in 1958. Bohr had visited India during January 1960 at the invitation of the Indian Science Congress Association. Both Homi Jehangir Bhabha and Mahalanobis had maintained close contacts with Bohr during their respective scientific careers. Also seen in the picture are Nirmala Kumari (wife of Mahalanobis) and Mrs. Bohr. Courtesy: Indian Statistical Institute Archives

Like all such computers of its generation, the HEC-2M was huge, occupying an entire floor at ISI. Getting an air-conditioned area ready for the machine that became operational in February 1956 was a task in itself, as centralized air conditioning was not commonplace in India yet. With memory of 1,024 words of thirty-two binary digits, the computer could perform two hundred additions or five multiplications per second.[26] Despite its limited computing power, HEC-2M attracted researchers from scientific institutions across the country—Indian Association for the Cultivation of Science, Calcutta; Indian Institute of Science (IISc), Bangalore; Indian Institute of Technology (IIT), Kharagpur; Tata Institute of Fundamental Research (TIFR), Bombay; and Physical Research Laboratory, Ahmedabad—as none of them as yet had any computer like HEC-2M.

The computer triggered nascent programming activity at the institute. At least a dozen scientists at ISI were able to learn how to program the machine and use it for applications designed by them within six months, even though BTM had not supplied a programming manual. A manual was written locally and formal training began soon afterward. ISI engineers also tinkered with the hardware of the British computer to improve its performance. For instance, the engineers improved the computer's speed by working with its magnetic drum and other adjuncts.[27] The computer had a punch-output unit to get the information in a form suitable for direct refeeding, which became necessary for large computations. This resulted in higher consumption of computer punch cards. ISI engineers incorporated a printing mechanism connected to a separate adding and listing machine in order to save punch cards.

Mahalanobis was constantly looking to add more computing power to speed up and widen research and national statistical projects at the institute. While the British computer was being built, he was in talks with the Soviet Science Academy for another computer. This effort resulted in another big computer, URAL from the Soviet Union, arriving at ISI in February 1958. It was gifted by the Soviet government through UNTAA.[28] URAL, manufactured by Counting and Analytic Machines (CAM) of Moscow, and was claimed to be a fully automatic, electronic digital computer capable of solving mathematical problems with speed and accuracy. It was constructed using eight hundred radio valves, three thousand germanium diodes, one magnetic drum memory, two tape decks, and an attached printer. Its ability to store large tracts of data made it suitable for ISI's statistical data processing work.[29] The computer could execute one hundred commands (addition, multiplication, etc.) per second. As with the British machine, ISI scientists made some changes to URAL's hardware. They installed a "magnetic drum memory system" and associated electronic circuits, which were considered core architecture of first-generation computers.[30]

Besides the electronic computer, ISI imported a range of equipment from the Soviet Union under the UN grant. This included machine tools, instruments and equipment for repair and maintenance of electronic computers, precision instruments, and accessories, all of which arrived at ISI between 1956 and 1958. Since the Soviet equipment was funded by the United Nations, among the supervising personnel were international experts including Americans. An in-house journal of ISI printed a picture in March 1957, showing an American kid—son of a quality control expert from the UN—switching on a Soviet tabulator installed at ISI. It was captioned "Soviet-American Cooperation at the Institute."[31]

While procuring powerful computers from the West as well as the Soviets, Mahalanobis continued to dream of an Indian computer. In 1961, ISI initiated a joint project with the newly set up Department of Electronics and Telecommunication Engineering at the Jadavpur University (JU) to design a second-generation, solid-state transistorized computer. The idea was to develop a "small-to-medium"-sized computer that was fast and versatile and yet cheap enough to be fabricated.[32]

Technical inputs for this project came from Nicholas C. Metropolis, first director of computing services at Los Alamos National Laboratory who had worked with John von Neumann in electronic computer research. Metropolis spent four weeks with the development teams at the invitation of Mahalanobis. Metropolis was director of the Institute of Computer Research at the University of Chicago when he was appointed to ISI as an expert by UNTAA, along with S. Y. Yong from the computer section of Philco Corporation. His main contribution was significant digit arithmetic (SDA) as an alternative system to floating point arithmetic normally used in modern computers. SDA was incorporated in hardware design of the computer developed by ISI and JU, a rare implementation of the idea proposed by Metropolis, according to Dwijesh Datta Majumder, a member of the development team.[33] Metropolis and Yong prepared "a detailed scheme of the logical design of the computer," working with the project personnel.[34]

The computer, named ISIJU-1, was finally commissioned in 1966 (figure 1.2). It was not a great success for various reasons, including its use of SDA, concluded Majumder, who was trained in computer system design at the University of Michigan under a fellowship from the United Nations Development Programme (UNDP) in 1964 and was influenced by lectures Norbert Wiener gave at ISI. ISIJU-1 was used at JU for teaching computer programming and circuit design and for solving moderate research problems. The original plan was to build two systems—one in JU and another in ISI, but the second system was never built. A radio data-link between the two centers was also designed and built but it was not made operational.

Even before ISIJU-1 was fabricated, ISI could command formidable computing power in the country's scientific community with two large computers in operation by 1959. The institute had been conferred the status of India's "national statistical and computational laboratory" through legislation passed by the parliament. Mahalanobis by then was an important policymaker in New Delhi charged with preparing the second Five Year Plan for the country. A new body of the government—Department of Statistics and the Central Statistical Organisation—had been established in recognition that statistical inputs were critical for India's national planning and

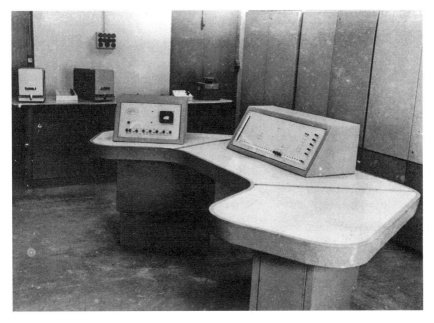

Figure 1.2
A view of the second-generation, transistor-based ISIJU-1 computer, jointly developed by the Indian Statistical Institute and Jadavpur University. The work on this system was initiated in 1961 and it was commissioned by Education Minister M. C. Chagla at Jadavpur on April 2, 1966. Courtesy: Indian Statistical Institute Archives

development. India, as Mahalanobis envisioned, was to pursue the path of planned development by "increasing the scope and importance of the public sector and in this way to advance to a socialistic pattern of society."[35]

Atomic Energy Group Moves Ahead

Computer development activity progressed in parallel in Bombay (now Mumbai) at the Tata Institute of Fundamental Research (TIFR). Bhabha founded the center in 1945 with funding from the Sir Dorabji Tata Trust run by the House of Tatas.

Son of an aristocrat lawyer, Bhabha first studied mechanical engineering at Cambridge and then theoretical physics at the Cavendish Laboratory. With several scientific papers to his credit in the early part of his career, Bhabha had proposed a theory to explain the process of electron showers in cosmic rays (known as the Bhabha-Heitler Cascade Theory) while working at Cambridge. In 1939, war broke out while Bhabha was on a short holiday to India. Forced to remain in India, Bhabha took up a teaching job at the Indian Institute of Science (IISc) in Bangalore and set up a laboratory to continue his cosmic ray research. But he soon discovered that the necessary financial support for scientific research was lacking in Indian labs. In 1944, he approached the Tata Trust again with a proposal to set up "a big school of research in the fundamental problems of physics, both theoretical and experimental."[36] This effort led to the birth of TIFR.

While pursuing research in the 1930s, Bhabha had traveled to research labs across Europe and forged bonds of "science and friendship" with leading scientists such as Ernest Rutherford, Niels Bohr, Enrico Fermi, Wolfgang Pauli, and Walter Heitler.[37] Bhabha knew Robert Oppenheimer from his Cambridge days, although when Bhabha arrived at Cambridge Oppenheimer had already passed through. The two remained in touch and Bhabha visited Oppenheimer whenever he was in America. Bhabha got Nehru to write formal invitations to Oppenheimer to visit India more than once after the Manhattan Project concluded, but Oppenheimer never accepted.[38]

The scientific elite had imagined a nuclear India even before the colonial rule ended in 1947. Bhabha's letter of March 1944 to the Tata Trust provides the evidence. He emphasized the need for research in fundamental physics, particularly nuclear research because "when nuclear energy has been successfully applied for power production in say a couple of decades from now, India will not have to look abroad for experts but will find them ready at hand." These words of Bhabha have proved prophetic because within three decades of beginning nuclear research India not only tested a nuclear bomb but also developed an elaborate program of nuclear power generation. In 1945, CSIR under Bhatnagar set up the Atomic Energy Committee to explore atomic minerals and to "suggest ways and means of harnessing the materials for production of nuclear energy." Indian physicists and political elite were also aware of the potential of an atomic bomb.

When India gained independence in 1947, historians believe, "more than a handful of scientists in India understood the physics of the fission process and grasped the implications of the successful projects in the United States and Canada."[39] Bhabha envisioned an elaborate plan for nuclear energy development and was negotiating for uranium with the British Atomic Energy Commission and the National Research Council of Canada even before the independence with blessings of Nehru. The first shipment of uranium oxide from Canada arrived in India a month before India was declared independent on August 15, 1947.[40]

Having founded TIFR with help from the Tata Trust, Bhabha could convince Nehru about the importance of nuclear research, promising him that nuclear energy could be a major source of electric power in a couple of decades. This gave TIFR a special status in the hierarchy of the Indian science establishment. The atomic energy panel of CSIR was recast as the Board of Research in Atomic Energy in 1947 to "plan and implement all atomic research and development in the country" and was finally replaced by an independent Atomic Energy Commission (AEC) within a year.[41] Bhabha persuaded Nehru that he needed an independent place of authority in the government free of bureaucratic hurdles to pursue his goal of developing nuclear power. As head of the Department of Atomic Energy as well as AEC, he reported directly to Nehru with secrecy maintained about nuclear research. High on his agenda was design and fabrication of an experimental nuclear reactor within five years.

Bhabha needed modern instrumentation and computers to implement his nuclear projects. He was feverishly looking for youngsters educated in science and engineering abroad. He used to meet and recruit people during his frequent travels to Europe and also within India. Bright youngsters sent abroad for higher education on fellowships granted by the Tata Trust were also a fertile talent pool. For instance, Bhabha hired Ayyagari Sambasiva Rao, an electrical engineering graduate from Stanford University, to help develop instrumentation for the balloon experiments.[42] The balloons flown to high altitudes used to carry battery-operated Geiger-Muller Counters to measure the total intensity and vertical component of cosmic rays.

Initially Rao assisted Bhabha in these experiments and was soon appointed head of the electronics unit at the Atomic Energy Establishment (AEE), which was by 1954 a separate organization from TIFR. All activities relating to reactor, materials, and metallurgy that were initiated at TIFR for development of the first nuclear reactor, Apsara, were transferred to AEE. Rao was sent for brief training, along with other scientists, in reactor control systems and health physics at Saclay Laboratories near Paris, France.

Like his contemporary Mitra in Calcutta, Rao had to scout junkyards and scrap markets in Bombay for war surplus material to fabricate electronic instruments in initial years.[43] In 1958, the electronics group initiated work on an analog computer capable of solving large mathematical problems related to control systems for nuclear reactors. The outcome of this effort was a self-contained general-purpose analog computer called EAC-62. Ten units of this computer were delivered to different research institutes and engineering colleges by 1965.[44]

Before the atomic energy groups started building analog computers in Bombay, an analog computer was built at the IISc in Bangalore during 1954–1956 by Vincent C. Rideout, a visiting professor from the University of Wisconsin–Madison. Rideout had brought with him several components and subassemblies including operational amplifiers required for fabrication of the computer, which he built along with faculty and students of the Department of Electrical Communication Engineering. It was named the Philbrick-Rideout Electronic Differential Analyzer, or PREDA for short.

A contemporary of Rao was another Tata Trust fellow recruited by Bhabha—Rangaswamy Narasimhan, who held an MS in electrical engineering from California Institute of Technology and a doctorate in mathematics from Indiana University. In the job interview, Narasimhan was asked if he was aware of the von Neumann report, a copy of which Bhabha had procured during his visit to Princeton. An affirmative answer ensured Narasimhan a job in the Instrumentation Group of TIFR and a project to design a digital computer. The group first focused on building an electronic digital computer with serial memory, starting with digital logic subassemblies (figure 1.3).

After some initial work in digital logic subassemblies, the group in 1954 decided to design and fabricate a "full-scale, general-purpose, electronic digital computer using contemporary technology." Six people—most of them postgraduates in physics with specialization in electronics—formed the core team. Except for Narasimhan, nobody in this group had ever used or operated a computer and none had trained or studied outside India.[45] The group had very little technical information available except for some information about the Ordnance Discrete Variable Automatic Computer (ORDVAC) designed at the University of Illinois, according to a member of the TIFRAC team.[46]

First a pilot machine was designed and assembled mainly to serve as a testing ground for ideas in circuit and logic system design. Based on this experience, a full-scale machine was built within two years and completed in 1959. Major components were imported, including control unit, arithmetic unit, drivers, memory units and core stacks, input console (tape recorder), teleprinters, and magnetic tape storage including tape drive.[47] The central processor consisted of 2,700 vacuum tubes, 1,700 germanium diodes, and 12,500 resistors. The machine used ferrite-core memory with a capacity of 2,048 words and memory cycle of fifteen microseconds. Its memory cycle time and forty-bit word length were both higher than the first-generation IBM 701 unveiled in 1952. It took forty-five microseconds for addition and subtraction, while multiplication and division took 500. The machine, commissioned for routine work in February 1960, was formally christened TIFR Automatic Calculator (TIFRAC) by Prime Minister Nehru in January 1962 (figure 1.4).

Figure 1.3
Dr. Homi J. Bhabha along with R. Narasimhan—who led the design team of TI-
FRAC—showing some circuits of TIFRAC to Nobel Prize-winning British physicist Sir
John Cockcroft and Lady Cockcroft at the Tata Institute of Fundamental Research,
Mumbai. Cockcroft was involved with the organization of science in India in the
initial phase. Courtesy: TIFR Archives

The TIFR team was greatly influenced by similar first-generation digital
computers built by universities and atomic energy groups in the United
States, including ILLIAC1 of the University of Illinois. Such systems were
built with vacuum tubes, semiconductor diodes, and ferrite-core memories.
The Illinois team made available to TIFR details of control logic design.[48]
Unlike the IBM 701, which used cathode ray tubes as memory units, TIFRAC
deployed three-dimensional ferrite-core memory. The decision to do so was
based on scientific journal discussions about the use of such memory in the
Whirlwind1 computer designed at the Massachusetts Institute of Technology (MIT).[49] The TIFR calculator design in 1957 was not yet far behind what
was being attempted elsewhere in the world, but it had become obsolete by
the time it was commissioned.[50]

Though not directly involved in computer development work, Bhabha
kept acquiring first-hand knowledge of contemporary computer technology.

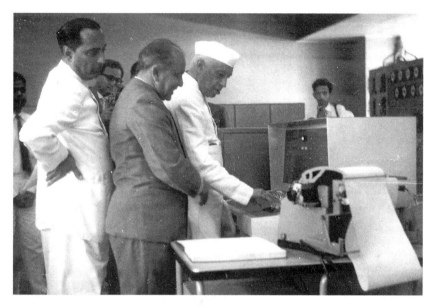

Figure 1.4
Dr Homi J. Bhabha (extreme left), director of the Tata Institute of Fundamental Research (TIFR), looks on as his colleague D. Y. Phadke shows Prime Minister Jawaharlal Nehru TIFRAC, the first digital computer designed by Indian engineers, after the inauguration of the new headquarters of TIFR on January 15, 1962. Courtesy: TIFR Archives

In 1959, he visited the University Mathematical Laboratory at Cambridge, United Kingdom, which had a first-generation computer and was designing a bigger machine. He invited the lab's director Maurice Vincent Wilkes on a lecture tour and also proposed training for the TIFR scientists in his lab. He had similar interactions with the electrical engineering labs of Manchester University, National Research Development Corporation, and the British Computer Society. Bhabha told his computer team back home that one of the best computer centers in America was at the University of Illinois and it might be useful to send some members to work with the Illinois team.[51]

National Computer Center: A Catalyst

Having demonstrated design and development capabilities with first-generation analog and digital computers at their respective research institutions, both Bhabha and Mahalanobis concluded they needed more powerful, standard, commercially available computers to meet computing needs of their respective research groups. The technology gap between indigenously made systems and those available commercially was large. Second-generation computers could be fabricated only in organizations with necessary industrial and production know-how, which India did not possess. In fact, the two leaders of modern Indian science had begun scouting for powerful computing machines even while their research teams were working on first-generation machines. Both of them were looking for contemporary, state-of-the-art computers and were in touch with leading computer labs and groups in the West. The drive for a higher-speed computer soon became a battle for supremacy in this newly emerging discipline with both ISI and TIFR staking their claim to the tag of national computing center.

Mahalanobis had already acquired two large first-generation computers from the United Kingdom and the USSR. He wanted to get larger, commercial machines but could not do so due to lack of government support.[52] His efforts to convince Americans to fund the purchase of a UNIVAC computer with grants from the U.S. Technical Cooperation Mission (TCM) met with similar fate in 1957. He had no option left but to install an IBM 1401 machine on hire and subsequently get a Honeywell 400 computer for ISI. Since many organizations had been using ISI's computer facilities for nearly a decade, Mahalanobis wished the institute to be declared a national computing center.

However Bhabha too was nurturing thoughts of getting TIFR declared a national computation center by acquiring powerful imported machines. He discussed the idea with IBM's Director of Research E. R. Piore, whom he had met while on a Paris- Zurich flight in June 1959. Piore advised "it would be wise to start with a fairly powerful machine, but not the most powerful available, as the programming of such [a] machine needed considerable experience and this could be obtained usefully on a machine which was fairly powerful."[53] The computer firm's first high-level contact with a top leader of India's scientific establishment and a key policymaker was purely accidental.

As a follow-up, IBM sent R. L. Garwin, a professor of physics at Columbia University, to evaluate TIFRAC and advise scientists on future activities in this field. Garwin supported the idea of acquiring a powerful computer to serve as the nucleus of a national computation center at TIFR. In Garwin's view, it was worth pursuing the goal of atomic energy scientists to use computers to design and run nuclear plants, on the lines of the Mercury computer at the European Organization for Nuclear Research (CERN), but he cautioned that Indians could face problems in programming such computers. Since TIFRAC was "a machine of limited speed and non-standard design" Garwin suggested purchase or hire of the IBM 704 computer being used in the United States to design nuclear reactors and also wrote a blue-print for the proposed computer center.[54]

IBM proposed the 704 as the first step, since importing a more pow-erful machine like the 7090 could take up to three years. Moreover, cost was another consideration. The IBM 7090 with 32,000-word memory was priced at $2.9 million or a monthly rental of $63,000, while the price of the 704 was about $2.19 million.[55] And education discount could bring down the actual price of the 704. When Bhabha went to attend MIT's cente-nary celebrations in early 1961, he discussed the IBM proposal with Jerome Wiesner, then advisor on scientific matters to President John F. Kennedy and earlier a professor at MIT's Research Laboratory of Electronics. Wiesner suggested Bhabha choose the 7090, which he said was ten times faster than the 704 and better suited for solving scientific problems.

M. Govind Kumar Menon, head of the physics group at TIFR and a close associate of Bhabha, was delegated in 1961 to visit IBM and UNIVAC division of the Sperry Rand Corporation in the United States. Menon was impressed with IBM, whose leaders did not want to miss an opportunity to further consolidate IBM's position in the Indian market. An outcome of this visit was the company's willingness to extend its 60 percent educational discount to the purchase of the 7090 too. Menon also met Wiesner who reiterated his recommendation of the 7090 for TIFR.[56] IBM promptly sent a formal offer from its Bombay office mentioning that the discounted price of the 7090 would be $518,560.[57]

Having zeroed in on a commercial machine, Bhabha began lobbying for external aid because the Indian government would have found it hard to spare so much foreign exchange just for one piece of equipment. He met John Kenneth Galbraith, America's ambassador in New Delhi, in August 1961 and handed over a note on computer activity at TIFR that included relevant portions of Garwin's report. Galbraith assured Bhabha of help to buy this computer.[58] Later the ambassador visited TIFR and promised to get financial assistance for the purchase under the TCM. Meanwhile, Maha-lanobis continued to make efforts to expand computing activity under his control. In February 1962, the Department of Statistics, acting on the advice of Mahalanobis, suggested setting up a large computer in New Delhi as a national facility similar to one established by the U.S. Census Bureau in 1955. The department supported the idea of buying an IBM 1401 or Univac 3 computer for the proposed national center.[59]

TIFR staunchly opposed the move. In July 1962, D. Y. Phadke wrote on behalf of Bhabha to the Department of Statistics, stating, "If only one high-speed electronic digital computing center is to be set up in India, it should be set up at TIFR. There may, however, be justification for setting up more than one center in India."[60] Phadke boasted of the design and development of the TIFRAC digital computer and other activities of the computer department at TIFR. He mentioned that the TIFRAC had a processing speed close to that of the IBM 704 and compared well in performance with contemporary computers developed in the East, including from the USSR and Japan.[61] IBM 704 was priced between 2.5 million and 3 million rupees.

Bhabha raised the issue with Mahalanobis himself, telling him that "we should jointly press for both computers, and I have a feeling that we will succeed in getting two from the Americans under TCM or under some other agency."[62] Bhabha argued that the UNIVAC that Mahalanobis proposed to get was much less powerful than the IBM 704 his own center was proposing to acquire, and "much less powerful" than the 7090 it planned to buy in two years. At the same time, Bhabha tried to downplay rivalry between the institutes by saying "in a big country like India I think there would be a legitimate case for having two computing centers, and getting two computers, one of the types that we have asked for it at Bombay, and the other of the type Prof. Mahalanobis desires."[63] This was not acceptable to Mahalanobis who replied that work relating to the National Sample Survey (NSS) needed electronic equipment for "speedy and adequate processing" of the large volume of data. In case, for some reason, two computers didn't become available, Mahalanobis said, "I should have no hesitation in giving higher priority to data processing equipment for NSS."[64]

The clash of two of Nehru's close advisors on a crucial high technology issue is intriguing. The computer projects of both Mahalanobis and Bhabha had the blessings of the prime minister. He was present for every important occasion—be it the inauguration of the analog computer at ISI or the naming ceremony of TIFRAC. Both scientists held key positions in the government. Yet Nehru chose not to interfere on the issue of a national computer center.

While the tussle was on, Bhabha decided to go ahead with the purchase of a large system. Since word had spread about the likely purchase, computer companies from the United States and the United Kingdom sent in their proposals to TIFR. In light of this, Bhabha thought of checking out all available options instead of placing the order with IBM. He handed the task over to TIFR engineers who were in the United States on different assignments and formed a panel headed by Narasimhan, then a visiting scientist at the Digital Computer Laboratory (DCL) of the University of Illinois at Urbana.

After visiting manufacturing and research facilities of major computer makers and a detailed technical and financial analysis of four large computers—IBM 7090, CDC 3600, Philco 211, and UNIVAC 1107—the panel made a surprise choice—CDC 3600. Factors like speed, logic design, and systems and engineering design tilted the decision in favor of the Control Data Corporation, despite the fact that only one such machine was in operation—at the company's plant in Minneapolis.[65] However, Argonne National Laboratory and other nuclear laboratories elsewhere were in the process of acquiring the CDC 3600. This provided "additional assurance of the basic soundness of the recommendation."[66] In addition, CDC was willing to offer a 40 percent education discount amounting to about $1 million. Though Indian scientists could not fabricate contemporary computers or get Indian companies to manufacture them locally, they had access to the latest computing technology via imports.

Bhabha applied to the U.S. Agency for International Development for a grant of about $1.5 million to acquire the computer. The CDC package also included a desk-size computer, 160-A, as a satellite system, card and paper tape readers with their respective punches, ten magnetic tape units, and one high-speed and one low-speed line printer. Five maintenance engineers and three programmers were sent from India to Minneapolis for training ranging from six to nine months so that they could get the site at TIFR ready and maintain the system afterward. From Urbana-Champaign, Illinois, Narasimhan coordinated training activity in such a way that "the maximum relevant know-how was transferred during the limited period of stay."[67] TIFR's maintenance engineers were present when the machine was being assembled and tested. The large computer arrived in Bombay on the morning of May 10, 1964, on a chartered Pan Am Boeing (figure 1.5).

Narasimhan arranged for all existing FORTRAN-63 library subroutines (subprograms or parts of programming code that can be used within a larger program to execute a specific task) to be sent to Bombay and suggested that once Indian programmers trained at CDC returned from the United States, they could take up the training of others. In addition, engineers were sent to other U.S. centers for training in computer programming with TCM grants.

From October 1964 on, the CDC system started functioning as a national computation facility open to academic and research communities. Computer time, programming help, and stationery were provided free in the first year. As in the case of TIFRAC, it was mandatory for all users to write and debug their own programs. A number of programming courses were organized to help users and also to disseminate programming know-how

Figure 1.5
TIFR got a modern computer from CDC to develop its own national computer center; large racks containing the CDC-3600–160A computer system, being unloaded from the chartered aircraft in Mumbai on May 10, 1964. Courtesy: TIFR Archives

in general. Nearly two dozen training courses (in 3600 FORTRAN, advanced 3600 FORTRAN, COBOL, COMPASS, and SCOPE) were conducted at TIFR, IIT Bombay, the University of Madras, the Bhabha Atomic Research Centre (as the AEE was renamed after Bhabha's death) and the Tata Electric Company. Individual researchers were allowed to spend time at TIFR to develop and test their own programs. An extensive library of subroutines was maintained and updated regularly. The programming staff developed several packages and utility programs, while standard packages such as Linear Programming, Integer Linear Programming, Sorting and Merging, List Processing Languages, and Network Flow Analysis were tested and made available to users.

In addition to the atomic energy and TIFR people, the CDC system attracted a wide range of users—academics and researchers, as well as commercial users like banks, public utilities, oil companies, and manufacturing companies. The list of users numbered close to 150 in the first five years of the computer's operation. This reflected growing interest in using computers for commercial applications in the 1960s. The computer was also used for space- and defense-related software development. In 1969, N. Seshagiri, a young programmer, wrote a program for sizing multistage rockets using computer-aided design (CAD). He developed a software package called SIMSPACE based on differential and algebraic simultaneous equations in numerous variables.[68] TIFR's computer scientists designed a three-week course in electronic computing and control systems specifically for the armed forces. The Indian Navy wanted to use the CDC 3600 to solve logistic problems relating to provisioning and supply of stores, and technical problems such as stability assessments and ship design.[69]

The CDC machine also helped TIFR scientists hone their skills in hardware and software maintenance. This was more out of necessity because the maintenance costs CDC demanded were rather prohibitive (almost $276,000 a year). Under the technical support contract the company would maintain two engineers on site primarily to train five TIFR maintenance engineers who could carry out regular maintenance work. When one of the memory drive lines got burnt, CDC suggested replacement of the memory stack at a cost of $40,000. But the TIFR maintenance team did not heed the CDC engineers' advice.[70] Detailed knowledge of the memory system helped them push faulty locations to one end of the memory by making hardware changes in the drive logic. Several mechanical replacement parts were fabricated in the institute's workshop and used successfully.

Modern Computers at IITs

The 1960s were pivotal for computer development and dissemination activity in India. Almost a year before the CDC computer arrived at TIFR, a fairly modern machine—IBM 1620—had been installed at the Indian Institute of Technology at Kanpur in the summer of 1963. This computer, along with another IBM 7044 acquired in 1966, became a hub of computer training, education, and commercial data processing activity in North India. The IIT Kanpur center helped initiate software writing skills on commercial machines in a whole generation of Indian citizens, and in forging future relations with the U.S. information technology industry.

Indian Institutes of Technology—which have acquired a global brand value—were conceived as modern, technical higher-education centers even before India became a nation. In 1946 the British Viceroy's Executive Council commissioned a panel of experts, under the chairmanship of Nalini Ranjan Sarkar, to draw a blueprint for higher technical education in India. Specifically, the panel was asked to explore "whether it is desirable to have (a) a central institution possibly on the lines of Massachusetts Institute of Technology, with a number of subordinate institutes affiliated to it or (b) several higher institutions on a regional basis."[71] The idea of patterning India's higher technical and engineering education after MIT was first proposed by Ardeshir Dalal, a former officer of the Indian Civil Service and an influential member of the industrial elite, after he led an industrial delegation to the United States in preceding years.

Bright Indians were already being sent to America for higher education under a government scholarship scheme, to address the shortage of skilled workers. For the long term, however, the country needed to develop its own higher technical education institutions. The panel suggested these be set up near large industrial areas to ensure "the right relationship between the public, industry and education."[72] Pre-independent India had some of the finest institutions in science such as the Indian Institute of Science, Bangalore, and TIFR in Bombay, but engineering education was pathetic. The country had forty-six engineering colleges with a total capacity of 2,500, and there was no postgraduate education in engineering. Colonial-era engineering education was designed to produce civil engineers and overseers—who could be employed in irrigation, public works, and railways. What independent India needed was a diversified technical workforce trained in a range of modern disciplines, for employment in large state-funded development projects as well as in private industries.

The idea of developing modern engineering education took shape after British rule ended. Nehru implemented the blueprint with the first IIT, established at Kharagpur in the eastern part of India in July 1951. Nehru wanted Indian engineering schools to be among the best in the world, so he enlisted some of the leading higher education institutions of the West to develop them. Seeking external technical and financial help was also inevitable as national resources were inadequate for the task. Help from different countries also meant a diversified engineering and technical education system would result. Politically, such an amalgamation fit with Nehru's vision of nonalignment with any superpower.

The first IIT did not receive any direct assistance from MIT though it did have international faculty drawn from the United States, the United

Kingdom, Ireland, France, USSR, Germany, Norway, Sweden, and Poland. For the second IIT at Bombay, the United Nations Educational, Scientific and Cultural Organization (UNESCO) arranged the donation of equipment and technical expertise from the Soviet Union and other Eastern bloc countries in 1956. The third IIT at Madras (now Chennai) was developed with German aid offered during Nehru's visit to West Germany in 1956.

Despite such varied international inputs, Nehru was still keen on direct involvement of MIT in development of IITs. In 1958, he requested that MIT send a team to India and help the government prepare a blueprint for an IIT at Kanpur, an industrial town in North India. Apparently, MIT refused, citing a shortage of staff, and instead it got the American Society for Engineering Education (ASEE) to send a group of six engineering educators to India. The ASEE team submitted to the Indian government a report outlining how engineering education could be developed. Subsequently MIT, responding to pressure from the Indian government, appointed a three-member team led by mechanical engineer Norman C. Dahl (1918–2004) to study how MIT could help IIT Kanpur grow. By then, three IITs were already functional. Upon visiting them and other colleges, the team found that the status of engineering education in India was similar to American institutes; as one member commented, "they pray to the same god as we do."[73]

MIT finally agreed to lead a consortium of nine U.S. universities to help set up the Kanpur institute. A formal ten-year program called the Kanpur Indo-American Project (KIAP) was initiated in August 1961. Members of this consortium were California Institute of Technology, Carnegie Institute of Technology, Case Institute of Technology, Massachusetts Institute of Technology, Ohio State University, Princeton University, Purdue University, University of California at Berkeley, and University of Michigan. Three major components of this project were: consortium staff working under a program leader at Kanpur; IIT faculty receiving on-the-job experience in consortium institutes; and procurement of equipment, books, and journals not available in India.

The consortium members sent highly experienced and specialized faculty to Kanpur. Although the curriculum and methods of instruction were not influenced by the ASEE report or members of its team, it was found that IIT Kanpur's first director P. K. Kelkar was already knowledgeable and influenced by the practice of engineering sciences followed in the United States.[74] IIT Kanpur thus took the engineering science route.

During the ten-year project, 122 American faculty members served a total of two hundred person-years at Kanpur, while fifty Indian faculty members were trained in U.S. institutes with five of them getting their doctorates there. A high-speed computer from IBM was among the equipment worth $7.5 million procured during the project.[75] When the computer arrived by a chartered DC7 plane in Kanpur, the IIT didn't have a department of computer science, or any courses in the field at all. The IBM 1620 had a central processor with core 40,000-digit storage, three magnetic tape units, and a card input–output unit (figure 1.6). The computer was received in Kanpur by a team consisting of Harry D. Huskey (University of California, Berkeley), Irving N. Rabinowitz (Associate Director, Computer Center at Princeton University), and Forman S. Acton (Associate Professor, Electrical Engineering, Princeton University). Huskey, a leading figure of computing in America, had worked on landmark computer projects such as the ENIAC and Bendix G-15 drum computer.

In the absence of any formal academic course in computer science, the computer center began its work in an "evangelical spirit" offering short-term,

Figure 1.6
A view of the IBM 1620 at the Indian Institute of Technology, Kanpur, the first such system to be imported into India in July 1963; the first set of Indian programmers were trained on this system, which became the nucleus for computer science education in India. Courtesy: Sandra I. Rabinowitz

intensive courses in computers basics and programming (mainly in FOR-TRAN II) for academicians, industry managers, and researchers.[76] Several thousand people benefited from these courses. The IIT Kanpur computer was also used by a large number of business firms and corporations for commercial data processing. Faculty members, encouraged to take up consultancy assignments with industry, made their first contacts with newly set up software firms like Tata Consultancy Services (TCS). The presence of a commercial machine in the IIT was critical at a time when IBM was aggressively expanding its operations among large users in India. Huskey organized an All India Computer Users Group—mostly users of IBM mainframes—which ultimately led to the birth of India's first body of computing professionals, the Computer Society of India (figure 1.7).

When the intensive courses started, faculty members noticed that they did not have any textbooks or course materials. In 1968, faculty member V. Rajaraman—who had a master's degree from MIT and a PhD from the University of Wisconsin—decided to fill the gap by writing the first set of Indian textbooks on Fortran programming, numerical techniques, and

Figure 1.7
Professor Irving N. Rabinowitz working with the IBM 1620 system at the IIT Kanpur.
Courtesy: Sandra I. Rabinowitz

digital logic. Prior to his IIT appointment, Rajaraman had worke
analog computer PREDA in Bangalore. Instant popularity of his u.c.,
priced books encouraged Rajaraman to write more and it also attracted
textbook publishers. Prentice Hall agreed to publish a new title, *Principles
of Computer Programming*, in 1969, on poor-quality paper to keep its price
affordable.[77] The second title, *Computer Programming in FORTRAN 77*, went
into forty print runs until August 2003. Several of Rajaraman's books sold
thousands of copies, filling a basic need of budding computer programmers
over the next three decades.

In 1965, an optional course in computer science was introduced in IIT
Kanpur for the M.Tech degree but it took another five years before a full-
fledged M.Tech course in computer science could begin. The B.Tech degree
in computer science was started in 1979.

Around the time IIT Kanpur got the IBM machines, IIT Bombay got a second-generation Soviet computer, Minsk II, for its computer center headed
by J. R. Isaac, an M.Tech from Carnegie Mellon University. The oversized
Minsk used discrete transistor-based circuitry and had paper tape input–
output devices. It needed almost one year for it to be installed and made
operational. All the manuals and technical literature was in Russian, which
faculty members had to learn to be able to use the computer. Though outmoded, the Soviet computer proved to be a blessing in disguise for the
nascent computer science faculty and its students who could tinker with
the hardware as they liked. This was unlike the situation at the computer
center in Kanpur where nobody—even engineers from IBM India—was
allowed to fiddle with the computer. In 1974, IIT Bombay got another
Soviet computer, EC-1030—a third-generation, integrated circuit-based
computer, comparable to IBM's 360 system.

The two Soviet computers gave the computer faculty as well as students
a very strong technical foundation in computer science and technology.
"I doubt if any computer has ever had its hardware and software modified
and enhanced as much as these two," Isaac said, of the institute's experience with the two machines.[78] This helped build a reputation of IIT Bombay
graduates for being proficient in both hardware and software, resulting in
their ready acceptance in American universities for higher studies despite
having been trained on Soviet machines. The interdisciplinary M.Tech and
postgraduate diploma in computer science began in 1973; while the B.Tech
in computer science was launched in 1980 at IIT Bombay.

Parallel to the growth of computer science education in the IITs, the
Department of Electronics (DoE) supported regional computer centers
that provided data processing services for commercial users in addition

to training engineers in programming. Technical and financial assistance for this initiative came from the United Nations Development Program, which felt that India needed R&D centers dedicated to software engineering skills. The UNDP then provided assistance to start a new outfit at TIFR: the National Center for Software Development and Computing Techniques (NCSDCT). The center was equipped with two powerful computers—DEC 1077 and PDP-11/40—in August 1975 for training and software development. The focus was on specialized areas like interactive graphics, CAD, and remote computing.

While courses in India's IITs were centered on computer science, NCSDCT focused on practical training in systems software. In the words of Srinivasan Ramani, its first director, NCSDCT trained "purely technical guys, the geeks of the business." The IITs had a strong academic orientation, whereas "we had a different view. If our students were not very good programmers, we would kill them," he asserted.[79] An early experiment in networking was conducted by linking up computers located at different locations via telephone lines, and doing similar linking up to conduct a one-year postgraduate course in software technology. The experience helped the NCSDCT launch India's first data communication network called the Education and Research Network (ERNET) for the research and academic communities. Know-how and software tools developed were transferred to industry and academic institutions. Technical assistance was extended to petroleum, banking, and financial firms to set up data communication networks.

Despite Nehru's intention to make Indian engineering education diversified with varied inputs, the U.S. orientation of the Indian technical elite ensured that the American system pervaded all IITs. P. K. Kelkar, who moved from IIT Kanpur to Soviet-aided IIT Bombay as director in 1970, sought to restructure the curriculum in line with American engineering education practices. IIT Kanpur faculty members influenced the purchase of a computer at IIT Madras in favor of an IBM machine. In these formative years of engineering education development, the U.S.-oriented technical elite played a central role in establishing computing education in India despite strains in political relations between India and United States after the 1971 Bangladesh war.[80] While some distinctive features reflecting traditions of donor nations were adopted in the initial stage, eventually all IITs settled for the engineering science approach pioneered by Gordon Brown at MIT, as veteran IIT teacher P. V. Indiresan recounted.[81]

The American model at IIT Kanpur did not yield desired results such as an "electronics park" to fuel industrial development similar to that triggered around MIT in Cambridge, Massachusetts, or Stanford University in

Palo Alto, California. Successful academic programs in aeronautical engineering, computer science, and material science merely "turned out Indian students overqualified for jobs at home and best prepared for graduate training and eventual employment abroad."[82] IIT Kanpur, in Dahl's assessment at the end of the ten-year Kanpur Indo-American Project, had proved to be an irrelevant factor in India's industrial and social progress and remained an isolated island of academic excellence.[83] In the short run, it actually accelerated rather than reversed "brain drain." The IITs emerged as islands of excellence in engineering education and a base to export bright graduates to the United States. It became the norm for IIT graduates to go to the United States for postgraduate and doctoral studies, and then stay on for teaching or industry employment. An oft-quoted joke about this trend: "When a student enrolls at an IIT, his spirit is said to ascend to America. After graduation, his body follows." The project's founders had intended to create an Indian MIT, not merely an MIT in India, as Stuart W. Leslie put it.

The deep connection of IITs with America, however, became beneficial in unexpected ways in India's post-liberalization period of the 1990s. IIT graduates who had migrated to America in the three decades since the 1960s had reached top positions in computer science departments of U.S. universities, participated in landmark projects such as MAC and ARPANET, were working in top companies like Intel and Microsoft, or had become entrepreneurs and angel investors. In 1998, Indian engineers were running several technology firms in Silicon Valley, employing a total of 16,600 people.[84] In December 1998, *Business Week* featured four IIT graduates on its cover calling them "Wiz Kids." Amazon had purchased the four IIT graduates' start-up, Junglee .com, for $160 million—one of the largest deals at the beginning of the dot-com era. Many of IIT graduates returned to India as their employer corporations opened offices, subsidiaries, and joint ventures in there. In this way, Indian students who had used an American-oriented system at IITs as a stepping-stone to higher education in the United States and to its technology became ambassadors of Indian skills and capabilities there.

Early Technical Capabilities

The initiation of computer technology development and manufacturing in mid-twentieth-century India was largely a subtheme of the development of modern science after the end of the colonial rule in 1947. The close links—personal and institutional—between Prime Minister Nehru and top scientists were essential in setting India on a path to scientific development and in seeding the information technology revolution. These links ensured that scientists played a decisive role in policymaking in electronics and computers as well as in developing related industrial infrastructure in the public sector in decades to follow. Nehru also nurtured higher technical and engineering education at IITs, which became centers of high-level engineering skills. These centers with their U.S.-style engineering education helped in forging close ties with the world of technology in the United States in myriad ways, in the decades to follow.

Mahalanobis and Bhabha got involved in computer development activity early on. Both did so to further their respective areas of scientific research—Mahalanobis for analysis of statistical data and Bhabha for nuclear research. In the years preceding India's independence, both the scientists were busy building scientific institutions in their fields of interest, which were to become national institutions in independent India. Both were educated in the West and had maintained their links with top scientists and scholars in their respective fields. Mahalanobis and Bhabha bonded very well with their Western counterparts while building teams of talented scientists at home. Such networking helped a great deal in their endeavors in the emerging field of computer technology as well.

A constant exchange of information, knowledge, and experience took place between Indian scientists and leading Western groups through education, training, lectures, and employment. Nehru depended on formal and informal advice from British scientists like A. V. Hill in matters of organizing scientific research in India. His scientist-advisors too leaned on Western scientists on several issues. Specifically in the area of computing, both Bhabha and Mahalanobis interacted with von Neumann. Bhabha consulted him in 1947 about reorganizing the School of Mathematics at TIFR.[85] On von Neumann's advice he appointed one of the postdoctoral fellows at Princeton, K. Chandrasekharan, as an associate professor in the school in 1949. Mahalanobis met von Neumann during a visit to the United States in October 1946 when the latter was developing an electronic computing machine at the Institute of Advanced Studies at Princeton. Per Mahalanobis's account of this meeting, the two discussed building a similar machine in India, and von Neumann assured him that "he would be able to come to India next winter if invited."

Top names of computing in America in the 1960s—Nicholas Metropolis, Norbert Wiener, Harry Huskey—directly contributed to imparting knowledge and building skills among Indians in the early phase. India acquired a good ensemble of modern computers including the CDC 3600, considered the "supercomputer of the 1960s." These computers provided opportunity to hundreds of Indian engineers to learn programming skills and gain first-hand experience in data processing.

Though Indian-made systems like TIFRAC and ISIJU were not technological breakthroughs, they served the purpose of helping Indian groups gain capability in various fields of computer design, fabrication, testing, operation, maintenance, and programming. Specialists had grown to maturity who could tackle with confidence the logical, circuit, system, and engineering design of a variety of digital equipment.[86]

TIFRAC helped spread computer consciousness among research scientists beyond TIFR. By 1964, the machine operated in two shifts as scientists from government laboratories, educational institutions, and private organizations from all over India used it for their computation needs. Perhaps the most significant contribution of this project was helping Indian engineers and scientists develop software programming skills. Several staff members were recruited and trained in programming. The availability of a functioning computer made it possible to recruit and train additional programmers. A programming manual was developed and an extensive library of subroutines was set up to help computer users write their own programs. In 1972, an institute report noted, "many of the current computer users in India handling highly sophisticated and advanced computational techniques had their first introduction to programming through the use of TIFRAC."[87] ISIJU-1 too was put to similar use but with only moderate success.

The CDC system gave Indian scientists and engineers tremendous experience in handling such a large system from its fabrication, installation, and testing, to solving complex problems. Specific capabilities were developed in hardware and software maintenance, software program writing, hardware troubleshooting, peripherals and components fabrication, and overall system management. Since large computers came under various grants and schemes, they had to be supported locally. Sometimes manuals had to be written and training programs conducted by Indian scientists and academics. For instance, lack of adequate support for updating of software from IBM forced undergraduates at IIT Kanpur to write a compiler that incorporated features implemented on newer versions of FORTRAN written for more recent hardware not available in Kanpur. Thus the problem of "producing up-to-date software for out-of-date hardware" spurred innovation.[88]

The experience at IIT Bombay with Soviet computers was similar. These very innovative skills came in handy when Indian companies took up work for U.S. firms in the years to follow. TIFR teams gained experience and knowledge through constant training, interaction, flow of documents and manuals, and visiting engineers and technicians from CDC. The knowledge thus gained was disseminated among others in India.

The computer centers at TIFR and IIT Kanpur not only helped scientific users of the atomic energy establishment and IIT respectively, but also a large number of academic and business users from all over the country. These two centers were particularly involved in helping build computer consciousness and software writing skills among several hundred engineers all over India. A great number of others were trained in computer use, FORTRAN and other computer languages, as well as software writing through a series of training programs. In the first phase of computer development, a good number of Indians worked on computers imported from the United States—some outdated and some contemporary; they were trained in American-style engineering schools that had U.S.-educated faculty members and were forced to innovate with hardware and software because of limited resources available. Out of all this emerged early capabilities in hardware design, software programming, maintenance, and training in the late 1950s and the 1960s.

Bhabha wanted to embrace the next stage of technology—integrated circuits—and both he and Mahalanobis wished to plunge into manufacturing of computers. Mahalanobis had a plan to launch commercial manufacturing of electronic calculators and other equipment through a company named Sankhya Yantra Private Limited, but officials in New Delhi shot it down. After visiting CDC production facilities in America, Bhabha set up a small group to work on printed circuit cards and also approached the Tata Sons to fund research on development of monolithic and hybrid circuits. Tata Sons, then in talks with Fairchild Semiconductor and other companies for microelectronics production India, were, however, not keen on funding research.[89] For manufacturing computers, Bhabha pursued the fledgling CDC, which showed great interest in India. CDC wanted to manufacture ferrite-core memory stacks—a labor-intensive product line—in India and ship them back to the United States for use in its machines. A similar unit was working for CDC in Hong Kong, and visited by executives of Tata Sons, which was to partner with CDC in the Indian venture. Despite detailed engagement for nearly three years, the TIFR-CDC-Tata Sons venture did not bear fruit because of Bhabha's untimely death as well as CDC management's apprehension about bureaucratic red tape and vacillating policies on foreign investment in India. A policy framework for development of computers and information technology and its use in the government and other sectors had still not emerged as of the late 1960s.

2 The Beginning of State Involvement

The very backwardness of the country in electronics and the smallness of the size of the present electronics industry could be turned into an asset, if early stages in the development of the industry in other countries are bypassed and the industry planned on the basis of the latest ideas and techniques. In no circumstances should India follow step by step the development of the electronics industry in the more advanced countries.

—"Report of the Electronics Committee," February 1966[1]

The 1960s represented a landmark in development of modern science and scientific institutions in India. All of the major scientific programs that India would make its mark in blossomed during this period—atomic energy, space technology, self-sufficiency in food production (the famous Green Revolution), information technology, and so on. While Bhabha was busy building nuclear reactors and research institutes in fundamental physics, another physicist, Vikram Sarabhai was engaged in launching sounding rockets. The launch of Nike-Apache—a NASA-built two-stage sounding rocket—in 1963 was a scientific project to study the ionosphere over the earth's magnetic equator that passes over Thumba on India's western coast, but it inaugurated India's entry into the space sector. Furthermore a string of Indian Institutes of Technology and Indian Institutes of Management were coming up that would produce modern engineers and managers. In hindsight, it looks as if India was trying to play catch up with the West in several sectors of science and technology.

For all their ambitious ventures, Indian scientists needed electronic components and modern data processing equipment and computers, among other resources. The computer building and acquisition activities initiated by TIFR and ISI were not adequate. In any case, large-scale dissemination of electronics and computers required a manufacturing base and capital that research institutes were not capable of generating, though they did make concerted bids to enter commercial manufacturing. A policy framework for electronics and computers did not exist.

The war with China in 1962 exposed the poor level of preparedness of Indian forces, particularly the lack of modern equipment. This prompted Prime Minister Nehru's government to take steps for reorganizing scientific research so that it could also cater to the needs of India's defense forces. Although a separate outfit—the Defence Research and Development Organization (DRDO)—existed, it was thought necessary by Nehru and others to involve scientific groups from other wings of the government in strategic research. As part of this exercise, Nehru appointed Bhabha to the National Defence Council in the aftermath of the war.[2]

The absence of an industrial base in strategic electronics was too glaring. Indian forces taking on the Chinese in combat reported a shortage of electronic components in the imported ware they were using. A specific instance was the shortage of transmit-receive switches used in radars. An SOS was sent to TIFR, following which its microwave engineering group delivered these switches to the military.[3] The microwave group was headed by an engineer who was trained at the British Atomic Energy Research Establishment at Harwell. It was difficult to procure key electronic items in the open market and foreign firms used to set unreasonable commercial terms for local production. When Atomic Energy Establishment (AEE) approached Philips in 1957 to set up a unit to produce electronics instruments for nuclear plants, Philips asked for permission to import capital equipment worth £60,000 for three years and wanted minimum purchase guarantees.[4] That's why AEE under Bhabha established an Electronics Division to ensure a steady supply of electronics for the nuclear development program. The atomic energy groups, by the mid-1960s, claimed familiarity with fabrication of reasonably sophisticated electronic instruments for their research needs. They supplied instrumentation to universities and medical institutes as well. Basic attributes of electronics manufacturing—scale, repeatability, and low cost—were, however, missing in operations of the Electronics Division.

Defense forces, however, depended mostly on imported electronics. Government-owned defense production units such as the Bharat Electronics Limited (BEL) in Bangalore then manufactured only communication equipment such as transmitters and receivers. The production of first-generation discrete devices at BEL started in 1962. During the same year one private-sector unit—Semiconductors Limited—was set up in Poona (now Pune) to manufacture germanium devices. Though many in the Indian defense establishment were in favor of either direct imports or technical collaboration with foreign companies, Bhabha prevailed in his stance that India should take the route of self-reliance in this field.[5]

The government too recognized that electronics was going to be a strategic sector impacting developments in atomic energy, defense, and communications. With a view to fix the type of shortage in electronics seen during the war with China, Nehru set up an Electronics Committee with Bhabha as chairman in August 1963. The committee was asked to assess the need for electronic equipment in various sectors and identify existing and potential sources of supply. Vikram Sarabhai, director of the Physical Research Laboratory at Ahmedabad, S. Bhagvantam, Scientific Advisor to the Minister of Defence, and A. S. Rao were nominated as members. This was the first time a group of scientists was called in to advise the government in an area that went beyond scientific research and involved industrial production. Until then, electromechanical and electronics production was confined to a handful of state enterprises such as Bharat Electronics Limited, Indian Telephone Industries (ITI), Hindustan Teleprinters Limited (HTL), and Hindustan Cables.

The overarching objective of the Electronics Committee was to prepare a blueprint for the "planned development of electronics, so that the country as a whole may become self-sufficient in this field in the shortest possible time." An attempt for "planned development" of an emerging and technologically dynamic sector such as electronics was a novel idea India was embarking upon. The government acknowledged electronics as "the nervous system of modern technology," which had "assumed an important role in monitoring and controlling the production process in engineering, chemical and metallurgical industries. It is vital for atomic energy, communication and defence."[6] The first exercise to develop national capability in electronics was, thus, initiated with strong strategic and defense implications.

The committee worked for close to three years (1963–1966), which was also the period when computer application activities were at their peak at research centers like TIFR and ISI as well as IITs. Multinational firms, mainly IBM and International Computers Limited (ICL), were expanding their sales and marketing in India, as discussed in detail in chapter 3.

One of the most significant recommendations of the Electronics Committee was that India should avoid the "step-by-step" development of electronics as seen in the advanced world and, instead, should leapfrog. The committee also recognized that building indigenous capability in electronics would require foreign collaboration in some areas. A time frame of ten years was given for development of an indigenous base in electronics that included R&D, design, training, and manufacturing activities. The committee ventured to quantify the numbers of equipment and components needed for different uses—radio receivers, wireless equipment, transmitters, navigational aids, microwave systems, transistors and semiconductors, and computers.

The estimate for the numbers of computers India would need was made on the basis of size and type of systems needed over ten years, by which time the Electronics Committee thought India would become self-sufficient in this field. In the committee's assessment, India needed ten large mainframe computers (such as the CDC 3600), five hundred midsized machines (costing up to five million rupees), and five thousand small computers costing less than half a million rupees each between 1966 and 1976.[7] The committee, however, did not define a midsized computer or a small computer in technology terms but went only by cost. While noting that necessary expertise existed in the country for design and production of analog and special-purpose digital computers, the Electronics Committee indicated India would need to depend on direct imports or foreign collaboration for large high-speed computer systems. It foresaw that computers would be needed for applications in academic research, industry and engineering, planning, weather prediction, space and defense research, inventory and retrieval (census, patents, insurance, library and hospital automation), traffic and scheduling (railways, airports, hotels, ports, etc.), and finance (cost accounting, payroll, purchasing, and banks).[8]

A robust electronics industry was projected as crucial for job creation and economic development of the country, making it a perfect pitch to the political leadership, as a potential wealth creator. The Electronics Committee's report compared the electronics industry with existing manufacturing industries such as steel. The size of electronics production in India in 1965 constituted just 0.15 percent of the gross national product compared to 3.5 percent in Japan, despite the fact that the return on investment in electronics was much higher than in the steel, chemical, or fertilizer industries, the report pointed out. In addition, investment in electronics to the extent outlined in the report could lead to creation of up to 400,000 new jobs. The small size of the industry, the report argued, could be turned into an asset if the early stages experienced in other countries were bypassed and the industry in India was based on the latest ideas and techniques.

The Electronic Committee's final report was ready in December 1965, but before it could be formally handed over to the government, Bhabha was killed in an airplane crash on January 24, 1966, while on his way to Vienna to attend a meeting of the Scientific Advisory Committee of the

International Atomic Energy Agency. The report had been circulated among committee members for review and Bhabha had told his colleagues before leaving for Vienna that he would sign it after his return.

Nehru had passed away in May 1964, after which the relationship between political and scientific leaders had somewhat soured. Lal Bahadur Shastri, who succeeded Nehru, was keen to promote agriculture research that had suffered benign neglect under Nehru. Shastri's tenure was rudely cut short with his death under mysterious circumstances in Tashkent while on an official visit to the Soviet Union. This sudden turn of events cata-pulted Nehru's daughter, Indira Gandhi, to the top job in January 1966. Bhabha had given an impression to his colleagues before proceeding to Vienna that he was looking forward to working with India's political leader-ship with Nehru's daughter at the helm.[9] But India's premier scientist died within a week of the country's first woman prime minister taking her oath of office on January 19, 1966.

With the exit of both prime movers of the electronics plan—Nehru and Bhabha—the onus of the report's implementation fell on Prime Minister Indira Gandhi, who swiftly appointed another Electronics Committee with Bhabha's successor at AEE, Vikram Sarabhai, as chairman. The idea was to outline a plan to begin indigenous production in electronics. It was not an easy task for atomic energy scientists because the subject of electronics had been put under administrative control of the Department of Defence Supplies (DoDS) while Bhabha's committee was at work. Owing to the divergent positions taken by the atomic energy and defense wings in the past, an intense turf war ensued to gain control of an emerging high tech-nology field.

DoDS had its own electronics production unit, BEL, and its leaders con-sidered the work of the two atomic energy-led Electronic Committees to be an academic exercise.[10] This attitude was reflected in the working process of the new committee that also included defense officials. The new Electron-ics Committee often witnessed "increasingly severe conflicts of philosophy, emphasis and interest" during its deliberations.[11] Broadly speaking, defense members of the committee were in favor of importing foreign know-how, while atomic energy scientists wanted industry to develop an "engineering and know-how base" through R&D.

However, the atomic energy group was happy with the success of its elec-tronics division, which was supplying analog computers, control electron-ics, and other equipment for nuclear reactors and other research projects. When the question of starting electronics manufacturing arose, the AEE launched itself into the arena. In 1967 its electronics division was spun off into an independent public enterprise called Electronics Corporation of India Limited (ECIL) in Hyderabad. The formation of ECIL was described by technocrats like M. G. K. Menon and Narasimhan as a perfect example of "government entrepreneurship," which meant commercializing technology developed in a government lab in a government-run enterprise. Such type of entrepreneurship was risk-free as public enterprises operated under government protection.

However, Sarabhai, who was not merely an academic scientist, had a different view. Coming from an influential industrial family in western India, he was well acquainted with how industry worked, having set up a number of chemical and pharmaceutical units. He applied his business acumen and concepts of cost-consciousness and profitability to his scientific endeavors.[12] When ECIL was formed, Sarabhai wanted it to be a commercial entity rather than the prisoner of inward-looking import substitution policy of the government. He believed that export-oriented electronics development would help India close the technology gap with the advanced world.[13] In fact, both Bhabha and Sarabhai were aware that high technology ventures, be they computers or nuclear reactors, could not be pursued in isolation. Early reactor development illustrates this approach. The Canadian-Indian Reactor, U.S. (CIRUS), as the name indicates, was built with technical assistance from Canada and the United States, while the Zero Energy Reactor for Lattice Investigations and New Assemblies (ZERLINA) was based on a design of a similar French heavy-water reactor called Aquilon. While the goal of self-reliance was worth pursuing, scientists felt it could not be achieved in isolation from ideas and technology from outside.

At the time ECIL was formed, the electronics division of AEE was working on the design of a digital computer for real-time applications like the control of nuclear reactors. This was a follow-up of the analog computers ECIL had developed earlier. The group developed logic circuits with the typical signal propagation time of fifty nanoseconds and an expandable memory system with a two microseconds-cycle time. A central processing unit was developed to provide hardware capability to handle a set of forty-five instructions.[14] The work on this system was completed toward the end of 1968, and the R&D information was transferred to ECIL. The system was named the Trombay Digital Computer or TDC-12 (AEE was located in Trombay near Bombay). Technologically, the TDC-12 was superior to the computers developed earlier in India because it was the first to deploy semiconductor devices and consist of standard components. The TDC-12—with a 4k ferrite-core memory and a 12-bit processor—was modeled after the commercially available—and hugely successful—PDP-8 computer of American computer maker, Digital Equipment Corporation (DEC).

TDC-12 represented a unique attempt by a state-run scientific laboratory to put one of its technologies into commercial production. Though
TIFR too had developed an online machine called Online Data Processor
(OLDAP), the group at AEE and later ECIL decided to develop its own version, as it found the TIFR approach to be academic. OLDAP was a near copy
of CDC 160-A, which had been imported along with CDC 3600 by TIFR and
was considered unsuitable for business applications. On the other hand,
TDC-12 had a more flexible design than OLDAP. TIFR scientists were more
interested in doing "path breaking (work) than in developing systems that
were actually required for scientific and other work," noted S. Srikantan,
the first head of the computer group at the ECIL.[15]

Following the launch of TDC-12 in 1969, ECIL came up with a third-
generation computer, TDC-312, and a later 16-bit microcomputer called
TDC-316. TDC-312 was said to be twice as fast as TDC-12 and was priced
much lower. Its size was one-third and power consumption one-fourth that
of TDC-12.[16] In all its computers, ECIL used indigenous components except
certain integrated circuits and core memories. The ECIL team wrote all
software including operating system software. The TDC series established
that modern digital computers could be designed and built in India, but
remained commercially unviable because one could import a correspond-
ing machine at a much lower price. This was because of DAE emphasis on
indigenous development regardless of cost. Most computers manufactured
by ECIL were supplied to atomic energy and defense and other government
labs, and had few commercial users. Subsequent review of ECIL operations
showed that its computers had very few applications packages, making
them unsuitable for business and even scientific applications.[17]

Formation of the Department of Electronics

As an extension of the work with the two Electronic Committees, the atomic
energy group pushed the idea of a new Indian Department for Electronics
to deal with all issues including industrial licensing. Sarabhai petitioned
Indira Gandhi in April 1967 and November 1968 to move the subject of
electronics to either the Department of Atomic Energy (DAE) or the Cabinet Secretariat with technical support coming from DAE.[18] Her top strategic
advisor, Parmeshwar Narain Haksar, agreed with Sarabhai on the need for
a separate high-level policymaking and executive mechanism for electronics. Atomic energy scientists suggested a two-tier structure—an Electronics
Commission (EC) along the lines of the Atomic Energy Commission with
all executive and financial powers and a Department of Electronics (DoE)

as an implementation arm. The idea was endorsed at a national conference on electronics hosted by TIFR in March 1970. Besides indulging in bickering with their defense counterparts, atomic energy scientists projected the newly established ECIL as the "national champion" in the field of computers and electronics.

By now reality had dawned upon the atomic energy community, with many members seeing the goal of total self-reliance in electronics and computers as unachievable within the ten-year time frame proposed in the Bhabha committee report. It was clear to them that everything from design to manufacture could not be attempted locally given the fast-changing nature of electronics and computing technologies. While advanced countries had embraced next-generation integrated circuits and multilayer printed circuit boards, India was still in the process of switching over from valves to transistors. In order to catch up, scientists wanted India's government to adopt "a liberal policy to allow fresh collaborations involving latest technology" and also set up a separate government agency to issue licenses for electronics production.[19] Foreign technical collaboration, the 1970 conference suggested, should be eased to boost local production capabilities while restricting technology imports to organizations with a strong R&D base, so that they could assimilate imported expertise and prevent imports of upgrades.

The domineering group of atomic energy scientists won yet again. The government established the DoE and the EC in 1970 and 1971 respectively, and as a natural corollary, passed on policymaking and implementation functions into the hands of atomic energy group. The new department functioned directly under the Prime Minister, much like DAE. Its secretary reported directly to Indira Gandhi, just as Bhabha used to report to Nehru. Bhabha's successor at TIFR, Mambillikalathil Govind Kumar Menon, was picked by Gandhi to head the new department at the suggestion of Sarabhai.[20] Menon, a solid state physicist, was actively involved in setting up and nurturing computer activity at TIFR.

The formation of the DoE reinforced the strategic importance of electronics against the background of worsening Indo-U.S. relations and another war with Pakistan that resulted in the creation of Bangladesh in 1971. The geopolitical arena had changed a lot since the period of Bhabha and the first Electronics Committee. India had signed a friendship and cooperation treaty with the Soviet Union in 1971, amid strategic ties between China and Pakistan with the United States backing such an alliance. The Nuclear Proliferation Treaty (NPT) had come into force in 1970. The fears of India facing technological sanctions because of its nuclear program were now more real. Technological self-reliance in electronics in the 1970s was more pressing for the government.

Achieving the goal of self-reliance, however, was not easy for the new DoE. Its stated purpose was the government's desire to promote industrial development, but while doing so it had to cater to the sensibilities around the greater use of technology, particularly computers. The overall political climate was not fully supportive of deploying computers for large-scale automation or computerization for fear of loss of jobs. For trade unions and left-wing politicians, computers symbolized loss of jobs and did not fit in the socialist pathway India was treading. When large computers were installed in state-run insurance companies and private mills, there were workers' strikes and computer installations were damaged. The overall industrial policy was in favor of import-substitution industrialization and not the labor-intensive export orientation.

At the same time, use of computers altogether could not be rejected. Industry was in favor of it. Banks, insurance companies, and private mills had been using unit record machines (URMs) and mainframes for a number of years now, primarily for automation of functions like accounting. Computers' use for higher applications such as inventory control, management of production processes, and project management reporting was at a nascent stage. Research organizations used computers for enhancing reliability and speed and to crunch large volumes of research data. Computers were not deployed as a tool for decision making, but merely for repetitive work and data processing tasks.[21] The government view was that automation could be introduced in industry on a selective basis and that technological advances should be regulated to make them consistent with the social good. Government permits for importing computers were subject to clearance from local government leaders, who were concerned about ensuring that the proposed import did not affect the interests of workers.

As a measure to quell mounting opposition to automation from trade unions, a government committee headed by economist Vinayak Mahadev Dandekar was tasked with deciding the criteria for introducing automation in industry. In its report submitted in 1972, the committee concurred that businesses could use computers for applications that were of a repetitive nature, but only after proper justification and prior approval of workers.[22] It also suggested that the state should set up computer centers for use by private companies. Such centers could be established jointly with private operators or solely by private companies only in cases where government-run facilities failed to deliver. The committee ruled that experts should examine individually all proposals for automation in industry. Industry representatives on the committee contended that automation and use of computers was an issue to be settled through an understanding between management and labor unions only.

Development versus Regulation

Self-reliance in electronics was the broad goal of the new DoE. Its mandate was to "make a comprehensive assessment, in both technical and financial terms, of national needs for all electronic products, and integrate such needs into a single overall framework" and "to initiate necessary promotional and regulatory measures required to ensure quality production of electronic equipment at satisfactory prices."[23] While the DoE's stated mission was self-reliance in electronics, the unstated objective was to reduce the influence of multinational corporations like IBM. As an immediate measure, foreign collaborations were restricted to export-oriented ventures and all computer users were told to meet their computing requirements either through locally available computers or state-run shared facilities called Regional Computer Centres (RCCs).[24] These centers were to be modeled after data processing centers run by multinational firms for use of businesses and others on a time-sharing basis. The government-run RCCs were also to act as centers for software development and data processing for national developmental projects.

In a bid to carve out a supreme role for itself, the new department also laid down a framework. For the use of computers, priority was to be given to programs of national importance in industrial and engineering fields, defense, export-oriented activities, and projects that had "a development catalyzing effect" on the economy.[25] Even for such projects, users were first expected to see if their computing requirements could be met with computers available indigenously or by state-run RCCs. Commercial applications did not figure at all in this scheme despite the fact that such applications were driving the computer industry in rest of the world.

Foreign computers were considered expensive items and their import had to be justified based on their relevance to national development. Importing computers for applications such as automation of accounts was discouraged. Applications to be encouraged were design automation, management-decision information systems, data banks, R&D computations, online controls that would directly increase productivity, and computation needed in export firms.[26]

The new policy focus on restricted imports, promotion of local production, and time-sharing operations was directly aimed at reining in the multinational computer makers—IBM and ICL—operating in India at that time. IBM had a near-monopoly of the data processing market in India. On June 1, 1974, the country had 224 computers of which 141 were supplied by IBM, 25 by ICIM (Indian subsidiary of ICL), and 10 by Honeywell.[27] Of the fourteen large computer systems installed in India by 1964, as many as twelve were in research and development organizations. In the next couple of years, about thirty computers were installed for commercial applications. After that, an average of twenty computers was installed every year till 1971.

IBM operations in India had come under scrutiny of several government departments and auditors for alleged irregularities, as elaborated in chapter 3. Atomic energy officials also felt that the company was dumping used machines and outdated technology in India. They were nurturing thoughts that ECIL could take on multinationals. This was a tall order, given the fact that ECIL with its TDC series was only a marginal player, having just 35 out of a total of 224 computer installations in 1974. All of the TDC machines—barring one—had been installed in government agencies such as the atomic energy labs.[28] The government corporation depended exclusively on local components in the early phase, ruling out production of contemporary systems. The shift to imported components later on helped it to bridge the technology gap to some extent. The computers it manufactured were unreliable in field operations due to the lack of modern production techniques and stringent quality control.[29]

The poor showing of ECIL coupled with restrictions on operations of IBM and ICL caused a shortage of computing power in India in the mid-1970s. Business and industry users were desperate to get computers. In order to ease the situation, the DoE decided to permit imports but wanted to control the process. It drew up an elaborate procedure for the "select import" of computers valued at more than 500,000 rupees. The central government in August 1975 designated the DoE as "the primary agency of the government for evaluation and approval" of all data processing equipment and computers required within the government and for import into the country.[30] In a Soviet-style control system, a Central Evaluation and Procurement Agency for Computers was set up within the Computer Directorate of the DoE to "coordinate imports."

The approval procedure was a nightmare. Every prospective computer user had to approach the DoE with a request, along with justification to import a computer. If it was convinced of the need to import the computer in line with "national priorities" as laid down by the Electronics Commission, in principle approval for the import would be given. DoE officials would then finalize configuration of the computer in consultation with the user and float a global tender to invite competitive bids. This would be followed by evaluation of bids by an expert committee. The user also needed to give his or her preferences to the committee, along with reasons for doing so. The experts would submit their report to an approval committee chaired by the EC chairman and with secretaries of other government departments as its members. Only after a nod from this committee could the user import a system.[31]

The different stages involved in this long procedure were: finalization of system specifications, financial and labor approvals, invitation of tenders, user comments, technical evaluation, price negotiations, final approval, finalization of purchase agreement, and placement of order and delivery. The estimated time required for all stages was fourteen to twenty-five months, but in practice it could take up to five years to import one computer. A study of eighty-two cases revealed that it took between one and fifty-four months for completion of evaluation and between six and sixty-four months for complete procurement of a computer.[32] In some cases, trials were conducted to benchmark systems to be imported with other computers. Public-sector companies, national institutions, and universities—and ironically, the DoE's own projects—had to wait for years to import computers. For Tata Consultancy Services—an emerging software player in the 1970s—it took three years to import a medium-sized digital computer for its New Delhi office.[33]

Minicomputers were emerging as a viable alternative to mainframes in the early 1970s, but the DoE allowed neither easy imports nor local production of such systems till 1978. A committee set up by Menon on minicomputers gave its report in 1973 but a policy pronouncement on the subject was made only in 1978. Not only had market conditions changed, but also computer technology had advanced to the next level. The delay appeared to be deliberate as Menon justified later: "If licenses were issued for minicomputer production earlier, companies would have gone in for assembly operations based on imported components. And this would not have been a meaningful operation in terms of foreign exchange outflow till the country had a program to manufacture basic components."[34]

Instead of acting in time to keep pace with market demands and technology, technocrats and scientists in the DoE waited for the technology to mature. The department's defense was that "technology relating to both processor and peripherals for minicomputers was in a state of flux in 1973 when experts gave their report." The department felt that "some stability in technology should emerge before deciding the technological basis and industrial structure on which our minicomputer industry should be built."[35] When technology had matured, the DoE funded "R&D projects on minimum range of peripherals and software needed for minicomputers, instead of issuing manufacturing licenses, so as to prepare the required base for an Indian minicomputer industry.[36]

While users were hungry for minicomputers and manufacturers were waiting for licenses, the DoE encouraged makers of electronic calculators to diversify into interim products such as microprocessor-based programmable calculators, cash registers, and accounting and invoicing machines.[37] Clearly, the thrust of DoE policies was a step-by-step approach rather than leapfrogging when technology was changing fast. This approach was diametrically opposite to what Bhabha had envisaged.

Eventually local companies were permitted to design and assemble computers using imported components but foreign collaboration was still not allowed. A production ceiling was fixed, in line with the prevailing industrial policy. No manufacturer was permitted to exceed annual turnover of twenty million rupees, effectively limiting production to fifty to sixty machines a year.[38] Each licensed firm was to be monitored and subjected to review every two years. Large computer systems could be imported but only after a strict technical review. All these restrictions, along with an impending shift to next-generation technology, effectively meant premature death of the minicomputer industry. By the time the DoE was ready to let Indians have minicomputers, the world had moved on to microcomputers and was close to the revolutionary era of personal computers or PCs.

The decision-making process was a long, drawn-out affair because Secretary Menon positioned the DoE as a scientific department like space and atomic energy. Policymaking of any consequence was based on a scientific approach—first studying the issue; discussing its different aspects among scientists; setting up a committee, if necessary; studying the committee report; and then taking a decision.[39] Such an approach delayed import of computers and also slowed the growth of the electronics and computing industry in its formative years. "In a country like India, the approach to computerization has to be very selective and that is why everything is officially controlled," was Menon's meek response to criticism in 1977.[40]

Menon cannot be solely blamed for unleashing an overly controlled regime. The actions of the DoE and the EC should be seen in the overall political and economic environment in which they operated. Indira Gandhi had taken a populist approach to economic policies—partly to improve her position in the Congress Party following the party split in 1969 so that she could win the elections on her own. The nationalization of private banks, trade controls, laws to curb private monopolies, and foreign exchange regulation are all examples of such measures. The foreign exchange became scarce following the oil shock of 1973 and could not be used for importing computers. The controlled economy regime—enforced through laws like the Monopolies and Restrictive Trade Practices (MRTP) Act and the Foreign Exchange Regulation Act (FERA)—meant that every industrial conglomerate had to obtain a plethora of government approvals for expanding production or establishing new capacity. Production had to be capped according to the ceiling fixed by the government. Such laws, coupled with restrictions on foreign capital and technology as well as high import duties on capital goods, effectively scuttled private enterprise and industrial growth. While public enterprises remained inefficient and unprofitable, private companies could hardly achieve any economies of scale.

The fact that Indira Gandhi had to depend on the support of the communist parties made any change in trade and industry-related policies difficult. As Menon, in retrospect, explained: "We were not the government. We were only a part of it. We were not the Parliament. It is Parliament that lays the route in which the country should go." He claims he favored a less-controlled regime with no caps on production capacities but could not find support from Gandhi.[41] In addition to the difficult political economy, the field of electronics itself was changing fast and these changes were taking place elsewhere, not in India.

The situation at the end of 1979, the Review Committee on Electronics pointed out, was one that "stifled initiative and enterprise of entrepreneurs and self-employed technocrats by subjecting them to time-consuming procedures and multi-channel scrutiny. Even when objectives such as limiting the growth of monopoly or dominance of multinationals did not come into play, proposals for computer import by industry were subject to needless and rigid control, strangling growth and causing frustration."[42]

The emphasis on self-reliance through excessive regulation and "uneconomic and arbitrary" limits fixed on production capacities were not conducive for industrial growth, the review observed.[43] Priority should have been given to minicomputer- and microprocessor-based systems with flexibility in the import of components. The committee suggested rational measures like duty-free import of certain components and subassemblies and higher duties for imported systems. It also proposed that software firms be allowed to import computers if they promise to export software worth a predefined value—a path-breaking recommendation that enabled the birth of the Indian software industry in the late 1970s and early 1980s. In Indian trade jargon, such an arrangement is called "export obligation."

Silver Lining in Dark Clouds

The objective of the DoE was to promote the electronics development needed for national programs in atomic research, space, and defense. Its thrust, however, was not on innovation and new technology development but on import substitution. This approach overlooked factors such as economic viability, volume production, availability of capital goods and tools as well as the threat of technology obsolescence—all necessary considerations in building an industrial base in electronics. Although the intention of overgrown electronics administration in the 1970s was to nurture India's indigenous electronics industry, it also meant concentration of government authority in a few hands. Multiple layers of applications processing and decision making were created.

The electronics department was mandated to be a developmental, promotional, and regulatory body. As far as the three core sectors were concerned—atomic energy, space, and defense—it was generously developmental and promotional. It doled out a large number of R&D grants in these sectors to research institutes and IITs. These projects led to development of skills and capabilities in those areas. However, in areas other than the core ones, the regulatory side of the DoE was overbearing. Commercial data processing and computers, where the government was largely dealing with needs of private companies, are examples of overzealous regulation.

The computer needs of government departments, mainly DAE, were met by ECIL. Those who did not want to go in for the ECIL systems—which in any case were nonstandard and unsuitable for commercial applications— were subjected to regulation perhaps unheard of in democratic governance: a centralized procurement system that required any company wishing to acquire a computer to let the government determine its configuration, vendor, price, and other conditions of purchase. The hapless importer could only sit and watch this whole procedure. This was so because the DoE did not consider the computer as a piece of office equipment or a tool for productivity enhancement, but as a symbol of power—computing power.

Menon's stint in the DoE was marked by several technology and critical infrastructure development projects, though the industry may have been unhappy over delays in importing computers and curtailment of local production capacities. Important national institutions were founded—the National Informatics Centre (NIC) to meet the informatics and computer applications needs of the central government departments and state governments; and the National Centre for Software Development and Computing Techniques (NCSDCT, which was later renamed National Centre for

Software Technology) to develop software techniques and train software technologists. States were encouraged to establish electronics development corporations, which triggered industrial activity in many of them.

Some of the national projects were executed with assistance from the United Nations Development Program. The UNDP provided financial and technical assistance for a number of IT-related projects, besides NIC and NCSDCT. These included the Education and Research in Computer Networking program, for which $6 million was given.

The end of Menon's tenure was followed by political turbulence in India as well as sweeping changes in technology in the computer industry globally. The arrival of the personal computer and the unbundling of software and hardware led to the advent of software as a separate business. The departure of IBM and licensing of Indian companies to make minicomputers, coupled with the arrival of other international computer firms, brought some dynamism in the sector. Restrictions on import of computers and software continued, along with giving primacy to public sector companies like ECIL. All this was somewhat stifling for private sector initiatives. The needs of commercial users were ignored altogether, while government agencies like DoDS with experience of electronics production were kept out of decision making.

Menon's most significant achievement was giving electronics a separate identity in the policymaking apparatus of India's central government, taking it out of the purview of the defense production and statistics departments. The situation might have been different had electronics and computers remained under the control of these two entities. Furthermore, Menon took a tough stand on the "As Is" programs of IBM and ICL and also conceived the idea of a Computer Maintenance Corporation (CMC) to take care of the maintenance of systems left behind by IBM. The refurbishing program of the two companies was terminated at the insistence of the DoE. Chapter 3 discusses this development in detail.

3 The Rise, Fall, and Rise of IBM

IBM thought that the Government of India machinery and the business and industry machinery would collapse if they walked out of India. This was their biggest folly. . . . They thought that the machines [they had installed] would collapse, nobody would be able to maintain, and the government would come on their knees and say, "Okay, please stay." Nations don't work like that.

—Om Prakash Mehra, Regional Manager, IBM World Trade Corporation India, 1977[1]

Calcutta was not only the birthplace of the earliest indigenous computers, it was also the entry point for computer multinationals. IBM World Trade Corporation (IBM WTC), a subsidiary of IBM Inc. that handled business outside the United States and Canada, started its India operations through a marketing and support office in Calcutta in 1951. A card manufacturing unit in Bombay followed a couple of years later to cater to the punched-cards requirement of IBM's data processing installations in India and other Asian markets.

A newly independent nation seeking to develop infrastructure and setting up heavy industries appeared to be high on the agenda of IBM WTC Chairman Arthur K. Watson. He first visited India in 1953, and among his various engagements was a formal dinner with employees at the Grand Hotel in Calcutta.[2] During his second visit in 1959, Watson met Prime Minister Nehru and inked an agreement to take up manufacturing in India.[3] This led to commencement of manufacturing operations in Bombay in addition to the punched-cards-making unit operational there. It would make India the eighth country in the world to have an IBM manufacturing operation. Previously, all commercial activities of IBM in India were based on imports. Nehru evinced personal interest in IBM's activities in India in the formative years and met the first batch of Indian recruits at the end of their IBM training program in August 1961 (figure 3.1).

Figure 3.1
India's first Prime Minister Jawaharlal Nehru with the first batch of IBM system engineers who got certificates from him on completion of their training in 1961. IBM was the first company to introduce commercial data processing and computing in India and was invited by Nehru himself to start business in the country soon after India won independence. Courtesy: Satendra (Dan) Gupta

Given stringent foreign exchange regulations in India, it was difficult for IBM to import punched cards or card stock for their production in sufficient quantities.[4] This forced IBM to explore other innovative options to ensure a steady supply of punched cards to its customers. Foreign exchange generated through data processing business was used to import special presses for manufacturing punched cards. The raw material for making punched cards was bamboo pulp available in plenty in northeast India. Cards made from this source were strong enough but did not have the rigidity or tensile strength of the usual IBM punched cards. India's version was slightly thicker too. That meant the feed throats of IBM punched-cards machines had to be adjusted to accommodate bamboo-made cards in the Bombay unit. In the end, the card operation was hugely successful, churning out some four hundred million cards annually within three years.[5] With the addition of high-speed rotary presses, the annual capacity reached 750 million cards by 1971.

The company established a full-scale Training and Education Center near New Delhi after it signed up its first Indian customer—Esso Standard Eastern Limited—for an IBM 1401. The machine had been introduced in U.S. markets in October 1959. The transistor-based system integrated all functions of data processing—stored program capability, high-speed card input/output, magnetic tape input/output, high-speed printing, and arithmetic and logical ability. It was a huge advance over the widely used electro-mechanical URMs. A 1401 was typically deployed for functions such as payroll accounting, sales and receivables accounting, and inventory accounting. This machine would come to dominate the Indian computer arena over the next two decades.

Over the next five years, IBM imported new 1400 series computers and 1620s for a small number of customers like Burmah Shell, Air-India, IIT Kanpur, University of Delhi, Roorkee Engineering College, Bombay University, Physical Research Laboratory (PRL) and Ahmedabad Textile Industry Research Association. PRL used the 1620 for advanced projects in space research, cosmic rays research, and ionospheric physics. It subsequently acquired System/360, which took fifty seconds to solve a problem in theoretical nuclear physics compared to five hours taken by the 1620.[6] A System/360 Model 44 installed at the Indian Institute of Science in Bangalore helped scientists solve problems relating to organic chemistry, x-rays and crystal structure analysis, fluid dynamics, heat transfers, diffusion, analysis of atmospheric data, design of microwave components, and optical data processing.[7] A similar computer was deployed at the Space Science and Technology Centre at Thumba for "measurement of rocket performance parameters by static testing, pressure testing of motor chambers, wind tunnel and rocket sled measurements on rocket models, measurement of aerodynamic heating by sock tube," among such tasks.[8]

The Rise of IBM

In the early 1960s, major customers, mostly top research institutions, universities, and government-owned companies, were supplied the new and latest machines imported from America. Manufacturing activity of IBM was limited to punched cards and reconditioning of punched-cards equipment for existing users. The Bombay unit's operation was expanded in 1963 to include manufacturing of data-entry hardware called 029 Key Punch and 129 Card Data Recorder for exports to IBM units in Southeast Asia.

A significant addition to IBM's Bombay unit was assembly of 1401s as the Indian market began to expand. The operation involved reconditioning old and discarded 1401s in advanced markets and renting them out to Indian users. The India branch earned 85 percent export entitlement, which meant it could use 85 percent of its export earnings to import disassembled 1401s and peripherals for reconditioning and renting or leasing to customers in India. The activity was permitted to allow Indian users to pay lease charges in local currency—the Indian rupee. A major flaw in this arrangement, however, was that IBM Bombay unit was importing used machines with zero book value. Such machines were referred to as "As Is" and "Refurbished" machines in government records, but IBM officials preferred to call them "Rebuilt" or "Reassembled" machines. In any case, these were not new machines.

It was not only in India that IBM was doing this, nor was IBM alone in following this practice. This was the norm prevailing in the computer industry in developing countries, probably as insurance against obsolescence. First, IBM resorted to this because the number of machines needed was very small, which did not justify investment in full-fledged local manufacturing. Second, the rate of obsolescence was very high in U.S. and European computer markets. When IBM was bringing in old URMs into India, they had already been replaced by 1401s in the United States. IBM started bringing in old 1401s in 1967–1968, when this model was outdated and replaced by the System/360, which had more than double its processing power. With new versions coming in and plenty of used 1401s available in the United States, the company decided to bring the old models to India and other such markets. Third, the sales strategy of offering computers on lease, rather than outright sale, adopted by multinational computer firms, allowed them to circulate discarded machines from one part of the world to another (figure3.2).

Soon after IBM began its "manufacturing operation" in India and recruited sales, support, and maintenance staff, the number of URMs and 1401s started swelling in India. Huge sales were recorded in the Western region that had a concentration of corporate firms, large manufacturing units, and financial institutions. Refurbished and recycled 1401s were supplied to oil companies, banks, insurance companies, public utilities, textile mills, steel plants, and airlines in several Indian cities. The list of customers read like a Who's Who of Indian business, industry, and public sector enterprises of the 1960s—Bombay Dyeing, Calico Hindoostan, Morarji Goculdas, Khatau Mills, Century Mills, Empire Dyeing, State Bank of India, Life Insurance Corporation of India, General Insurance Corporation, Brihanmumbai Electric Supply and Transport Undertaking, Ahmedabad Electricity Company, Indian Airlines, DCM Mills, Escorts Limited, and so on. After

Figure 3.2
IBM engineers giving a demonstration of the IBM 1401 computer to Prime Minister Nehru during his visit to the IBM training center in Faridabad in 1963.While nurturing computer design activities by Indian groups, Nehru was open to induction of foreign technology. Courtesy: Satendra (Dan) Gupta

winning over scientific and academic institutions, IBM had conquered a bulk of commercial data processing market in India within a short span of time.

The company's largest customer in India was the Indian Railways (IR).[9] In 1963, the Railways signed a deal with IBM to install URMs in all seven of its zones. The use of these machines continued in the Railways till the production unit of IBM started churning out reconditioned 1401s in 1967. Three of them were installed in the zonal offices at Calcutta (Eastern and South Eastern zones) and Guwahati (Northeast Frontier zone). By 1971, IR was said to be the largest computer user in India having fourteen computer centers—one in the Railway Board office, one in every zonal headquarters, one in Mugal Sarai yard, and one each in the three production units. These were all 1401 computers. The computer at the Railway Board office in New Delhi was connected to all major broad gauge inter-railway interchange points, through a national teleprinter network. Some of the applications research projects Railways pursued related to developing train running rules, marshalling yard simulation, locomotive utilization, and other research projects aimed at improving efficiency.

It was IBM's philosophy to work very closely with its customers. "I rather liked working with IR and almost considered myself part of their team," recalled Joe Cleetus, systems engineer assigned to the computer center at the Railway Board.[10] Another contemporary in Bombay, K. R. Trilokekar, noted, "Our association with customers was well respected and recognized by them. The department where IBM's data processing equipment was housed on customer premises was known as the "IBM Department.'"[11] This appeared to be a deliberate practice to inculcate among users a sense of dependence on IBM's machines, as Om Prakash Mehra, a PhD from the University of Wisconsin who was Branch Manager first in Calcutta and then in Bombay, recalled: "I said wherever we have our machines, we must push psychologically or by request that the EDP (electronic data processing) department be called the IBM Section. Later this became a common practice. We did so because earlier this section was called the Hollerith Section."[12] EDP departments in companies having ICL machines were named Hollerith Section.

ICL was IBM's sole competitor during the 1960s. The British firm was specifically formed to counter the growing influence of IBM in data processing markets in the UK and the Commonwealth. In India, it began its manufacturing operations in 1963 through a fully owned subsidiary, International Computers Indian Manufacturing Company Limited (ICIM), building on existing marketing efforts. ICL, like IBM, manufactured peripherals—nonprinting key punches, verifiers, duplicators, and interpreters—at its Poona facility for export markets. It was also permitted to use its export earnings to import used machines like the 1004, 1902, and 1903 for resale in India. ICIM had a contract with the defense public sector unit in Bangalore, Bharat Electronics Limited (BEL), for assembling computer systems.

The rentals charged by IBM were steep. A study of computerization in the Western region (which had a high density of computers) in the 1960s showed that the annual rental of a medium-sized computer with its peripheral equipment ranged from $32,500 to $39,000. The cost of maintenance was about $13,000 a year. The average yearly maintenance for some models from Honeywell and Minsk, which cost less than IBM and ICL machines, was $10,000.[13] The rental fee charged by IBM included maintenance for a fixed number of machine hours per month. The company's engineers also helped customers in designing and developing applications, besides helping in other tasks such as recruitment of personnel for programming and operations.

In 1970s when multinational companies were installing mainframe computers like IBM 1401 and ICL 1901 in India at very high rentals, equivalent minicomputers were available in developed markets at much lower prices. In 1975, a computer slightly more powerful than the 1401 was available at $1,200, while IBM in India charged $20,000 or more as annual rental for similar machines.[14] When IBM's marketing executives would confront their senior managers on the issue of high rentals being charged for used "reconditioned" machines, they would be told that the company was charging for the service and not the machine.[15]

IBM could succeed in marketing its outdated systems in India because no institutional framework existed in the 1960s to guide the introduction of computers in government departments and state-run companies. In many cases, ministries and other agencies, which leased machines from IBM or ICIM, had little say in the choice of configuration and features as they lacked necessary expertise. Expensive hardware was bought or leased without proper analysis of needs, identification of priorities, and coordination with other departments, mainly due to the pressure of having a "computer facility" available and the enthusiasm of individual officials. This resulted in the creation of islands of automation within the government, an analysis later revealed.[16]

The growing use of computers in the government sector without a formal policy gave rise to the suspicion that it was a direct consequence of aggressive marketing tactics of multinational companies. IBM was said to be in the practice of hiring well-educated and connected people for various positions, paying them handsome salaries. The company's public relations exercises included luxurious seminars for prospective customers, media reports of the period alleged.[17] This was also the perception in official circles as echoed later by M. G. K. Menon, that "somehow they (IBM) had tremendous influence on a lot of our senior people in educational institutions, defense, banks, airlines. They followed the traditional pattern of offering people trips abroad (to government officials), employing their children, and so on."[18]

The use of computers in large government utilities and private mills caused a backlash against automation. IBM consciously started strengthening its image and cultivating influential people in 1967 when its managers felt that people in the government, trade unions, and the press were misunderstanding its role. Workers led by fiery labor leader George Fernandes in Bombay were staging protests against the installation of computers. IBM, therefore, decided to hire Kanwar Rajendra Singh, a journalist with *Hindustan Times*, as a public relations officer in 1967 to handle all its external communication and image building.[19] He cultivated journalists and organized educational talks and workshops on the benefits of using computers for them. This helped create a positive buzz about IBM with favorable stories about its activities appearing in newspapers. The PR office was also deployed to counter the impression among workers' unions that computers were meant to replace human workers, causing job loss. IBM sponsored a trip to India of Joe Glazer, a U.S. trade union activist and avid computer user, who delivered lectures on the benefits of computers.[20] The PR office also regularly organized seminars for EDP managers and government officials and held events like photography and art exhibitions.

Beginning of the Fall

IBM had a good run of the Indian market for two decades following its entry in 1951. Bringing in discarded machines, refurbishing them locally, and leasing them out to Indian users was a profitable business, as marketing executives of the period would recollect. Shashi Ullal, who worked in the Western region of IBM India, recalled how "the company imported used machines which probably would have been dumped here at $100 or $200 c.i.f. (cost, insurance, freight). They used to rent one of such machines—say, an accounting machine, for the rupee equivalent of one thousand dollars per month. I would call it profiteering, considering the fact that we had 70–80 percent share of the market."[21]

The first signs of trouble for IBM appeared in the wake of devaluation of the Indian currency by 57.5 percent in response to the unfavorable balance of payments in June 1966. This devaluation first turned out to be a windfall for IBM, but soon landed it in deep trouble. The lease agreement signed by IBM with its customers prior to rupee devaluation had prices quoted in dollars (though the payment had to be made in rupees) even for products that were "manufactured" in India with condition that "all payments are required to be made in Indian Rupee at the official exchange rate." As a consequence of this clause, prices of all machines leased under such agreements went up overnight, increasing the liability of IBM customers substantially.

The Comptroller and Auditor General of India (CAG) spotted this glaring anomaly in contracts during a routine audit of the Railway accounts in April 1968. The auditor pointed out to the government that IBM quoting prices in dollars for products manufactured in India was not justified.

The government soon discovered that many government departments were paying huge sums of money to IBM because of this irregularity. It was found that IBM was quoting maintenance charges also in dollars. In addition, it had increased prices of locally made items as well as maintenance by 57.5 percent on the pretext of the devaluation of the rupee. Normally prices of products made with indigenous content should not have been hiked after the devaluation. Following a reprimand from the Commerce Ministry, IBM agreed to return to the Railways part of the additional money it had collected up to December 31, 1968. At the same time, it tried to justify price hikes on the grounds that its data processing business in India had been making cumulative losses since 1951 and that it was returning the money only as a gesture of goodwill.[22] Obviously, the computing giant did not want to be seen as bowing to pressures from the Indian government.

More skeletons tumbled out in the final audit report of Railways for 1971–1972. CAG noted that the utility had leased URMs and other equipment from IBM without analyzing the need for such equipment, resulting in their underutilization. More seriously IBM had billed the Railways an inflated amount of 3,712 rupees ($490) for each Disc Pack, while the prices disclosed by the firm in the bills of entry to Indian customs ranged between $66 and $69 and had been assessed to be no more than $125 each. This matter was also raised in the Indian Parliament and referred to its Public Accounts Committee for further investigation.

While investigation continued into its post-devaluation price hikes, IBM applied for a new industrial license in December 1968 to market its System/360 series of computers. The Department of Industrial Development sought the opinion of the Electronics Committee chaired by Vikram Sarabhai. The committee set conditions for IBM to continue its operations without altering its ownership pattern and system of export obligation. First, the company was asked to slash the price of the System/360 series because Indian officials felt "such computers would have outlived their technological and commercial usefulness" by the time they were imported into India. Second, IBM was not to link the sale of its computers with maintenance contracts and supply of spare parts. It was to allow its Indian customers to service their own machines and maintain their own inventory of spares. Third, IBM was to establish a fully owned or jointly owned company for software development activity in India.[23]

This was the first time an Indian government agency was trying to set terms for IBM. This must have been a cause of further discomfiture for IBM, which was used to deciding both the level of computer technology it wanted to bring to Indian markets and the commercial terms for doing so.

The operations of both IBM and ICL came under another level of scrutiny during the hearings held by the Committee on Automation, which was set up by the Ministry of Labor, Employment and Rehabilitation in 1969 to establish criteria for automation in industry, particularly the use of computers. The committee noted that the computers IBM and ICIM sold in India were "obsolete in the sense that either they belong to a distinctly earlier technology in terms of hardware and software design or they are no longer in production."[24] As a follow-up to the audit report by CAG, the government decided in July 1973 to examine the costs of leases and maintenance charged by IBM and ICIM, including export/import prices and intercompany pricing, through an inter-ministerial working group. The group reported in July 1974 that there was a prima facie case for reduction in leasing rates by 25–30 percent and recommended that the DoE should discuss the matter with the two companies to reduce the rates as of January 1969.

In 1973, the government amended the Foreign Exchange Regulation Act (FERA) to regulate foreign equity, in response to the oil shock. It was aimed at conserving foreign exchange resources and ensuring its utilization for economic development of the country. The law required foreign companies working in India with more than 40 percent foreign equity to obtain fresh approval from the Reserve Bank of India (RBI) to continue their operations. This gave the DoE a legal mechanism to leash multinational firms. It promptly recommended that IBM and ICIM should be told to cease their trading activities over the next two years, while diluting their equity levels from 100 to 40 percent. Both the firms approached RBI and were allowed to continue operations for another two years, subject to the condition that they would finally dilute their equity.

In the meantime, the Public Accounts Committee (PAC) of the Indian Parliament—to which the matter had been referred after the CAG audit—gave a preliminary report in which it observed "the firm (IBM) has been imposing its own terms and conditions on the government." This became the ground for the committee to launch a full-scale inquiry into the functioning of IBM and ICIM in November 1975. Representatives from twenty-five government departments, ministries, and agencies deposed before it. A 435-page report was presented to the Parliament on April 28, 1976, by its chairman Hirendra Nath Mukherjee, a member of the Communist Party of India, which was an ally of the Congress Party of Prime Minister Indira Gandhi.

The PAC report held IBM guilty of unfair practices and fraud. It observed that "IBM, with its near-monopoly position in India, has defrauded the country of enormous revenues by resorting to various unfair practices like transfer pricing under the garb of inter-company billing system, misuse of import entitlements, exaggerated claims of drawback, underpayment of excise duty, exaggerated claims of depreciation, development rebate, head office expenses, etc."[25] All these practices, it noted, had enabled the firm to reap high profits at the cost of the exchequer as well as the technological development of the country.

The import entitlement facility given to IBM to the extent of 85 percent of its export earnings, PAC noted, made it possible for the company to "dump in India what was largely junk," that which had hardly any market value elsewhere in the world. Such business practices helped IBM earn "excessively high profits without making any substantial or significant contribution towards India's attainment of self-reliance in critical areas of computers."[26] IBM was also found to be claiming huge tax exemptions under "head office expenses," amounting to as much as 78 percent of the book profits. In 1974, the company made a voluntary disclosure that it had made excess claims on head office expenses from 1966 to 1970 to the extent of $450,000 and submitted amended tax returns.

Rental income made up for 61.10 percent of operating revenue of IBM in 1969, which fell to 53.39 percent in 1974. Only 9 percent of its income in India was derived from data processing operations in 1974. Both IBM and ICL were indulging in under-invoicing. Huge differences were found in the prices shown by IBM to customs and what it charged from its Indian customers and users.[27] Similarly, tax treatment of "As Is" machines was arbitrary. Serious gaps were found, as refurbishing of these junk machines was treated as manufacturing activity by various departments, including the income tax department.

IBM was reluctant to stop marketing its obsolete machines in India, offering only small concessions in response to the mounting pressure. When its plan to introduce System/360 series computers was rejected by the DoE on the grounds of obsolescence, it conveyed to the government in 1971 its willingness to manufacture 370s in India. When the pressure to dilute its equity mounted, the proposal was revised in 1974 with new offers like an export-oriented unit to manufacture computer peripherals and dilution of equity in data centers and card manufacturing. In 1976, it made a proposal that included a plan to set up a software development laboratory for 100 percent export. IBM said half of these exports would be done through local Indian companies. In response to the demand for transfer of technology, IBM offered to "license all its patents (related to components and subassemblies for peripherals) to Indian companies at a royalty of less than one percent," according to Dan Gupta, a top executive of IBM in India then.[28]

The 1976 proposal included an offer to split Indian operations in two—one for card manufacturing and data center services with 60 percent Indian equity as required under FERA; and the other for fully owned export-oriented manufacturing. In the export unit, IBM wanted export "entitlement" to retain 80 percent export earnings and use it to import computers to be sold to India in rupees. However, IBM did not want to dilute its equity in its marketing and maintenance business, which the company considered its core strength globally.

All the while, IBM was talking to officials appointed by the Electronics Commission to informally negotiate with the company. As this process was not making any headway, EC Chairman Menon appointed his confidant Seshagiri to conduct informal dialogue with IBM to avoid its exit from India. Given the unfavorable political atmosphere, these talks were kept under wraps. Seshagiri worked out a compromise formula that would let IBM remain in India and at the same time ensure conditions of the foreign exchange law could be fulfilled.[29] He proposed that IBM set up a fully owned company for manufacturing equipment and software for export and a 40 percent owned company (as required under FERA) with a non-IBM name to carry out Indian operations. The two companies, in turn, would be subsidiaries of a fully owned holding company. This would have saved the day for both IBM and the government. The government could then say that Indian operations were only 40 percent IBM-owned as required under FERA rules, while IBM could have continued to have 100 percent control over its Indian operations through a holding company.

While on an official trip to New York to attend a UN meeting, Seshagiri informally discussed the proposal with senior officials of IBM Americas/Far East who gave a positive response. Back in New Delhi, a follow-up meeting took place with the general manager of IBM India, T. Brian Finn, but he stuck to the "no dilution of equity" stand taken by the company all along.[30] It is possible he did not have the go-ahead from the headquarters to negotiate on this issue.

Some senior executives of IBM India got the impression that Finn had come to India with a brief to close down local operations, as all hopes of an agreement with the government had failed. This assessment gained credence due to some of Finn's actions like announcing a voluntary retirement scheme (called the Special Opportunity Plan) in early 1977. However, executives close to Finn pointed out that he made all efforts to rescue the situation. The reason for Finn's tough stand in final negotiations with the DoE may have had something to do with the falling clout of IBM India in the company's headquarters due to certain unethical dealings by Finn's predecessor Alex Taylor. Versions given by senior executives of the period indicate that Taylor had favored an Indian realtor and other suppliers.[31] Gordon R. Williamson, then president of IBM Americas/Far East Corporation, however, recounts that Taylor was shunted out of India for making a donation of $5,000 to the Congress Party in violation of the company's business practices.[32]

The Department of State was kept in the loop about the negotiations IBM was holding with the Indian government about the future of its operations. Ralph Pfeiffer, chairman of IBM Americas and Far East, told State Department officials in Washington prior to his visit to New Delhi in April 1976 that IBM was prepared to be reasonable, but was not willing to stay in India at any cost. Size of operation ($25 million) and annual profit ($1 million) were not significant enough for it to compromise on what it considered its basic business principles. The strategy drawn for Pfeiffer's visit to New Delhi was "to try to talk reasonably with M. G. K. Menon and others without acrimony or ultimatums. If this ploy fail[ed] he [would] return within a month to try to see Mrs. Gandhi or Finance Minister Subramanian in last attempt to negotiate agreement whereby IBM can remain in India on acceptable terms."[33] State Department officials were of the view that "India wanted IBM to remain in India, but on Government of India terms" and that the position of IBM as a major transnational operating in the country "was likely to prejudice IBM efforts to obtain a reasonable concession."[34]

Although both the government and IBM had hardened their positions considerably by the end of 1976, some hope was still lingering. This hope turned into potential opportunity for IBM when Indira Gandhi's Congress Party was defeated in parliamentary polls in 1977. A newly formed pro-socialist Janata Party, formed by the merger of four parties opposed to Indira Gandhi, came to power. Several longstanding critics of Indira Gandhi became government ministers. Among them was George Fernandes, a trade union leader who had led anti-computer workers in Bombay in the 1960s. He was nominated communications minister but soon shifted to the industry ministry. In the run up to the elections and later as a minister, Fernandes had declared that India did not need "foreign technology for making brassieres and tooth paste." He was particularly targeting Coca-Cola, and wanted the multinational to share its so-called secret formula if it wished to continue operations in India. By then, a few multinationals had already made their intentions known to cease their operations in India rather than dilute their equity to meet the provisions of FERA.

The technology import restrictions imposed during the tenure of Indira Gandhi were reflective of the shift in India's stance toward foreign investment beginning in 1969. The thinking that India needed foreign technology and not foreign capital had led to the cap on foreign investment to 40 percent and rules discouraging foreign technology in certain areas, repetitive imports, restrictive clauses in collaboration agreements, and management control of foreign companies in their joint ventures in India.[35] This shift, in effect, marked the end of the Nehruvian era of a liberal attitude toward foreign investment that had attracted multinationals like IBM to India.

Soon after the change in government, IBM had begun making contacts at the highest level hoping for a review of its case under FERA. Pfeiffer and Finn met the new Prime Minister Morarji Desai twice in 1977 but he gave no assurance on any exemption from the foreign equity cap.[36] Desai directed IBM officials to Industry Minister Fernandes when they met him for a second time. The meeting with the minister turned out to be decisive. This is how Fernandes described the meeting later: "IBM was very cocky. They went to the extent of telling me that they have refused to accept what the French President, General Charles de Gaulle, had told them (to dilute their equity). So I told them, 'if you think the General succumbed to you, I am telling you that I am not succumbing to you. You get out.' Yes, I said 'You get out.'"[37] In any case, he said, in his view computers deployed by IBM were taking away jobs of Indian workers.

A news report in the *New York Times* on October 1, 1977, quoted IBM officials saying the demand of diluting equity in marketing and after-sales service operations was unacceptable.[38] IBM Chairman Frank T. Cary blamed the Indian government for forcing the company to close its Indian operations.[39] The firm decided to sell its rented computers to customers over the next three months while disposing of data center services, card manufacturing, and data processing maintenance operations.[40] IBM officially exited from India on June 1, 1978.

On a visit to the United States during June 1978, Prime Minister Desai, fielding questions on the IBM dispute, asserted that the company had left on its own and that the government did not ask it to fold up.[41] Desai did not link IBM's leaving with the foreign exchange law, but said it had more to do with its unwillingness to share its technology. For him it was an issue of India's dependence on foreign technology. Desai was probably echoing the stand taken by policymakers like Menon, who would recall later, "I had any number of discussions with them, trying to persuade them to manufacture in India, train people here, because this system of leasing and maintenance meant we remain dependent on them. It was like hiring a car. But they were not prepared to do any of these things."[42]

IBM believed till the end the government would make an exception, according to accounts given by insiders. Saurabh Srivastava, then working in the corporate office of IBM India, explained, "Since they had 80 percent of the market, there was an air of arrogance. Government was responsible because it was too rigid. There wasn't enough trust on both sides."[43] Some commentators believed that the Indian government was unnecessarily inflexible while dealing with IBM. By rejecting IBM's 1976 proposals, they felt that India lost the opportunity to host new services, an export unit, as well as its standards-setting services.[44] However, disclosures about efforts made by the DoE to find a solution while maintaining a tough public posture show that the government was willing to accommodate IBM's concerns. Top management of IBM also understood the Indian government's stand.

Life after IBM

Fears had begun to be expressed about the future of IBM installations across India while the issue of foreign equity was lingering. This was because maintenance of URMs and mainframes was a key component of the company's operations. Servicing of existing machines, in the event of IBM folding up, was causing concern among its customers as well as the DoE. The centralized import policy had led to delays and a shortage of computer systems. In order to ease the situation and bring in new technology, import of computers by expatriate Indians was permitted. It was thought that along with the computers some expertise would also come in. In all, eleven import licenses were issued and five new 1401s were imported. The Indian office of IBM installed these imported systems but refused to provide maintenance services since these machines had been imported directly. This way the company also wished to send a signal to the government that its existing as well as imported systems would meet the same fate if it was forced to close down its operations in India.

This is how an IBM insider O. P. Mehra saw the situation: "IBM thought that the Government of India machinery and the business and industry machinery would collapse if they walked out of India. This was their biggest folly. All the railways were on IBM, steel plants were on IBM, both the airlines were on IBM, [a] substantial part of Life Insurance Corporation was on IBM, defense was considerably on IBM. They thought that these machines [they had installed] would collapse, nobody would be able to maintain, and the government would come on their knees and say, "Okay, please stay." Nations don't work like that."[45]

The five directly imported IBM 1401s were installed at commercial data centers in Bombay for use on a time-sharing basis. It was a high-cost operation for owners of these centers—the total cost of each computer and import duties was about $35,000. For one hour of computer time, users had to cough up the rupee equivalent of $100. Owners of these five systems panicked when IBM India refused to provide maintenance services, saying these computers were imported directly and not through the Indian unit. They came together and made a unique offer to Ramesh D. Grover, a senior maintenance engineer of IBM. He was offered the equivalent of five years' worth of his salary in advance to start an independent company to maintain the five systems. Grover was a sharp engineer having serviced thirty-odd 1401s in Bombay. He quit IBM in 1976 to found Computer Maintenance Services (CMS), India's first third-party computer maintenance company. CMS chose the Indian Independence Day—August 15, 1976—to launch its operations as a symbolic gesture to denote the first cracks in IBM's monopoly in India.

The DoE bent the rules to let CMS operate because it was also keen to break IBM's monopoly in maintenance. The government had set up its own maintenance company—Computer Maintenance Corporation (CMC)—to look after machines left behind by IBM. It was made legally binding on IBM to transfer its maintenance business including its central stores in Bombay to CMC. The store had about one million spare parts of 30,000 different types. In addition, IBM kept stocks of spares at eighty-four locations in the country to meet routine requirement of spares locally. When it closed down, IBM had several thousand machines running at one hundred locations across India.[46]

IBM was also told to give an option to its employees if they wanted to join CMC. The nonproprietary business of IBM—data centers and card manufacturing—was inherited by International Data Management (IDM) floated by a group of IBM employees. The continuation of data center operations was crucial as they supported over 360 large and small customers in New Delhi, Bombay, Calcutta, and Madras. The manufacturing unit of IBM was taken over by yet another set of IBM employees. All this ensured there was no break in maintenance, spare part supplies, data center activities, and card manufacturing after IBM's exit.

MNCs and National Governments: International Perspective

India was not alone in being harsh with multinational computer companies. Other developing countries like Brazil and even developed European countries like France faced the predicament that India faced in the 1960s and 1970s with regard to the operations of computer multinationals, particularly IBM. Their approach in tackling the situation was different though the objective was the same—curbing power of U.S. corporations in an emerging high technology field so that indigenous capability and industry could grow. U.S. corporations were dominating this field and wanted to do business on their terms, while countries with a base of technical and scientific expertise wished to develop technology and an industrial production base on their own.

Many countries nurtured local industries through liberal government grants and favorable procurement policies as they calibrated relations with U.S. computer firms. Serious attempts were made to develop so-called "national champions" in the area of computing. Governments provided huge grants to computer companies, both state-owned and private, in order to develop local industries. The R&D support given by the French government from 1966 to 1975 was £139 million. In Germany, it was £365 million during the same period. In the UK, £18 million was given to ICL and £13 million to other computer companies.[47] Besides liberal grants, national champions also got preference in government purchases. In India, ECIL was positioned as the national champion in electronics but research grants it received were insignificant compared to its European counterparts. Brazil's experience with American companies was similar to that of India, but Brazil did not oust multinationals. Instead, it made them conform to a certain set of policies designed to benefit Brazil and to boost exports.[48]

In the developed world, France was the first country to experience the technological hegemony of American computer firms. The U.S. government vetoed the sale of a powerful CDC 6600 machine to France for fear of its use in nuclear development programs. This made France realize the strategic significance of this technology and a program, Plan Calcul, for development of computers was set in motion there. Funds were pumped into development of its indigenous computer industry and the French government's purchasing system was tweaked to favor local products.

The British government too established a state-funded enterprise—International Computers Limited (ICL)—to compete with American firms like IBM. However, both France and Britain did not fully shut doors to foreign technology. After a decade, the French government allowed Honeywell-Bull, an American computer maker, to buy out Compagnie Internationale pour Informatique (CII), while ICL in Britain formed a joint venture with CDC and National Cash Register, both American firms, to make computer peripherals.

Nixdorf in Germany benefited from government purchase policies and grants for technology development. In the early 1960s, the German Research Council ordered four computers for use in German universities—manufactured one each by four German companies. In 1967, the government launched an electronic data processing program with funding of DM387 million. Nearly three-quarters of this money went to Siemens and Telefunken-AEG. This was a deliberate attempt to create a German computer industry. The German Ministry of Research spent large amounts on training. Siemens received $120 million to design its own computer technology.[49] The experience of Japan and some Western European countries showed that protectionism in the form of restrictions on imports as well as local manufacturing by MNC subsidiaries was required for developing an independent computer industry.[50]

This only shows that even developed countries like France and Britain have had to restructure their ties with American multinationals and provide a favorable environment for their own industries to grow. India did try feebly to restructure its relations with IBM and ICL, but did not succeed because of socialist policies it pursued in the 1970s. While countries like Brazil and France encouraged local private firms on their own or through joint ventures to replace multinationals, Indian government wanted public sector firms only to play a major role.

IBM: Mixed Bag for India

The episode of IBM having to wind up its operations in India after dominating the market for close to twenty-five years also denotes a power struggle between a multinational firm and the government of an independent nation. With a market share of 80 percent, the firm was in a position to dictate the industry's growth both in terms of size and sophistication by deciding products to market or manufacture in India and their time of introduction.

The contours of this power struggle emerged when the Electronics Committee headed by Sarabhai set conditions for letting IBM continue its operations in the country. This was the first time any government agency talked tough with IBM. Scientists in the government wanted IBM to bring in the latest technology and share it with Indians. In the words of Menon, "IBM really never responded to national aspirations. They were interested in a 100 percent company that would get to a very dominant position in the computer market to sell their systems. They wanted to dictate terms on how the market should grow based on their systems."[51] In this battle for supremacy, FERA and findings of parliamentary committees only became handy weapons.

The DoE came into being with an objective to take command of the sector. Its charter clearly articulated this goal by saying it wanted to see that "the key segments of the computer industry are under national control, free from monopolistic influences or trends or domination by foreign companies."[52] In addition, it wished to make sure "the direction and pace of setting up productive capacity for computers and allied equipment, as also the availability of computational facilities, are determined by national needs and priorities."

IBM's business practice of dumping used equipment in India also clashed with the national goal of bringing in the latest technology and developing an indigenous program of design and development as well as production of computers. India had a good potential demand for data processing machines in every sector of governance, in addition to research and academic infrastructure that was in the making. IBM took advantage of early entry into such an unexplored market with huge potential. All it had to do was to bring in systems, refurbish them, and rent them to government departments and academic bodies at rates that were often very high. The absence of any policy for computerization in government departments and the lack of clear objectives for data processing facilitated IBM a great deal.

Had IBM and ICIM progressively brought in the latest technology and shared it with Indians, it would have helped meet national objectives in this sector. IBM justified selling outmoded equipment saying it wanted India to grow step by step in computer technology, almost setting the policy agenda for India. This was totally at variance with what the Bhabha-led Electronics Committee had prescribed: it wanted India to leapfrog and not take a step-by-step approach. Another reason IBM cited for bringing in old machines was that the Indian data processing market was not ready to absorb latest technology. The idea behind selling and renting out discarded computers in India, according to IBM officials, was not revenue generation.[53] They argued that it was a conscious decision based on the thinking that the best way to help India develop its data processing industry was to build up a network of skilled vendors who could supply high-quality components to IBM in India. And this goal could not have been achieved if IBM brought in the latest computers to India. In such a situation, the argument that IBM's departure—just before the start of the personal computer revolution—meant a major technology loss for India does not hold water.

While some may blame the scientific establishment for its misplaced technological nationalism leading to IBM's ouster, the same establishment should be credited for foreseeing dangers of continued dependence on a multinational corporation in a crucial high technology sector. This establishment realized that if these corporations, particularly IBM, were allowed to guide the destiny of the computing industry in India, as they had done for nearly twenty-five years, it would harm national interests. The IBM system of lease and maintenance resulted in a culture of dependence and hindered the natural growth in India of engineering and programming skills among users.

At the same time, IBM's contribution to creating a computer culture in government and business in early years can't be undermined. This helped in developing a favorable environment for the introduction of computers on a large scale in the years to come. IBM introduced top government and public sector officials to the use of computers through training programs. It was due to IBM's aggressive marketing that computers were introduced in large industrial sectors such as textiles, jute, and steel. All this was done at a time when computers were considered job snatchers.

In addition, IBM helped develop a pool of highly skilled computer professionals in systems engineering, programming, and maintenance. Engineers and marketing executives who worked in IBM at various times later joined the Indian computer companies that emerged in the 1970s. IBM used to employ fresh graduates from Indian universities and engineering colleges and train them in all aspects of business. Formal training was imparted to customers in business sectors. In academic and research institutions, people trained by the company then took up training of more people. This multiplied the number of persons exposed to computer use and those having basic knowledge of programming. The data centers the company ran in the four metros led to software development skills, as programs had to be written for every customer. A major disadvantage, however, was that this generation of programmers was exposed to just one platform—IBM.

All these benefits are incidental because whatever IBM did—training of customers, education programs for government officials, or grants to educational institutions—was only to boost its business in this vast market. It is not as if others were not willing to do the same, but IBM had the early mover advantage. CDC gave an educational discount to TIFR and trained its engineers. Like IBM, other U.S. firms too were eager to play a deciding role in the Indian market. In the 1960s, the CDC was planning a joint venture with TIFR and the Tata Group so that it could develop a computer manufacturing industry in India. When the DoE approached Burroughs to start operations in India, it also wanted terms similar to those under which IBM operated in India.

The Phoenix Rises Again

IBM's journey back to India began very soon after it left. The company shut its operations in June 1978 and began exploring business with India again in 1980. Dan Gupta was appointed to a committee set up in 1983 to explore marketing of computers in India. CMC, which was set up to maintain IBM computers in India, became its first customer in the post-1977 period, importing three large systems. The DoE allowed these imports on the condition that imported computers would be used for predominantly promoting software exports. This was so because the DoE was aware that the bulk of software export potential was dependent on IBM or IBM-compatible systems.[54] Given the changing market demands, IBM was exploring low-cost resources in Asia for software development. India was an obvious choice. A small office was opened in India to get software work done through vendors. In 1986, a software development and training institute jointly managed by IBM and the Indian government was proposed. Around the same time, some Indian companies approached IBM to propose setting up joint ventures. After long deliberations, IBM and the Tata Group set up a joint venture company, Tata Information Systems Limited (TISL), in February 1992.

In 1997, TISL was renamed Tata IBM Limited as IBM equity in the venture went up. Another joint venture, IBM Global Services, was launched the same year with 20 percent equity from the Tata Group. In 1998, the IBM Research Laboratory was established on the campus of IIT Delhi. The Tata Group divested its equity from both the companies in 1999 and a fully owned IBM India was born. In April 2004, IBM took over the business processing outsourcing firm, Daksh. With this, IBM India could claim presence in every segment of the Indian IT market—hardware, software, research, business process outsourcing (BPO), and consulting. In 2014, the company had nearly one hundred thousand employees in India, said to be the largest number to be employed by any foreign company in India. The company held its annual financial analysts meeting in Bangalore in June 2006 for the first time to send out signals that "places like India do not simply mean cheap labour."[55] As IBM's chairman and CEO Samuel J. Palmisano observed, "If you are not here in India, making the right investments and finding and developing the best employees and business partners, then you won't be able to combine the skills and expertise here with skills and expertise from around the world, in ways that can help our clients be successful."[56] It was full circle for IBM.

4   The Dawn of the Computer Age in India

It had all the markings of a Silicon Valley success story. Young, blue jeaned computer programmers pulling all nighters, walls peppered with PERT diagrams, weekend retreats, employee counseling programs and performance-linked awards. But it is not Silicon Valley, it is India; it is not Apple Computer it is C-DCOT, the government funded Center for Development of Telematics.

—Pyramid Research report on Indian telecom industry, 1987[1]

Computer or information technology touches lives of millions of Indians in ways they may not be fully aware of. Nearly one million tickets are booked on the Indian Railways (IR) everyday using its extensive, computerized passenger-booking system. Half of these tickets are booked online by passengers from the comfort of their homes and offices or from cybercafes. Millions of Indians withdraw, deposit, or transfer money from their bank accounts across the length and breadth of the country irrespective of the bank or branch they patronize, courtesy the network of ATMs and the National Financial Switch connecting major banks. Identification data of over 560 million Indians including their biometric details are deposited in a database maintained by the Unique Identification Authority of India (UIDAI). Nearly half a million poor Indians get government subsidies directly into their bank accounts that are linked with the UIDAI database daily. The wide-ranging benefits of technology are reaching millions of Indians despite a low base of personal computer (PC) ownership and broadband connections in the country.

All these applications of information technology would have been unthinkable in the 1970s and 1980s for most Indians, but for a small band of technologists and policy planners who foresaw applications of computer technology for the public good. Several major projects such as computerization of train reservation and banking operations, networking of government offices, and modernization of the telecom infrastructure were initiated during the 1980s. In addition to far-reaching economic and technological changes, the 1980s was also a period of political turmoil. Indira Gandhi, who had returned to power in 1980 after a three-year hiatus, was assassinated in 1984 and her elder son Rajiv Gandhi was chosen as a replacement by the Congress Party. The tenure of Rajiv (his first name has been used in order not to confuse with Indira Gandhi), the youngest person to have become prime minister, is ingrained in public memory as India's computer age and dominated by his close circle of aides nicknamed "computer boys." This was a critical period in India's emergence as a low-cost destination for software development.

Grooming of a Technophile-Politician

In India, the new technologies of computers and informatics were the domain of scientists till about 1980. These technologies were seen more as helping scientific and academic work, with some applications in business and industry. In the 1980s, computer technology saw mass application in different sectors and came face to face with common users—though India as a whole was at least five years behind the age of home and personal computing that was unfolding in the United States.

Bulk of the credit for this transformation goes to Rajiv who was a trained commercial pilot and a technophile. For thirteen years he worked as a pilot in the government-owned carrier, Indian Airlines, having joined it soon after obtaining a commercial pilot license in 1968. The job of an apprentice pilot with the airline at age twenty-four was a dream come true for the young man who had always been fascinated with flying machines. His maternal grandfather Jawaharlal Nehru had introduced him to flying as a young adult in New Delhi. Rajiv continued to pursue his interest in aviation while studying in Cambridge and had enrolled at the Wiltshire Flying Club at Thruxton, where he used to train on a four-seater version of a Tiger Moth.[2] On his return from Cambridge he became a member of the Delhi Flying Club and continued training.

Soon after the induction course, Rajiv was posted as a copilot on Fokker Friendship planes of Indian Airlines and was promoted to fly an Avro—HS-748—as copilot in 1970. In another two years, he attained the rank of captain and became a commander in 1975. As an employee of the state-owned company, he was treated on par with others and carried home a modest pay packet of about $4,000 annually.[3] He made sure that no special favors were showered on him and always kept a low profile while at work. Rajiv's devotion to duty and meticulous handling of his job as a pilot were rewarded through quick promotions. He was made a check pilot in 1977 and he graduated to the post of an instructor in 1980. His dream was to command a Boeing, which became a reality when he qualified as a Boeing copilot in January 1981. But this turned out to be his last year in the airline. His life was about to change forever.

While Rajiv was busy in his flying career, his mother rode a political rollercoaster in the 1970s. After the split in the Congress Party in 1969, she had initiated a number of economic policy changes. Prominent among them were the nationalization of private banks and an end to the privy purse of former princely states. Such seemingly tough measures helped her win the elections in March 1971. The pinnacle of her tenure was India's victory in the war with Pakistan and the creation of Bangladesh in December 1971. This made Indira a leader of stature at home and abroad. However, the political situation had worsened for her in the mid-1970s, mainly due to student protests led by socialist leader Jayaprakash Narayan. She suffered another blow when her election to Lok Sabha (Lower House of the Indian Parliament) was declared invalid by a court. Instead of resigning from her post, she imposed a state of internal emergency in June 1975. Press censorship was enforced and all political opponents were put in jail. In early 1977, she declared elections but lost miserably to a newly formed opposition coalition called the Janata Party. This party was in power for barely three years. Indira rode back to power after midterm elections in 1980.

All through these tumultuous years, Rajiv maintained a studied distance from politics. He pursued his interests in music, electronics, and amateur radio. He had always enjoyed tinkering with engines and machines, cleaning and fixing them. In 1974, he assembled his first radio set from a do-it-yourself kit using a Japanese-made Yaesu transmitter.[4] His flying schedules forced him to spend almost twenty-four-hour-long breaks in Bombay. When in the city he used to frequent Cosmic Radio, a company dealing with hi-fi audio systems because of his interest in music systems. During one such visit, the shop's proprietor Manubhai Desai introduced Rajiv to another entrepreneur, Prabhakar Shankar Deodhar, who had just bought a ZX Spectrum microcomputer from the United Kingdom.[5] Common interest in new gadgets drew the two to each other (figure 4.1).

Rajiv came face to face with on-the-ground realities during his frequent visits, almost every week, to Deodhar's electronics manufacturing unit in an industrial enclave on the outskirts of Bombay. His interest in gadgets gradually diversified to include electronics industry- and policy-related issues. On the one hand, this was the time when Korea and Taiwan were emerging as suppliers of electronic equipment and components. On the

Figure 4.1
Electronics buff and entrepreneur Prabhakar Shankar Deodhar (right) showing Rajiv
Gandhi (who was an elected member of the Indian Parliament then) the ZX Spectrum, 8-bit personal home computer that he had bought in London soon after its
launch, in October 1982. Two years later when Gandhi became prime minister, he
appointed Deodhar his key advisor on electronics and chairman of ET&T Corporation, which launched a "People's PC." Courtesy: P. S. Deodhar

other hand, India had inward-looking policies that restricted imports and
was focused on self-reliance. An export-promotion industrial area called
Santa Cruz Electronics Export Processing Zone (SEEPZ) had been set up in
Bombay but restrictive policies still continued. India's electronics industry
was lagging behind latest research and production technologies by at least
three generations or fifteen years. With the prevailing duty structure, modernization of any sort in the electronics industry was very difficult.

Rajiv was exposed to the problems small-scale industries faced due to
bureaucratic hurdles and business-unfriendly policies pursued by bureaucracy in New Delhi, particularly scientist-bureaucrats in the DoE. These
policies encouraged production of components locally while discouraging
imports, unlike other Asian countries. "Rajiv's formative ideas about Indian
electronics and computer industries were formed during those days . . . by

the time he had to participate and take part in politics, he had enough information on what is on the ground and he was not blinded by merely living in Delhi and not being aware of what the world was like outside," Deodhar would later recall.[6]

In January 1980, Indira Gandhi returned to power after victory in the midterm elections. Her younger son Sanjay, who was elected to the Lower House, began playing a bigger role in the affairs of the ruling party and the government. Political circles were rife with speculation that Indira was grooming Sanjay as her successor. But destiny willed otherwise. Sanjay died in a tragic crash of a small plane that he was flying on the morning of June 23, 1980. This event changed Rajiv's life. He started spending more time with his mother, but kept at bay sycophants who wanted him to take Sanjay's place. His Italian-born wife, Sonia, was also against his joining active politics.[7] But he could not resist these pressures for long. He quit his job at Indian Airlines on May 5, 1981, to run in a parliamentary election that he won with ease. Rajiv was thus formally inducted into Indian politics at the age of thirty-six.

Rajiv was soon surrounded by like-minded professionals who were new to politics like him. Arun Nehru, a third cousin of Rajiv, was president of the paint firm Jenson and Nicholson before he plunged into politics. Arun Singh was working with a British multinational, Reckitt & Coleman, when he decided to quit and join Rajiv. Satish Sharma, a few months senior to Rajiv in Indian Airlines, also gave up his job to help out the young Gandhi in politics. This bunch of Rajiv's friends was nicknamed "computer boys" as they were all highly educated, technology savvy, and used computers in their work.

Restrictions on importing computers imposed in the 1970s were not only affecting business users but also companies and entrepreneurs who wanted to take up software development as an independent activity. To help this segment of users, a review panel (headed by technocrat Mantosh Sondhi) had earlier proposed an innovative solution—allowing import of computers against the obligation to export software. Computer imports were somewhat eased and companies were encouraged to use such machines to take up software export projects. This recommendation was accepted by the government, and it became official in January 1981. Also accepted: another recommendation of the panel to simplify procedures for industrial approvals and make the DoE the sole authority for clearing proposals for electronics manufacturing.[8] These were early indicators of a liberal approach in this sector.

This new twist in India's electronics policies came as a relief to industry, which was suffering because of restrictive policies and the socialist approach hich state-owned enterprises played a key role in industrial activity. The ......structure needed for industrialization was woefully inadequate. Power shortages were common. India's telephone system was archaic, undependable, and corrupt. The waiting list for getting a landline phone connection was over half a million entries long. The waiting period for getting a telephone connection was up to five years in a metropolitan city. The "license-permit" Raj—a sobriquet for all this red tape—was at its peak.

Indira had begun thinking about some of these problems after her return to power in 1980. The years she was out of power perhaps made her ponder such issues. She set up a committee to review the telecom system, which recommended migration to digital electronic switching systems from the aging analog switches. She directed expansion of the state-owned television network and permitted private companies to manufacture TV sets. A new policy on electronics components was announced by her government in 1980, recognizing for the first time the need to step up production to make manufacturing economically viable. Technology imports were also eased in order to improve the quality of products. In the run-up to the Asian Games hosted by New Delhi in November 1982, Indira gave the go-ahead for the liberal importing of color television sets, ignoring opposition from the DoE. Some 50,000 color television tubes were imported through a government agency and made available to private manufacturers. This was a precursor to a liberal import policy for the entire electronics sector.

The 1982 Asian Games also gave Rajiv a public profile as Indira asked him to help the organizing committee. Given his penchant for technology and computers, Rajiv proposed that computers be used for operations, guest coordination, athletes' registration, compilation of results, and announcement of the medals tally. The task for developing necessary software for results announcing was entrusted to the government agency National Informatics Centre (NIC), which had a computer network operational in the national capital and connecting some government offices. Planning a real-time computer network for a major sports event was still a challenging task for NIC.

NIC engaged about 120 engineers to develop software for monitoring of stadium construction activity, player registration, games conduct, and results. Team members had to interact with officials of different games associations to understand how each game was conducted and scored. A network was set up connecting seventeen stadiums in New Delhi and one in Bombay where aquatic events were hosted. The software—including network protocols—was developed indigenously. The network consisted of an imported Hewlett Packard (HP) server and nodes supplied by a local firm,

DCM Data products. For the first time in the history of the Asian Games, international press could access results in real time at a centralized press-room. Later, officials from the Seoul Olympic Games Committee came to see the Indian system. The Computer Maintenance Corporation (CMC) used the know-how it gained to develop a Games Event Management System, which was deployed first in the Mediterranean Games held in Syria in 1987.

Rajiv had worked closely with NIC on this project and it resulted in intellectual camaraderie between him and N. Seshagiri, the head of NIC and a policymaker in the DoE. They shared a common interest in computers and technology. It was this acquaintance and Rajiv's own interest in computers that were to prove fruitful in the years to come. Seshagiri had arranged for importing a late-model Toshiba laptop for Rajiv from Japan through a NIC officer who was posted at the Indian embassy in Tokyo.

After color TV imports were liberalized for the Asian Games, industrial licensing for consumer electronics was abolished and import tariffs were slashed in a new policy announced on August 16, 1983. The policy was a break from the socialist approach that treated consumer electronic products as luxury items that needed to be taxed heavily. Both import and excise duties on electronics products were slashed in some cases to zero. Import duties were particularly high, up to 158 percent on some products. Large-scale industries were allowed to manufacture products that were earlier reserved only for small-scale units. Liberal access to foreign technology too was permitted with a view to modernize a range of electronics and communication industries.

The new electronics policy was based on a detailed framework prepared by Deodhar and vetted by Rajiv. This was a watershed event in policymaking. For the first time, Indira effected a major policy change on the advice of a nongovernment technocrat distancing herself from her advisors on science and technology–related matters in the 1970s. Deodhar could convince Indira that electronics manufacturing in India was suffering because duty structure made imported components costlier than finished products. In the absence of local manufacturing, people were smuggling in products from other countries. Deodhar was given a formal position in the government—he was made chairman of Electronics Trade and Technology Development Corporation (ET&T) in January 1984 and later chairman of the Electronics Commission. Subsequent to the new electronics policy, the 1956 Industrial Policy Resolution was amended to permit private companies to manufacture telecom equipment either on their own or jointly with the government.

In January 1984, the Congress Party also began computerization of its operations under the guidance of Rajiv, who was its general secretary. Its youth wing, Youth Congress (I), installed a computer at its headquarters to computerize information about its members and activities. A cadre of Youth Congress workers was also trained to handle data processing machines.

Crafting a Liberal Computer Policy

Encouraged by the unshackling of the electronics sector, Seshagiri in the DoE advocated a liberal policy framework specifically for the computer industry. The suggestion that the direction of the new policy should be liberal came from Rajiv, who was consulted by the Minister for Science and Technology Shivraj Patil.[9] The much-delayed minicomputer policy of 1978 had not yielded desired results. Over eighty companies were given manufacturing licenses, but only six had gone into production by 1981. As a first step toward opening up India's computer industry, import duties were brought down by 15 percent in August 1983.

Seshagiri was the lone proponent of liberal policies in the DoE. Top officials did not favor drastic changes in computer policy. CMC managing director Prem Prakash Gupta, who was now also secretary of the DoE, wished continued dominance of public sector units like CMC. The first draft of the proposed computer policy reiterated the dictum of "national control over computer production" enunciated by atomic energy scientists in 1971. This would have meant continuance of the public sector-oriented and highly restrictive regime for computers. Gupta's idea was that CMC should become a national champion in every segment of the computer industry—hardware, software, and maintenance.

Aware of the realities in the electronics sector globally, Seshagiri knew that the kind of centralization envisaged by the old guard in theDoE would be disastrous. He could not make DoE bosses agree with his view that state control and import substitution in a fast-changing and technology-driven sector would be futile. He identified "progressive" elements in the higher echelons of the government informally and tried to convince them of merits of a liberal framework to promote electronics and computer technology. "I intentionally became close to them. For example, I put Dr B. K. Gairola, who was working with me in NIC, to tutor Rajiv Gandhi in computers. . . . Using NIC, I not only befriended the Nehru-Gandhi family, but also people [senior cabinet ministers] like V. P. Singh, P. V. Narasimha Rao and others. I used to go to their houses, talk to them. I was logically trying to convince them," Seshagiri said of his strategy.[10]

The new computer policy (NCP) was finally approved by Indira's Cabinet.[11] However, before it could be made public, she was killed by her own bodyguards on October 31, 1984. Rajiv, who was sworn in as prime minister the same day, chose her birth date (November 19) shortly after to announce the new policy. This gave the impression that the NCP was the work of the new government. The widely held notion that a new, liberalized computer policy was hurriedly brought in soon after Rajiv became prime minister was wrong.

In fact, at the time Rajiv took over from his late mother, groundwork for a liberalized regime in the electronics, computer, and telecom sectors had already been done. The new electronics policy had been announced. The Cabinet had approved the NCP; it had cleared the formation of the Centre for Development of Telematics (C-DOT) to develop a digital switch, and opened up telecom equipment manufacturing to the private sector. In order to boost diffusion of computer technology, the government had also decided to introduce computers in its various ministries, educational institutions, and public sector units. The forces of change that came to a head under Rajiv's regime had already been unleashed under Indira with Rajiv fully in the picture in his personal capacity. Indira—and later her son—went ahead with liberal electronics and computer policies. Ironically, trade unions dubbed 1984 the "Anti-Computerization Year," though the opposition was weak compared to that witnessed in the late 1960s.

Under Prime Minister Rajiv Gandhi, his young friends-turned-politicians and technocrats close to him acquired new clout. The club of "computer boys" now included Sam Pitroda, Ashok Ganguly, and Sanjeevi Rao, besides Deodhar, Seshagiri, Arun Nehru, and Arun Singh. This was the first time private sector executives and techies—not politicos or bureaucrats belonging to the elite Indian Administrative Service (IAS)—found a place in the inner circle of an Indian prime minister. Since this was Rajiv's first official post, he had no favorites in the bureaucracy. It was also for the first time India had a prime minister who was not a career politician but a professional previously employed in a commercial firm.

Rajiv's love for technology and gadgets continued after he became the prime minister. He used two Toshiba laptops for organizing a database on various party and government matters, appointments, travel schedules, and speeches.[12] He would carry a laptop with him while traveling within the country or abroad. Rajiv reportedly was one of the first Indians to own a Sony portable compact disc player; he even had a CD player installed in his bulletproof Range Rover. In addition, he had a shortwave radio, which could be tuned by pushing buttons—a novelty then.[13]

The NCP opened up imports but retained some elements of protectionism. Import procedures were simplified. The objective was to promote manufacturing of computers based on the latest technology, while spurring progressive indigenization. The manufacture of microcomputers and minicomputers as well as personal computers, including those based on 32-bit chips, by wholly owned Indian companies or those with foreign equity up to 40 percent, was permitted. Restrictions on production capacities were lifted but manufacturing of CPUs of mainframes and super minicomputers was reserved for the public sector. Import of software was allowed, but emphasis was on the import of source code and on centralized purchase (for distribution within the country) of software. For import of computers, the policy recommended "sufficiently high import duty" for protecting local manufacturers, besides retaining some controls over imports.

Software development was recognized as an "industry." A Software Development Promotion Agency was set up to boost software exports. Special low duty was proposed for the import of computers meant for developing software for export markets. The most notable element of the policy was to facilitate software exports through satellite-based data links with overseas computers—a development of great significance discussed in detail later. It was the first time software exports appeared on the radar of Indian policymakers in a promotional policy framework. With all these steps, software exports were expected to reach $100 million per year within three to four years.[14] The final outcome was subject to cooperation from the Posts and Telegraph Department, which controlled all communication networks including satellite links. Rajiv's government also initiated administrative changes in the British-era Posts and Telegraph Department by carving out a separate Department of Telecommunications (DoT) and by converting the Overseas Communication Service into an autonomous corporation called Videsh Sanchar Nigam Limited (VSNL). These changes were crucial to improve inland and overseas communication links.

The NCP achieved its desired results in the hardware sector. Within a year of the policy, computer production grew by 100 percent in unit terms and 65 percent in monetary terms, while prices fell by 50 percent.[15] This was in contrast to the situation a decade ago, in 1975. Since then, from being a net importer, the computer hardware industry had become a net exporter with much-reduced participation from multinationals. Software exports also kicked off. In 1985, software exports were estimated at $30 million, mainly accounted for by three firms—government-owned CMC and two Tata firms (Tata Consulting Services and Tata-Burroughs Limited).

Although the 1984 policy was progressive and a break from the past, other ministries in the government were yet to ease restrictions and controls. Companies interested in software exports still faced problems in getting satellite data links due to restrictive policies of the telecom department and an archaic telegraph law. This frustrated companies genuinely interested in software exports.

With a view to promote an indigenous software industry, a separate "policy on computer software export, software development and training" was announced in November 1986. A specific policy objective was to "capture a sizeable share in the international software market." Foreign exchange rules for importing computers and software tools for developing software for exports were simplified. Export obligations for foreign exchange used still continued, which means companies could buy imported systems only out of the foreign exchange they earned from exporting software. The import of licensed software was liberalized, bringing it under a category called Open General License (OGL). Computers meant for software exports could be imported without any duty, provided they were used in a custom-bonded area. Foreign collaboration in software development was also permitted, subject to a cap of 40 percent on foreign equity. But it could exceed 40 percent if the unit was solely for exports.

The definition of "software export" was broadened to include exports via satellite data links and "consultancy delivered at the location of foreign clients abroad by Indian computer expertise." This was the official recognition of a uniquely Indian phenomenon called "body shopping," in which local consultancy firms recruited IT workers and sent them to foreign clients to work on software projects and temporary assignments. In effect, these firms acted as "body shops," and hence the term "body shopping" (see chapter 6 for fuller explanation of "body shopping"). A new group—the Inter-Ministerial Standing Committee (IMSC) housed in the Computer, Communications and Instrumentation wing of the DoE—was set up to facilitate implementation of the new policy and to act as a single authority for clearing proposals. Software firms had to register themselves with the DoE in order to avail of export promotion assistance and other benefits.

The import liberalization had mixed impact. Several thousand PCs came into the country, enlarging the base of computers to a great extent. The shortage of computing power witnessed in the aftermath of IBM's exit was finally over. The critical factor, of course, was the advent of PC technology. The availability of a large number of computers gave rise to small-scale software firms to cater to the software needs of new computer owners.

The flip side of import liberalization was erosion of technological and design capabilities gained during the 1970s and early 1980s. The flood of foreign collaborations meant practically an end to R&D in Indian companies. Pioneering hardware firms like DCM Data Products, HCL, and Wipro (whose stories are discussed in detail in chapter 5), which had invested a great deal in design innovation, faced hardships. Their development teams slowly frittered away and local firms were forced to either opt for joint ventures with foreign companies or reselling arrangement with multinationals. Local capabilities in component manufacturing were hit due to lowering of duties on components. Imports made kit assembly operation more viable than indigenous production. This trend, however, helped in developing capabilities in systems integration and assembly operations.

During the tenure of Rajiv Gandhi, India moved toward a favorable environment for introduction of computers in the sense of technology diffusion, unlike the 1970s, which had witnessed a hostile attitude toward large-scale computer application. However, resistance to the introduction of computers continued in bureaucracy and among the political classes, barring a few progressive elements. Rajiv was preoccupied with pressing domestic issues such as unrest in Assam and Punjab, defeat of the Congress Party in by-elections, and defense purchase scams in the second half of his five-year term.

Because of his noticeable interest in computers and electronics, charges of elitism were flung against Rajiv and his government. Within the party, the "computer boys" became the target of ridicule and attack for promoting high technology projects. Yet it was during his tenure that two major technology projects got off the ground, touching the lives of millions of ordinary Indians—the railway reservation system and digital telephone exchange. The two projects are discussed here in detail, following a section on the development of networking. They proved to be game changers for software development and set the pace for diffusion of information technology in the decades to follow.

The Beginning of Networking

The history of computer networking in India is not very old. It begins in 1977, with a link that connected the Colaba campus of TIFR with an engineering college, Victoria Jubilee Technical Institute, located in downtown Bombay. The National Centre for Software Development and Computing Techniques (NCSDCT) established the link using TDC 316, leased telephone lines, and networking software written in-house. Scientists working on the project were influenced by their previous exposure in the late 1960s to ARPANET in the United States.

Srinivasan Ramani, who led the team at NCSDCT, explained, "We realized that the strength of ARPANET was not that it worked on perfect communication systems. It worked on imperfect communication systems. It could work even when links failed. And it was a very logical thing to believe that in India you needed the technology because our communications infrastructure was poor." This was the thinking that led Ramani to pursue further work in networking.[16] NCSDCT was started with seed funding from the United Nations Development Program (UNDP) and had on its review panel eminent computer scientists including Maurice Wilkes and William Wulf.

The next step was to try out the feasibility of a multipoint network using satellite links instead of leased telephone lines. This was a joint project with the Space Applications Centre, Ahmedabad, and the Telecom Research Centre, New Delhi. A network connecting computers in Bombay, Ahmedabad, and Ghaziabad was realized via a link provided by an experimental geostationary satellite called Ariane Passenger PayLoad Experiment (APPLE) launched in 1981. A 32-kilobits-per-second (kbps) modem was designed and built by TRC while the satellite terminal consisted of a twenty-feet-diameter dish antenna. The network was called COMNEX (Computer Networks Experiment). Ramani considered it the precursor to the VSAT technology that was to dominate satellite communication in years to come.

A chance to extrapolate from this experience in networking came when the DoE proposed to set up a larger academic and research network in 1984, on the lines of ARPANET. It was called the Education and Research Network or ERNET, and connected five IITs (Madras, Kanpur, Bombay, New Delhi, and Kharagpur) and the Indian Institute of Science in Bangalore, besides NCSDCT. It began as a multiprotocol network—using both Open Systems Interconnect and Transmission Control Protocol/Internet Protocol, on dialup as well as leased lines. Initial applications included electronic mail, mail fax, and file transfer. This network was connected to the global Internet via an analog 9.6 kbps leased line with the UUNet (Unix-to-Unix Network Technologies) hub in Falls Church, Virginia. The link was upgraded to 64 kbps in 1992.

That's how the Internet came to India in 1989. Commercial Internet services were introduced much later, in 1995, by VSNL. By then, ERNET had connected three hundred educational and research organizations in India as well as in Nepal and Bangladesh, and had about twenty thousand users.

Another major networking effort was mounted by NIC, which had demonstrated a real-time, multipoint network during the Asian Games in 1982.

The center's original objective was to introduce the use of computers in government offices at various levels beginning with the central government in New Delhi. It created a pool of trained software professionals in the government sector and databases that helped in planning and decision-making processes.

NIC director and one of Rajiv's "computer boys," Seshagiri figured that micro earth stations could be used to roll out a national network rapidly rather than depend on leased telecom lines. A Dutch firm, Equatorial Pacific International Company, was the only one then with a functioning network based on micro earth stations. It refused to share technology but agreed to form a joint venture with an Indian government agency, ITI, given the size of the order (1,000 satellite terminals over five years). NIC took up the job of writing software for this network, which was rolled out from 1988 onward. Four NEC SX-1000 mainframes were imported from Japan, as there was an embargo on importing such large computers from the United States and allied countries. Outside the United States, this was said to be the first VSAT network in the world and remained the largest government network for some years. Over 2,500 NIC engineers developed applications for various government departments and public sector companies.

The Train Reservation Project

One of the most visible and high-impact projects of the 1980s was computerization of the passenger reservation system of the Indian Railways. Like other high-technology projects associated with this period, it was met with long bureaucratic delays before becoming a reality during the tenure of Rajiv Gandhi.

The IR, a legacy of the British Raj, had a complex passenger reservation system involving ten fare types, 130 coach types, ten classes, forty quotas, and 120 types of concessions in the 1980s.[17] In 1984, about 4.5 million passengers traveled every day in two thousand trains crisscrossing the country. Almost 75 percent of reservations of seats and berths was handled in four metropolitan cities with nearly fifty thousand requests for reservations made daily at these stations. Seats and berths in different trains were reserved manually at train-specific reservation counters at major stations. If a berth was not available in a particular train, the passenger had to move and queue up in front of the particular window for an alternative train. This process not only led to crowded reservation counters and hardship for commuters, but also left room open for corrupt practices.

IBM and Tata-Burroughs at different times in the 1970s made proposals to the Indian Railways for computerization of its passenger reservation system. An internal IR committee too had suggested this. But the IR bureaucracy did not act until the World Bank set improved efficiency through modernization and computerization as a precondition for advancing a large loan. The World Bank even suggested the U.S. Southern Pacific Railroad as a model worth replicating. An IR team sent to study different systems in Europe and the United States suggested that computerization of freight operations along the lines of the Southern Pacific Railroad operations, using imported hardware and software. Another inter-ministerial committee then studied computer systems of railways in France, the UK, Germany, the United States, and Canada, and recommended the Canadian system as the most suitable model for India.[18] Software developed by Canadian National (CN) was selected but the freight computerization project could never take off in India due to several technical and bureaucratic problems.

For computerization of passenger reservations, the Directorate of Operations Information System (DOIS) of the Indian Railways prepared a plan based on proposals submitted earlier by IBM and Tata-Burroughs. Lower-ranking officials in the finance section raised several objections despite the fact that it would cost just a fraction of the money needed for the Canadian freight system. The Indian Railway Board opposed the passenger reservation system on the ground that it gave no returns on investment. Several such hurdles were placed to ensure the proposal made no progress, frustrating N. C. Gupta, head of the DOIS. He decided to break official protocol and approached Deputy Minister for Railways Y. Mallikarjun directly. He convinced him about potential benefits of computerizing passenger ticket booking in terms of the enormous benefits to passengers as well as the Indian Railways booking staff.[19] Mallikarjun took the case up with senior minister Prakash Chand Sethi and the project got a go-ahead despite fierce opposition from the top brass of the Railway Board.

CMC, which had earlier worked with the IR on a UNDP-funded project on software development for freight movement, was already working on a pilot passenger reservation project in Secunderabad. It seems CMC got interested in computerizing train reservations after its chairman, Gupta himself, had to wait for hours in a queue to book a ticket for his sister to travel to Bombay from Hyderabad. The contract for the reservation project given to CMC in November 1984 covered delivery of the required computer hardware, system software, application system, special hardware (developed at its R&D center), site preparation (air conditioning, false roofing, power back-up, etc.), training, operation support, and maintenance warranty.

Handling a software project from scratch posed unique problems. The Indian Railways handed over to the CMC team the IR's commercial manual and a one-line brief: "Develop a reservation system that meets [the] requirements of all these rules." Most of the rules in the book were 150 years old and every rule had ten to fifteen exceptions. For instance, there was a rule that passengers could take a mule with them but only with a set of conditions. Naturally, the CMC programming team could not make heads or tails of this book. Arvind Sharma, manager of the reservation project, described the initial phase thus: "It took us three days to arrive at the conclusion that we are building this system for the passenger and not for CMC or the Railways."[20] Sharma decided to follow principles of software engineering, an emerging discipline then, to move ahead with this project. Two computer science professors from IIT Madras and IIT Kanpur served as external experts. It took development teams six weeks to write some 1,400 pieces of software, which were then integrated and tested. A simulation model was built and software behavior under different volume conditions was tested. From concept to testing, the project took twelve months.

The next question was the choice of hardware for rolling out the system for IR. Digital Equipment Corporation (DEC) in the United States had just announced cluster architecture for its VAX system. After a detailed review of this design, the CMC team chose the VAX cluster architecture and its load sharing between different processors as the project's hardware platform. A cluster provided for a common database that could be accessed by different central processing units. FORTRAN-77 was selected for coding application programs to enable subsequent porting of the software from one machine to another. An optimum configuration of systems was selected in order to avoid restrictive trade clauses of the U.S. government, although this would have meant upgrading the system very soon. This was said to be the first online transaction processing application on a VAX cluster, and the first computer application with direct interface with customers in India.

Railway officials had the fear of losing authority in an important area of their operation, while some workers thought they might lose their jobs. The CMC team, however, got the support of the operational staff—including booking clerks and reservation supervisors. They would tell N. C. Gupta, "Everyone thinks we are corrupt; we are making people stand in queues. But we know how the system is working. It is bursting at the seams. If this system can give some relief, we will use it. After our eight-hour shift, we have to spend 2–3 hours with accounts people trying to reconcile the day's sales. Sometimes we don't get sleep at night."[21]

CMC and the Indian Railways took care to involve workers' unions very early in the development process, in view of stiff resistance toward computerization in Indian banks. Trade union leaders were brought to the R&D center in Hyderabad and were given demos on system objectives, functionality, and benefits. The leaders gave valuable inputs that were also incorporated. IR also agreed to give special allowances to operating staff. An air-conditioned environment and special uniforms gave the reservation staff a better status within the organization. These initiatives helped ready acceptance of computerization among employees.

By 1990, the software application was made available in twenty-two cities—accounting for 66 percent of the IR's reservation requirements. Several smaller stations were connected to bigger ones as satellite terminals and reservation offices were opened at different places within a city to decongest the main reservation complex. The software had many unique features such as the capacity to issue tickets from any station to any other station, reservation on different segments of a train's route, online changes in train profiles and route structures, the ability to define different advance reservation periods for different trains, online aggregation of data such as revenues or berth utilization, and compatibility with hardware from multiple vendors. The software could be adapted to not just fare revision but also changes in business rules. Soon different cities were interlinked into a real-time, all-India, year-round reservation system.

For the Indian Railways, computerization of passenger reservations yielded substantial reduction in the cost per ticket issued, a 40 percent increase in transactions handled per day, higher productivity, and fewer errors in computation, concessions calculations, and more. It was also a major image booster for IR. In a larger context, it created a positive image for computer applications in different sectors, including banking. For passengers, it meant savings in reservation time and transportation costs, reduced corruption, and new convenience. The mean waiting time for passengers making reservations went down from seventy minutes to twenty-four minutes, resulting in an average annual saving of 100 million rupees for the economy.[22] The greatest benefit for employees was a reduction in shift duration from eight to six hours owing to faster post-shift reconciliation of accounts. A study commissioned by the IR in 1990 reported that it would have needed 33 percent more staff to handle additional volume of work at 1985 service levels.[23]

Unlike computerized booking introduced by Indian Airlines in the 1980s, the Indian Railways system was more successful because it integrated all services—reservation, ticketing, and cash transactions—at a single counter.

This experience led to improvements in the airlines system and also became a model for computerization in many road transport systems.

Meanwhile, freight computerization suffered time and cost overruns, as software supplied by Canadian National was found unsuitable for the Indian system. Finally in January 1998, the IR asked the Centre for Railway Information Systems (CRIS) and CMC to work together to develop a new freight management system, beginning in the first phase with a wagon management system. In the second phase, a terminal management system was deployed all over the country. This helped the IR to meet its loading targets due to the increased availability of wagons, and to improve the handling capacities of freight terminals during 2004–2005.

The IR did not want to give the contract to CMC in 1983 on the grounds that freight movement was a vital function and its running could not be entrusted to an external agency. Therefore it decided to buy the Canadian software and customize it; but after a decade IR was forced to go to CMC again. This episode points to tendency among different ministries of rejecting Indian technological capabilities without proper evaluation and going in for the easier option of imports. IR's rejection of CMC was surprising in view of the fact that the London Underground Limited had trusted the same company to develop its time-tabling and signal data generation software.

The IR passenger reservation project served as a showcase for other public services such as banking, where trade unions were against automation. Computerization in banks was first discussed before the National Industrial Tribunal in 1981 during hearings over an industrial dispute between the Reserve Bank of India (RBI) and its workers. The tribunal favored use of computers and other sophisticated machines, provided it did not result in displacement of more than 10 percent of the staff. The central bank then computerized clearinghouses and also installed ledger-posting machines.

In 1983, three major bank workers unions signed an agreement with the Indian Banks Association (IBA) to let banks initiate "selective automation." For instance, it was agreed that banks with less than five hundred branches would not install large computers, no accounting machines would be used in rural branches, and no electronic machines with memory would be installed in semi-urban branches. Gradually ledger-posting machines, microprocessor-based systems, and mainframe computers were deployed at branch and zonal levels. The RBI also developed a national banking network to facilitate interbank fund transfers, national clearing of intercity checks, and connectivity between branches. All these developments augured well for the Indian computer hardware and software firms and brought computers face to face with the India's banking customers.

IBA signed another agreement with the employees' unions in March 1987, specifying the configuration of electronic accounting machines to be used and listing several other conditions including payment of a special allowance of 350 rupees per month to machine operators. In September 1989, about 4,500 advanced ledger-posting machines had become operational in branches of nationalized banks. Technical specifications of computers to be used in banks were also established. UNIX was chosen for the operating system, and Microfocus Cobol and X.25 as protocol support. The hardware was to be IBM PC-XT/AT-compatible machines with 256 kilobytes of random access memory and 16-bit word length. Several Indian computer vendors were able to meet the specifications.[24] For networking, Open Systems Interconnection Standards were recommended.

The idea behind these specifications was to promote multivendor standards and prevent banks from getting locked in with proprietary hardware and software. It is this one recommendation that gave rise to a whole industry in the mid-1980s, as most of the vendors aligned to these specifications and developed solutions for UNIX. Familiarity with UNIX gave the Indian programmers an edge in the 1990s when they began to work for U.S. customers.

The Leap to Digital Telephony

Another technological milestone of the period was development of an indigenous rural telephone exchange under the aegis of the new Centre for Development of Telematics. The condition of the telephone system in India at the beginning of the 1980s was pathetic. The government had decided to change from analog to digital telecom exchanges, but it was possible to do so only with imported equipment. Local production was not feasible because technology for digital switches was not available freely and very few countries possessed it.

India's transition to digital telephony had three distinct strands, which came together to deliver a new technology. The expertise for this project came from three different backgrounds—a government-run telecom lab, an autonomous research center engaged in basic research, and an Indian technocrat-entrepreneur from the United States.

A project to develop an Indian electronic switching system had been initiated at the Telecom Research Centre (TRC) in the 1960s soon after Bell Telephone Laboratories announced commercial trials of the world's first such telephone exchange in the United States. The technical details published in the October 1964 issue of *Bell Technical Research Journal* formed the basis of this effort, which went on for a decade with meager funding and no political backing. A hundred-line electronic switch was developed and demonstrated in November 1973. At this point, only nine countries had this technology. This was followed by a thousand-line exchange called Stored Program Controlled No 1 Exchange or SPC-1, which was commissioned in June 1981. SPC-1 remained a research switch because the government decided to go in for digital switches and selected E10B of Alcatel of France.

Parallel to efforts of the TRC in the 1970s, another research team was working on a telecom switch at TIFR, along with engineers from IIT Bombay. It was a classified project to develop a digital automatic electronic switch (AES) for the Indian army. The project involved development of a rugged processor, electronic switching systems, necessary controls and software, and self-diagnosis features.[25] It was designed for both fixed line and wireless communication. However, no efforts were made to make a commercial version of this military communication system.

Far away from TRC and TIFR efforts, an engineer-entrepreneur of Indian origin, Satyanarayan Gangaram Pitroda, was working on telecom technologies in Chicago. Pitroda—later known as Sam Pitroda—had developed and commercialized a digital switch called DSS580 with innovative multiprocessor control. Pitroda, a postgraduate from the Illinois Institute of Technology, had worked at length with the telephone company GTE. He had to his credit over two dozen U.S. patents—one of them for an "electronic diary." When Toshiba started marketing electronic diaries, Pitroda filed a patent-violation claim and won $80,000.[26] In 1974, he launched his own switching company, Wescom Switching Inc., with venture capital funding and two partners. This company was sold to Rockwell International in 1979 for a whopping $40 million.[27]

Pitroda had lived the American dream and wanted to return to India to help improve its archaic telephone system. His eagerness had something to do with his early life In India when he had personally experienced lack of communication facilities in villages. Pitroda first saw and used a telephone when he was twenty-two. That's why as a telecom entrepreneur he wanted to help his homeland. But he had no contacts in the Indian government except for G. B. Meemansi—leader of R&D teams at TRC—whom he had met during a conference at Japan in 1976. When Indira Gandhi set up a committee to review the telecom system in 1980, Pitroda wrote to its members outlining his ideas on telecom development, particularly the need for India to go digital. Subsequently he wrote to the prime minister herself offering to return to India to help develop a modern telecom system.

Indira Gandhi asked Rajiv's friend Deodhar to go to Chicago to determine the genuineness of his offer, specifically "why he (Pitroda) want[ed] to return to India." Deodhar did so and reported to the prime minister that Pitroda was a bright entrepreneur who had just sold his company and appeared to be genuinely interested in India. The way Indira personally commissioned a background check showed her interest in the man. Pitroda first met Rajiv in 1981 and subsequently Indira, who directed the DoE to pursue Pitroda's idea of developing an Indian digital switch.

After the usual bureaucratic wrangles and turf war between the DoE and the DoT, it was decided to set up a National Centre for Electronic Switch R&D—subsequently renamed the more modern-sounding Centre for Development of Telematics. It was set up as an autonomous body, modeled after TIFR to provide for freedom and functional autonomy. In 1984 the TRC team that developed SPC-1 and the TIFR team that developed the switch for armed forces in the 1970s were regrouped to form C-DOT's core development team. It was given thirty-six months and a budget of about $30 million to develop a digital switch. Such target-oriented technology development, conducted in a mission mode, was a new experience for Indian scientists and technologists.

The challenge was to develop a rugged telecom switch that would work without an air-conditioned location in rural areas. The existing analog electromechanical switches based on crossbar technology required air conditioning and were designed for Western networks with fewer calls per line. In Indian situations, such switches would fail because of high call volume.

The switch designed by C-DOT was based on low-power-consuming, complementary metal oxide semiconductor (CMOS) circuits. It could function properly in temperatures as high as 45 degrees Celsius and humidity of 80 percent, with no air conditioning. In addition, it could work under high BHCA (busy hour call attempt) conditions. The design started with a basic switching module of 128 ports that could operate as a private branch exchange (PBX). Its modular design switch meant that it could be deployed as a rural automatic exchange (RAX), trunk automatic exchange (TAX), or main automatic exchange (MAX) with capacity ranging from four hundred to forty thousand lines. It was a pulse code modulation (PCM) switch from which one could make calls anywhere in the world. Millions of lines based on the C-DOT switch have been installed in India and dozens of developing countries since 1987 (figure 4.2).

Several new hardware and software technologies and tools that were just becoming available went into the making of the Indian switch.[28] It deployed the concept of distributed processing using 8-bit and 16-bit

Figure 4.2
Sam Pitrodra, technology advisor of Prime Minister Gandhi, explaining features of
new rural telephone exchange developed by C-DOT to communications minister
Arjun Singh (extreme right) in 1987. The spread of C-DOT technology ushered in
telecom revolution in India in the 1980s and 1990s. Courtesy: Sam Pitroda

microprocessors with interconnection between them over the switched
networked path. The design allowed for replacement of these processors
with enhanced versions later, if needed. The software was programmed in
high-level language—initially in C and then in CHILL (CCITT High Level
Language).

Pitroda's connections with suppliers in Chicago ensured access to components not available in India. Ease of production was another factor kept
in mind while designing the switch so that the technology could easily be
transferred to industry. The investment required for setting up a production
unit with annual capacity of a half million lines was estimated to be $20
million in 1989. This was eight to ten times less than similar plants based
on other technologies.

The C-DOT project was a resounding success. Not only did it develop
a rural electronic switch tailor-made for Indian conditions, but its technology was transferred to several private manufacturers. It was a unique

public-private partnership in India's history: the state funded research to develop a technology and then transferred it to private sector for manufacturing without any fee. This was the kind of strategy countries like Korea and Taiwan had followed in the 1970s, to take a lead in electronics hardware production. With licensing of the C-DOT technology to private companies, the public sector monopoly in telecom switch manufacturing was broken, and the benefits of public-funded research were made available to the private sector at no cost. This project helped a great deal in expanding the telephone network to rural areas, both through personal ownership of phones and through privately operated phone booths known as Public Call Office—or PCO booth—that Pitroda implemented.

For Pitroda, the rural telecommunications project was more than a technical challenge: it was an exercise in "national self-assurance," just as space and nuclear programs had given Indians pride in their country's scientific capability. "India like most of the third world was using its foreign exchange to buy the West's abandoned technology and install obsolete equipment that doomed the poor to move like telecom snails where Europeans, Americans and Japanese were beginning to move like information greyhounds," Pitroda noted in an article in the *Harvard Business Review*.[29] India and countries like her, in his view, "were falling farther and farther behind, not just in the ability to chat with relatives or call the doctor, but much more critically, in the capacity to coordinate development activities, pursue scientific study, conduct business, operate markets and participate more fully in the international community." Pitroda was certain that "to survive, India had to bring telecommunications to its towns and villages; to thrive, it had to do it with Indian talent and Indian technology."

The project helped in technological capability building in terms of innovation, production system management, investment, component procurement, marketing, engineering, technology diffusion, skill development, production process improvement, and vendor development.[30] It had a profound impact on the software development industry. The digital switch and other projects were software driven. These projects helped develop necessary skills and a set of professionals trained in telecom software development. The work culture in C-DOT was open, was nonhierarchical, and promoted innovation and new ideas (figure 4.3).

Conclusion: New Alliances Emerge

The science and technology policies pursued by Rajiv Gandhi were a continuum of the policies of Nehru and Indira Gandhi. Yet there were significant

Figure 4.3
Prime Minister Gandhi (third from left) speaking at the national conference on telecom mission in New Delhi in February 1987. His advisor Sam Pitroda is on the extreme left. Courtesy: Sam Pitroda

differences. Clearly, his focus was on technology and its wider application rather than on basic research and import substitution–led technology development. His stress was not on expansion of science and technology infrastructure, in contrast to the approach in Indira Gandhi's time.

If Nehru was the political patron of Indian science, Rajiv played the same role for Indian technology. The way science developed in the Nehru era was through politician-scientist alliances, mainly links that Nehru built with leading scientists. This resulted in the birth and growth of science conglomerates like the Council of Scientific and Industrial Research (CSIR), Defence Research and Development Organization (DRDO), and the Department of Atomic Energy (DAE). The focus of this era was scientific research for national development. As far as technology-based production was concerned, the public sector had a supreme role. During Rajiv's era, technology development and diffusion took place through the politician-technocrat alliance. Scientists had a role to play but it was technologists and technocrats who called the shots. Technocrats were key participants in the new alliance with India's political leadership. The focus was on technology and not on the esoteric goal of scientific research for national development. And, as far as production was concerned, the private sector was given a major role to play.

In the Nehru era, scientists like Bhabha, Bhatnagar, Mahalanobis, and D. S. Kothari built alliances with the political leadership and earned unstinted government support for their own areas of work and research conglomerates they set up. Technocrats like Sam Pitroda, Seshagiri, Deodhar, and S. Ramachandran and scientists like C. N. R. Rao played a similar role in the Rajiv period and got support for their pet projects like NIC, C-DOT, ET&T, tissue culture, and superconductivity. Yet another example of Rajiv's support for domestic generation of technology was the development of supercomputers in the wake of the American embargo on such systems. He gave ready approval to the suggestion to establish the Centre for Development of Advanced Computing (C-DAC) for the purpose. On the lines of C-DOT, the new center was allocated about $35 million to develop a prototype of a supercomputer based on parallel processing in two years (figure 4.4).

Figure 4.4
In the 1980s, the American government denied India access to supercomputing technology for fear of its use in nuclear weapon designing. In late 1988, the U.S. administration cleared import of a Cray supercomputer for weather forecasting purposes with a number of conditions. The system (seen in the picture)—Cray X-MP/14—was installed in early 1989 at the National Centre for Medium Range Weather Forecasting (NCMRWF). Meanwhile, the Rajiv Gandhi administration in India had set up a dedicated national agency, the Centre for Development of Advanced Computing (C-DAC), which delivered India's first supercomputer PARAM 8000 (PARAllelMachine) in 1990. Courtesy: NCMRWF

A clear shift in focus and motivation took place in this period—from a unified and centralized system of scientific research in public sector laboratories to a problem-solving, mission-oriented model of developing technology. The very structures of the Nehru era were bypassed to facilitate technical innovation. Private enterprises—not the public sector—were made the beneficiary of technologies developed in public-funded agencies. Unlike the TDC computer technology, which was developed at AEE and transferred for production to public sector ECIL, C-DOT technology was not automatically transferred to public sector units like ITI but given freely to a range of private companies.

Rajiv linked poverty directly with technology. He believed that poverty by definition was the lack of use of technology by an average person. In his view, "as long as we prevent average people from using better technology, we are inadvertently or deliberately continuing his level of poverty and not allowing him to get out or break free from that burden of poverty."[31] The type of technologies Rajiv referred to was not the so-called appropriate or rural technologies, but the likes of C-DOT's digital telephone exchange, tissue culture, genetic engineering, solar power, and so on. According to Rajiv, "Appropriate technology is only appropriate for those who are exporting it to us and those who are trying to get rid of old, redundant units which they cannot use anymore anywhere else; it is appropriate for them and not appropriate normally for us."[32]

The path of self-reliance followed by Nehru and Indira Gandhi also got a new meaning in the Rajiv era. Rajiv redefined self-reliance as "indigenous efforts and alertness to outside technological progress. It means developing (on) imported technology, making the next technological breakthrough ourselves, closing the technological gap."[33]

All along, this politician-technocrat nexus influenced policymaking and investment in computers, electronics, telecommunications, biotechnology, and alternative sources of energy. Rajiv's interest was notably greater in such sunrise technology areas, rather than basic research. Rajiv gave practical and industry orientation even to traditionally nurtured areas of scientific research like space and atomic energy. He did not want the nuclear power sector to grow on a reactor-to-reactor basis, but wanted nuclear power to grow in an industrial sector.[34] And in doing so, he was not averse to the import of larger reactors. That is why talks began with the USSR for the import of reactors, but the deal got derailed due to the break-up of the Soviet Union.

The 1980s, encompassing the Rajiv era, was a significant period in the development of India as software and services giant. The policy changes in this period marked an ideological shift from self-reliance, and the state-driven and import substitution approach to the market-led, private-sector driven liberal approach in the communication and computer sectors. IT networks developed, and the use of IT went up. An environment that was hostile to technology earlier was converted into the one conducive for change. The policy thrust was specific to boosting computer hardware and software industries. In the software sector, the export focus thrust was carefully built through domestic capabilities. These policies had a mixed result in both the hardware and software industries. Since economic liberalization was not full-fledged, but only partial, full benefits could not be reaped.

5 Discovering a New Continent

The ad campaign opened up [the] first time user market. I think this was a turning point for industry as a whole. There was huge latent demand in the market. What we did was primary marketing. It was like discovering a new continent.

—Arjun Malhotra, cofounder, HCL, on selling 8C, India's first mass-marketed microcomputer, in 1980[1]

The departure of IBM from the Indian market in 1977 came at a critical juncture. The computer industry was undergoing a tectonic shift from mainframes to minicomputers and microprocessor-based systems. But Indian companies could not take advantage of this change fully because of high import duties on components and capital goods, restrictions on import of technology, and caps on industrial capacities. In order to meet the demand for computers in the country, entrepreneur-driven companies had no option but to develop their own design capabilities. Some of them could introduce near-contemporary machines in the local market. This gave birth to an indigenous computer industry in the 1980s, though the groundwork for it was already underway in the previous decade.

From Textiles to Calculators

The pioneer among Indian computer companies was DCM Data Products, a unit of the DCM group, North India's largest industrial conglomerate. Delhi Cloth Mills (DCM) was founded as a small cotton yarn-spinning mill in 1889 but over the first half of the twentieth century it grew to become a large industrial conglomerate with interests ranging from textiles to engineering products. When a new generation of foreign-educated members of the clan entered the family-run business, change was inevitable. Vinay Bharat Ram, grandson of the group patriarch Lala Shri Ram and son of Lala Bharat Ram, had obtained a management degree from the University of

Michigan in 1960. Initially he managed DCM textile mills in Delhi, but he soon started exploring new avenues of manufacturing under an aptly named initiative—New Projects Organization (NPO)—within the group. Electronics, which was flavor of the season, was an obvious choice.

Sometime in 1969, business magazine *Fortune* had featured an electronic four-function desktop calculator developed by Sharp Electronics of Japan dubbing it "the star of business machines." It was the first electronic calculator incorporating LSI (large-scale integration). The magazine article caught Vinay's imagination (use of his first name is to avoid confusion with his father Bharat Ram) and he decided to import one of the calculators. Though not an engineering graduate himself, he was keen to acquire knowledge in electronics, which he thought could be a potential new area of business. No sooner had the Japanese gadget costing about $400 arrived when Vinay marshaled a team of engineers and asked them to take it apart. The idea was to see if it could be assembled locally. He also began corresponding with U.S. and Japanese companies to propose collaboration. He managed to obtain a provisional license to manufacture 2,000 calculators a year with foreign know-how. Calculator technology had moved from transistors to large-scale integrated circuits and microprocessors, making some high-end calculators as powerful as first-generation computers. Another Japanese firm, Busicom, followed with a calculator based on Intel's 4004 microprocessor in 1970.

Keen to collaborate with a Japanese corporation, Vinay dashed off letters to several Japanese companies. Mere acknowledgment of his letters from Sony and Toshiba were enough for an enthusiastic Vinay to proceed to Tokyo. After his persistent calling, a reluctant Sony official gave him an appointment. A tall man received Vinay at Sony headquarters in Tokyo and announced, "Yes, I am Akio Morita." The name didn't ring a bell in Vinay's mind because Morita was yet to achieve the kind of global name recognition that the Sony Walkman would later bring him.

Morita was accompanied by a group of executives dressed in navy blue uniforms. When Vinay told them the purpose of his visit, the Sony officials were skeptical. They were unwilling to collaborate because DCM had no experience in technology business whatsoever; its focus had been on textiles, cement, sugar, and so on. However, just before the meeting was to wind up, Vinay mentioned that his father Lala Bharat Ram had just become president of the International Chamber of Commerce (ICC). This unrelated but important information about the patriarch of the Indian industrial house impressed Morita and other Sony executives because an Asian had not occupied the ICC post before. Bharat Ram's predecessor at

ICC was Arthur K. Watson, chairman of IBM World Trade Corporation. The ICC connection to the DCM chairman clinched the deal. Morita accepted DCM's proposal to assemble Sony electronic calculators in India. Bharat Ram, who was in Montreal attending an ICC meeting, came to Tokyo to wrap up the agreement. It was agreed that DCM would pay a royalty of $100,000 to Sony for assembling 2000 calculators annually in India. The first industrial collaboration for making a high-tech electronic product in India was thus begun.

Vinay was overjoyed as his dream of assembling the "star of business machines" in India was finally becoming real. For the house of DCM too, it was a turning point. Back in India, however, Vinay's joy was short-lived. Per government regulations, he filed an application for foreign collaboration and for conversion of the Letter of Intent into a manufacturing license. Shockingly, the government refused to convert the provisional license into a manufacturing permit because the policy at that time, he was told, did not allow such collaboration. The government was closely looking at promoting the electronics industry but was not keen to let a private company enter such a strategic field. "Here we had a prestigious collaborator like Sony and the government said 'no.' This was socialist India," Vinay would later recall.[2]

The decision was taken at the highest level in the government. Parmeshwar Narain Haksar, principal secretary and economic advisor to Prime Minister Indira Gandhi, was known to hold pro-state and socialist views. It was on Haksar's advice that Indira Gandhi had begun projecting a socialist image of her government.[3] The key decisions that the prime minister took to bolster her socialist image were nationalization of private banks and abolition of the privileges of ex-princes. Allowing a leading industrial house to enter a new area of economy like electronics with foreign collaboration would have gone against the socialist scheme of India's development. So, the first private sector attempt to launch manufacturing of electronic products with foreign technology ended in a fiasco.

The government under Indira Gandhi had accepted recommendations of the Industrial Licensing Policy Inquiry Committee, which had observed that "outflow through royalty and restrictive collaborations" was adversely affecting the government's "long-term import substitution efforts." In its members' opinion, foreign collaboration should merely be "instruments to further as well as exploit the industrial and technological base that had already been established."

Refusal to approve foreign technology or proposals for joint ventures with foreign companies was not unusual in India in this period. For example, the government had denied permission to Fairchild Semiconductors to set up a manufacturing plant in India in 1963. The Far East was yet to emerge as a destination for offshore manufacturing by U.S. companies. Fairchild President Robert Noyce—later to cofound Intel—was looking at possible locations in Asia, particularly India, to take advantage of cheap labor. While on a tour of Asia with the idea of setting up a facility, Noyce and colleagues visited India and returned via Hong Kong.[4] In the Indian capital, Noyce met officials at the Directorate General of Technology Development (DGTD), which was a centralized agency to review all proposed imports (of machinery, raw materials, manufacturing plants, etc.) that could even fix royalties as well as set production ceilings based on its own judgment. This is what it did with Fairchild.

Noyce was asked to keep Fairchild equity in the joint venture below 50 percent and pay royalty of 4 percent. In addition, Fairchild was asked to limit production to 0.6 million devices, instead of its proposed 10 million.[5] Agreeing to a regulatory ceiling on production would have been absurd for a manufacturer that was looking to achieve economies of scale by leveraging cheap labor. Fairchild finally decided to set up a plant in Hong Kong in early 1965 with a production capacity of five million planar transistors annually.[6] The wages were $1 per day, lower than what American counterparts earned per hour. Later it set up production facilities in Korea where wages were even lower. The Fairchild episode helps explain how India lost an opportunity to be part of the manufacturing business that would make the Far East a favored destination for U.S. semiconductor manufacturers.

The presence of international names like Fairchild, Sony, and CDC (which too was exploring the Indian market around the same time) in the 1960s would have helped India access much needed foreign know-how, skills, and manufacturing techniques. IBM, which used to manufacture data processing equipment such as key punches at its Bombay plant, had helped develop a base of vendors and component suppliers.

In DCM's case, Vinay decided to do the next best thing—reverse engineer the Sharp calculator. In 1971, a team of engineers, one of whom one had a PhD in electronics from Tokyo University, was ready with a working prototype of a "four-function calculator." As the name indicated, it could perform four functions—addition, subtraction, multiplication, and division. It had no memory and had a LED display. The calculator was fabricated in the garage of a DCM textile mill in Delhi. A new wing—DCM Data Products—was then set up within the textile division to manufacture calculators. This was the first attempt by an private Indian firm to manufacture calculators and computers. Until now, the market had been dominated by multinationals—IBM and ICL—and the government company ECIL.

Vinay expanded his NPO by picking up bright young men from different DCM mills across the country who had been recruited for the "DCM Senior Management Training Scheme"—a kind of in-house management development program. Arun Joshi, a management graduate from MIT, was specially hired to run this program. Those selected to join DCM Data Products (DCM DP) included S. Raman, an industrial control engineer; Shiv Shankar Nadar, who was in charge of marketing readymade shirts (Lord Jim brand) in the textile division; and fresh engineering graduates such as Arjun Malhotra from IIT Kharagpur.

DCM DP was a spin-off of a large industrial house, but it had all the trappings of a start-up. It operated out of a garage, had little money to begin with, attracted young talent on the promise of a rosy future, introduced a completely new product, and made money in the short term. Vinay depended on the parent company to fund his venture as the concept of risk or venture capital was then nonexistent in India.

Vinay realized his dream with the launch of DCM's locally made desktop electronic calculator in August 1972. Importing components was difficult and only a few local firms made reliable components and parts. The DoE had fixed a ceiling on "import content" of electronic calculators which was initially 400 rupees (about $55 in 1972) and progressively brought down to 150 rupees ($20).[7] Manufacturing processes were archaic. Parts inside the calculator were hand-wired and, therefore, could easily malfunction. The calculator had to be housed in a wooden case since importing ABS (acrylonitrile butadiene styrene) plastics was prohibitive. This made the DCM calculator slightly bulkier than a briefcase. Yet it was displayed as an example of indigenous technology at the annual India International Trade Fair and shown to Prime Minister Indira Gandhi.

From rudimentary four-function calculators, DCM DP moved over to programmable calculators, also called scientific calculators as they could perform tasks such as square root calculations. The calculator group, now almost entirely consisting of freshly recruited graduates from IITs, was attached to the unit engaged in making programmable calculators using MOS (metal oxide semiconductor) chips. In 1974, the company released a new calculator model—the 1080 PS. It had a capacity of eighty programming steps and ten data storage steps. DCM could sell hundreds of units within a short period since only smuggled calculators were available in the market, at highly inflated prices. Development engineers were surprised when Nadar with his aggressive marketing skills could sell several units with just a mockup.

Innovative ways were devised to market the calculators. Two members of the marketing team—Ajai Chowdhry and Yogesh Vaidya—developed "applications" for calculators. They created an "estimation formula" which could be used by government departments to assess farmlands irrigated by any irrigation project. Top officials in the irrigation department of Maharashtra state liked it and suggested the use of DCM calculators in irrigation projects all over the state. Encouraged with this marketing "breakthrough," the team came up with a similar formula for estimating sugar production and was able to sell a number of calculators to cash rich sugar mills in the same state. "This way [the] calculator became a precursor to a computer and this experience helped us a lot in future," Chowdhry said of the unique marketing pitch.[8]

The success of calculators encouraged Vinay to venture into more ambitious line of products—mini- and microcomputers. This was a logical next step. India was still in the mainframe era and only large corporations and government companies could afford to use computers. The market, however, was about to change as American minicomputer makers had started exploring the Indian market in light of uncertainty about the operations of IBM and ICL. In December 1975, DCM launched India's first microprocessor-based computer—DCM 1101—built using the PPS4 chip from Rockwell. It was a 4-bit computer and came in two versions—scientific and statistical. An IBM 360 computer at the University of Delhi was used to develop software for this machine. With all these products, Shiv Nadar and his marketing team proved their mettle by selling the products all over the country.

Despite this initial marketing success, the DCMDP faced financial problems and was constantly at war with bosses in the textile division of DCM. The group's management did not fully appreciate the potential of this new line of business. It was reluctant to fund development work on new products. Nadar suggested a novel way to beat the cash crunch—offering a multiple-year warranty for calculators instead of the standard one year. Advance maintenance fee collection could generate cash immediately. An advertising campaign was launched, showing a baby with just a locket hanging around his neck, with "three year warranty" inscribed on it. Sales teams were given aggressive targets to get customers to sign up for the three-year warranty. This generated some cash and the nascent venture survived.

The cash crunch and running battles with managers in the textile division left the young marketing team of DCMP DP bitter. Nadar and his team members were increasingly feeling restless and frustrated. Thoughts of exploring a future of his own occupied his mind all the time. His experience with marketing calculators was a proof enough that there was latent demand for locally made technology products in India. Occasional market surveys and other research reports published by the Electronics Commission helped Nadar get a sense of the larger picture. Armed with his field experience and rudimentary techno-commercial inputs from government reports, Nadar zeroed in on two potential areas for entrepreneurship—medical electronics and computers. Ultimately he settled on the unexplored area of computers. The next task was to build a team and generate necessary seed money.

A conference of sales and marketing executives of DCM DP, held in October 1975, provided an ideal backdrop for Nadar to informally discuss his idea among like-minded colleagues. He persuaded ten of them to part ways with DCM and float a new company. In a dramatic move, they all resigned en bloc the very next day. Finally six of them—Shiv Nadar, Arjun Malhotra, Ajai Chowdhry, Subhash Arora, Yogesh Vaidya, and D. S. (Pammi) Puri—stuck together to launch a new firm. A few months later, DCM DP technology head S. Raman, also joined the team. Nadar had the cream of DCM DP—engineers, marketing, technology and HR people—on his side.

Birth Pangs of a Garage Start-Up

The six young men pooled their savings as well as loans from family members to start a new company—Microcomp—with a total capital of about $21,000 (187,000 rupees). Initially it operated from Nadar's residence in Safdarjung Development Area in South Delhi, but soon shifted to a *barsati* (rain shelter on the rooftop) of a bungalow in Golf Links owned by Malhotra's maternal grandmother. An address in the posh Golf Links gave the new company instant respectability and an impression that "these guys have family money," as only the rich could afford a house in this neighborhood adjoining the Delhi Golf Club. Microcomp decided to start by producing calculators, which was a familiar territory for its founders.

Microcomp—short for microprocessor and computer—was actually the code name of a 4-bit microprocessor-based computer that DCM was developing when Nadar and team walked out. The start-up simply appropriated the name as DCM had not bothered to register it.

The company had limited capital, no manufacturing facility or a license to start manufacturing, and little design and development experience. It was largely a bunch of enthusiastic marketing and sales people. Designing or developing a calculator for manufacture appeared to be a tall order.

While the team was contemplating its next move, Televista, makers of a popular television, made an interesting offer to Microcomp: to market its calculators on a profit-sharing basis. Microcomp snapped up the offer as it could provide an opportunity to raise much-needed capital for the microcomputer project.

Aggressive marketing tactics of Microcomp soon propelled Televista to the top position, ahead of big brands like DCM, Nelco, Weston, ECIL, and Devidayal. All India-made calculators used chips imported from Electronic Arrays, NEC, Hitachi, Texas Instruments, GI, Mostek, National, and Rockwell. The demand was so high that Televista could not keep up with it. Meanwhile, Microcomp started sourcing calculators from another company and selling under its own brand—Omron. It was a pocket calculator and was aggressively priced at 199 rupees. In yet another marketing first, Nadar and colleagues roped in a general retailing shop, Akabarallys in Bombay, to sell their pocket calculators. Till then, calculators were sold only through direct selling. Omron soon outsold Televista calculators; that company ultimately terminated its contract with Microcomp.

The calculator business generated some cash within three months for the microcomputer project. Getting necessary capital and a manufacturing license was still a hurdle for the start-up. Nadar looked for a way out. He was aware that government-owned electronics companies in many states had been licensed to manufacture a range of electronic products including computers, but were making only television sets. The Uttar Pradesh Electronics Corporation Limited (UPTRON) was one such company. Microcomp approached it with a proposal to float a joint venture to manufacture computers in a new industrial township, New Okhla Industrial Development Authority, or Noida, which was coming up near Delhi. An agreement between the two was inked in August 1976 (figure 5.1). Normally, such a venture would have been funded this way: 26 percent by the UP government, 25 percent by private partners, and the rest raised by the public. Since the cost of going public was too high compared to the total equity of $225,000 (two million rupees), it was decided to let Microcomp own 74 percent. A joint venture by the Uttar Pradesh state government would succeed on the heels of poor performance by several public sector undertakings.

The joint venture was named Hindustan Computers Limited (HCL). Microcomp had to try hard to get the title registered because only large companies were allowed to include "India" or its Hindi language equivalent like "Hindustan"' or "Bharat" in their name or logo. The name had several advantages—it sounded pan-Indian, gave the feel of a large corporation or a public sector undertaking, and clearly mentioned the word "computers."

Figure 5.1
Entrepreneur Shiv Nadar (seated at right) signing the agreement with the state-owned Uttar Pradesh Electronics Corporation Limited in August 1976, establishing the joint venture Hindustan Computers Limited to manufacture computers; HCL became a major player in microcomputer manufacturing as mainframes were gradually phased out after the exit of IBM in 1978. Courtesy: HCL

It denoted "largeness, it was Indian, it was patriotic, it was perfect," to use the words of one of the founders.[9] The logo was also designed to give the feel of a "solid company." An important-sounding name was crucial for the start-up because its promoters were conscious that Indian consumers, who were accustomed to big names like IBM, ICL and to some extent DCM, would not trust buying a high-tech—and high-cost—product like a computer from an unknown little firm (figure 5.2).

Within four months, HCL introduced its first major product—a 4-bit microprocessor-based computer called Micro-2200 for scientific and engineering applications. The first unit was sold to IIT Kharagpur on November 25, 1976, for about $3,100 (27,772 rupees).[10] It was actually a "me too" version of the DCM 1101 system launched nearly a year ago. Both deployed Rockwell's PPS4 chip and had similar architecture, given S. Raman had designed both. However, HCL founders contended that their machine was an advance over the DCM 1101 because it had a magnetic card reader unlike

Figure 5.2
HCL's first microcomputer—Micro 2200—launched in 1976. It was a 4-bit micro-processor-based (PPS4 of Rockwell International) computer targeted at scientific and engineering applications. The first unit was sold to the Indian Institute of Technology Kharagpur. Courtesy: HCL

the DCM 1101, which had a cassette storage device.[11] Though Micro-2200 entered the market much later, it overtook DCM 1101 very fast because it was priced low.[12]

Old timers at DCM feel that HCL benefited from development experi-ence its engineers gained while at DCM. It is alleged that some people left the company with designs, drawings, and software codes of the DCM 1101 to join rival firms. HCL benefited in other ways, too, as elaborated by a DCM software engineer: "They (HCL) came up with exactly identical product. Only some packaging was different. For instance, in our system, 'insert' feature was not there. This allowed users to insert a step at any point in the program. In DCM, marketing people used to ask the development team to introduce this feature. Raman did not do it here, but introduced this feature in the HCL machine. This made a big difference for users."[13] The incident merely echoed what was happening with computer makers in the Silicon Valley then. Edison DeCastro, who designed a 16-bit minicomputer at Digital Equipment Corporation, walked out and formed Data General and launched a successful machine based on his 16-bit system design.

After Nadar and colleagues walked out, DCM DP had started working on a minicomputer—a copy of PDP 11 of DEC launched in 1970—and was ready with a 16-bit computer named Galaxy. But when the company came to know about rival HCL preparing for the launch of an 8-bit machine, it hurriedly started working on a similar system with help from engineers hired from IBM India and other companies. DCM's 8-bit computer was based on Intel's 8080 microprocessor and came bundled with a locally developed operating system and software for applications such as inventory management. It was sold under DCM's Spectrum series and advertised as a "business management system."

The Spectrum series, which competed directly with TDC-312 and TDC-316 systems manufactured by ECIL, demonstrated the growing technological sophistication of computers fabricated in India during this period.[14] In some respects, DCM computers were better than those from ECIL. The per-bit cost in rupees of the main memory used in the TDC-316 was equivalent to $0.14, while that of DCM system was $0.06. The technology gap between systems introduced in advanced markets and those in India too was narrowing compared to the situation in 1960s when the market was dominated by old computers from IBM and ICL.

The technological sophistication of computers being fabricated by companies seeking to get a slice of the post-IBM market—ECIL, DCM, HCL, and others—was a result of imported components and peripherals. ECIL computers had components from Intersil and Motorola, floppy-disk drives from Shugart, BASF, and Pertec; hard-disk drives from Memorex, Pertec, and BASF, and printers from BASF and Dataproducts.[15] DCM computers incorporated Kennedy magnetic tapes and hard-disk drives, Shugart floppy-disk drives, and printers from Centronics. HCL sourced its microprocessors from Intel and peripherals from Shugart and Centronics.[16] Clearly, India's fledgling computer companies were capable of plugging into global supply markets to overcome the lack of an ecosystem for technology products at home.

The Systems Software Division of DCM collaborated with Tandy Corp in Fort Worth, Texas, for software development. "It began with support for Tandy's TRS-DOS, and then proceeded to doing higher skill tasks such as writing drivers to adapt MS-DOS to the hardware of Tandy and customizing MS-DOS itself. For this, our engineers had access to source code of MS-DOS," said Joe Cleetus, who headed the division then.[17] DCM also worked for Microsoft at their Bellevue software office, and developed branded products as well. Mactran—a full FORTRAN-77 compiler system with a fully symbolic source-level debugger for Apple Macintosh based on 68000 and other processors of Motorola—was a successful product of DCM. The company sold about one hundred copies of Mactran a month at $99 each. In the mid-1980s, DCM's overseas software business grossed $1.2 million a year.

Discovering a New Continent with 8C

HCL announced its 8-bit microprocessor-based computer, 8C, powered by Rockwell's PPS-8 microprocessor in August 1977. The use of a 5.25-inch floppy-disk drive from Shugart Associates as a storage device was the most notable feature of this machine because eight-inch floppy-disk was the prevailing industry standard then.[18] Prior to the introduction of the eight-inch floppy-disk by IBM in 1971, paper tapes and cassette recorders were used for data storage. HCL engineers had established contacts with Alan Shugart during a visit to the United States in 1977.[19] For an Indian start-up to launch a microcomputer almost at the same time as was happening in U.S. technology hubs was certainly impressive.

The use of the 5.25-inch drive made 8C highly suitable for Indian conditions. A floppy-disk could store 80 kilobytes, and its drive had auto restart function in case of power failure. It could be run with a car battery in case of power shutdown, unlike the AC-operated eight-inch drive that required regular power supply. Since data entry usually took a lot of time and power failures were common in India, a drive running on battery power was critical. For Indian customers interested in cheaper alternatives to card punch systems, this 8C feature proved very attractive. The computer had external hardware and a special software facility which ensured that the program, if interrupted by power failure, would restart exactly where it had stopped. Mainframe computers offered no such feature. 8C's hardware consisted of a central unit, a floppy disk read/write unit, and an alphanumeric keyboard. It had a twenty-character green fluorescent dot-matrix display.

Yet another highlight of 8C was an operating system written in Business BASIC (Beginners All Purpose Symbolic Instruction Code) language and a series of applications such as financial accounting and payroll and inventory control packages. Business BASIC contained elementary statements necessary to write simple programs and features like "file handling" statements. As cofounder Ajai Chowdhry later described the effort, "We decided to write everything from scratch. We wrote a BASIC Interpreter and some very good utilities, which were valuable for commercial computing. We wrote a product called SuperSort. Sorting was very big deal in any commercial data processing system. Our operating system was built into ROM so that it would give it a better speed."[20] The microcomputer was targeted at small companies, the lower end of the market. The upper end was comfortable with mainframes from names like IBM, and later on, minicomputers from other U.S. manufacturers.

The early introduction of novel features such as the 5.25-inch floppy-disk drive in HCL's first microprocessor-based system shows that Indian computer firms were attempting to deliver contemporary systems using new components and peripherals no sooner than they became available in the United States. But the local market's small size, and lack of a manufacturing base, meant that Indian companies lagged behind in the race. Apple-2, introduced in April 1977, had a cassette interface and a 5.25-inch floppy drive was incorporated in Apple Disk II released in July 1978.[21] Apple and HCL computers were totally different in their physical appearance and applications—Apple's was a desktop, while HCL was a floor standing unit; the Apple machine's console was integrated, while 8C had a separate console; Apple was a general-purpose machine, while 8C was a business computer. Both systems used BASIC and ran on proprietary operating systems. The DoE's official journal described 8C as "a commercial microcomputer system, the first of its kind in Asia."[22]

By a quirk of fate, the day HCL announced the launch of 8C through a full-page advertisement in newspapers (August 8, 1977), their front pages carried the news of IBM folding up its operations from June 1, 1978. This helped the company build a perception that it was a new corporation that the government had set up to replace IBM. Perhaps people confused HCL with Computer Maintenance Corporation, which the government had incorporated for maintenance of IBM machines, but it was not yet in public knowledge as it had not placed any advertisements in newspapers until then. When buyers confronted HCL executives, asking whether it had been set up by the government to replace IBM, they just shrugged, leaving the question unanswered. In fact, even in DoE reports of the period, HCL's name figures under the heading of public sector organizations along with BEL, ECIL, and Hindustan Teleprinters Limited because it was a joint venture with a government entity, UPTRON. The image of HCL as a govern-ment-supported computer manufacturer was thus not entirely misplaced.

A price tag of $10,000 (83,500 rupees) for 8C may have appeared exces-sive (one could buy a car for about $2,000) but it was reasonable compared to the costs of leasing an IBM or ICL mainframe. In a typical data center, one hour of data processing time could cost in rupees the equivalent of about $85. That's why when HCL announced 8C, a number of enterprises placed their orders. HCL would take 30 percent in advance and 70 percent on delivery. The advance covered the bill of materials and the rest was the profit margin. Initially 8C was labeled in documents filed with the govern-ment as an "accounting invoicing machine" for tax purposes because a sep-arate classification for a microcomputer did not exist in the tax regulations. HCL had earlier imported an electromechanical accounting and invoicing machine from the East German manufacturer, Robotron, so HCL founders knew that a classification for such a machine existed in tax schedules.

Selling microcomputers in a market bred solely on mainframes was not easy. Manufacturers who were trying to target users of obsolete URMs left behind by IBM met with little success. This was because data processing operators, and not programmers, ran URMs, and these people were scared of learning the ropes of programming required for microcomputers. HCL gained an insight into the latent market from a project report written by an Indian intern from an American management school in 1979. The project gave an idea of how an organization makes the decision to buy a computer. Based on this, HCL decided to focus on the entrepreneurial organizations where the decision maker was an individual and not a process. All mar-keting executives were told to identify in their prospective users an orga-nizational need—a sort of "hot button"—for which a computer could be deployed for higher productive gains.

Armed with this insight, HCL launched an aggressive advertising cam-paign with the theme "Breaking the Common Computer Myths." This opened up the markets for HCL dramatically. The first myth that the series of ads exploded was "Too Complicated, My Staff Cannot Handle It." The ad boldly declared: "For the first time in India, HCL introduces a computer which even your typist can operate." This was to break the myth that only businesses having Electronic Data Processing (EDP) departments with dedi-cated technical staff could use computers. All of a sudden, HCL's sales rose to one thousand computers a year, while other manufacturers were stuck at two hundred or so. Competitors started slashing prices and luring HCL's marketing executives with fabulous offers. In a way, the company created a new market segment—that of first-time users—which did not exist earlier and was not targeted in the mainframe era. The company also appealed to cost-conscious buyers by selling peripherals like printers, electric typewriters, and key-to-diskette data terminals separately as "add-ons." Users could first buy the computer and stagger the purchase of peripherals.

Malhotra recalled, "That ad campaign opened up the first-time user market. I think this was a turning point for the industry as a whole. There was huge latent demand in the market. What we did was primary marketing. It was like discovering a new continent."[23] In June 1980, HCL surpassed DCM Data Products in terms of revenue and profits. HCL management attributed this success to "an excellent feel of the lower-end markets, strategic advertising and a sales team that does not believe in giving up."[24] In 1981, HCL launched System2, based on Intel's 8080 chip. This machine was marketed through road shows in smaller towns—yet another marketing innovation. The very next year, another new machine—WorkHorse1—was introduced, again targeting small businesses. This was dubbed "the first indigenously developed single board desktop computer" (figure 5.3).

Figure 5.3
The newswire service United News of India collaborated with Hindustan Computers Limited to pioneer instant analysis by computers of the results of the 1980 elections to Lok Sabha (the Lower House of the Indian Parliament). This was a first-of-its-kind computer application in India. Courtesy: HCL

Though HCL took the lead in developing proprietary hardware and operating systems and application packages initially and did well in the market, it had to change its strategy after IBM introduced the PC in 1981 with the Disk Operating System (DOS) developed by Microsoft. In fact, before DOS was introduced, HCL had introduced a standard operating system—Control Program for Microprocessors or CP/M—in newer versions of 8C. It was a single-user operating system developed by Gary Kildall of Digital Research Inc. (DRI). The CP/M was popular among microcomputer makers between 1975 and 1981 as applications written for this could be ported between computers of different makes. WordStar, a popular word processing program, and dBase, a database program for smaller machines, were originally written to operate with CP/M. Many basic concepts and features in DOS developed by Microsoft were patterned after this operating system.

In fact, initially DCM's computers were also based on CP/M. A number of utilities such as sorting were extended so that larger amounts of data that could be stored on multiple floppy-disk machines. A compiler for BASIC was developed to replace the interpreter that came with CP/M. Later CP/M was replaced with Intel's iRMX86, which was released as the developer's OS for developing software. At DCM, iRMX underwent a revamp with only its core elements (kernel, memory management, interrupts, etc.) preserved. An additional layer of software was added to allow manual intervention to run high-speed peripherals such as magnetic tape drives and fast disk drives.

When imports were liberalized in 1984, a number of companies started assembling PCs from imported kits. HCL, too, got into the PC segment right away launching its product range under the brand name of BusyBee based on Intel's 8086 chipset. For this PC, the company developed an operating system equivalent of Microsoft's DOS. The micro code was written in such a way that it could run two commonly used applications—Lotus 1-2-3 and Word Perfect—and much faster than other PCs. Because it could run Lotus despite not being an IBM-compatible machine, BusyBee was priced almost 10,000 rupees higher than similar machines.

Prior to this stage, HCL was stuck with proprietary systems. As demand grew for standard products like PC compatible and UNIX-based computers with standard languages like Micro Focus COBOL, the company looked for suitable technological options. It first worked with the UNIX7 operating system, which was available free, and then it bought the source code of UNIX5 from AT&T and built utilities around it. The capability gained in developing proprietary operating systems and applications as well as in hardware designing at HCL was not wasted. It came in handy for HCL when it forayed into outsourced R&D and services as the market matured.

By 1986, HCL had become India's largest computer manufacturer. In 1988 the company made it to the top of the DQ 20, a listing of computer firms published by the Indian trade magazine *Dataquest*, surpassing revenues of DCM, Wipro, ICIM, and ECIL.

Exploring America via Singapore

The success of 8C on home turf encouraged HCL to explore export markets in 1980. It ventured into manufacturing 8C in Singapore for Southeast Asian markets, taking advantage of tax breaks and subsidies offered by the island government under its Pioneer Status Scheme. The unit, Far Eastern Computers Pte Ltd (FEC), manufactured microcomputers using components and parts imported from India. Taking a cue from the success of an aggressive marketing campaign in India, the company placed full-page advertisements in *The Strait Times* announcing the launch of its system with the tagline "Computerization, Not Just Computers." Rebranding 8C as Abacus for Southeast and Far East Asian markets was also a clever idea, given predominance of Chinese-origin businessmen in Singapore. In five months—August to December 1980—the company booked orders worth 1 million Singapore dollars. "The whole idea of FEC was that we didn't want to be a big fish in a small pond. We were willing to be small fish in a big pond. Singapore was our window to the world," as one of the founders put it.[25]

HCL devised a novel way to supply software for its microcomputers sold in Singapore. In order to develop customized applications for computers sold in Singapore, a Software Exports Division was set up in Madras in South India. Since commercial data links for software export—satellite or undersea—were not yet in vogue, a complex system was followed. FEC engineers would conduct systems analysis in Singapore, then send details to Madras, where programmers would write the software and put it on a floppy disk and courier it to Singapore. But this model had inherent pitfalls. Floppies were unreliable. Often, the data sent via floppies became corrupted or simply vanished by the time it reached Singapore. Enquiries revealed that outmoded x-ray scanners at Madras airport were to blame for this software vanishing trick. Eventually, the system had to be disbanded, but it had helped demonstrate a new model for software exports and marked the beginning of a new line of business—dedicated offshore software development—for the company. The experience would prove useful when HCL returned to software development and services in the 1990s.

The Singapore experience was crucial for HCL's initiation into UNIX technologies and for partnerships with U.S. companies. The subsidiary had begun dabbling with UNIX early on and that experience trickled down to the parent back home.

When Singapore's government called for bids to supply computers for its polytechnic and engineering colleges, Chowdhry lobbied officials to let UNIX-based systems also to compete for the bid. He traveled to the United States to talk to various companies making UNIX systems and zeroed in on the Apollo Computer Corporation, which was marketing workstations for academic and engineering institutions. Chowdhry also went to the UK to meet Apollo system users in Brown and Oxford universities. Armed with all this newly acquired knowledge, HCL won the bid in Singapore despite stiff competition from products like IBM's PC.

The success became a turning point for FEC and parent HCL. It introduced them to the advantages of UNIX as well as to an American partner, Apollo. HCL decided to bring Apollo workstations to the Indian market and began joint manufacturing activity in India, making it first company to launch workstation production in India. Apollo's Domain Series was marketed in India as Nexus 3000. In 1989, Hewlett Packard (HP) bought Apollo. This made HCL a partner of HP and the two floated a joint venture company—HCL HP—in December 1991 to manufacture computers based on RISC (Reduced Instruction Set Computing) architecture. This was the first joint venture between an Indian and a U.S. computer firm—ahead of full-fledged economic liberalization unveiled in 1992.

The partnership with a leading American firm gave HCL a window to the larger information technology world. As Chowdhry says, "we learnt what a global company was. We were very Indian till then. We learnt what processes are. They are very important. How passion and process go together. Till then we only had passion. It also gave us positioning in the world. [People said] if a staid company like HP could partner with HCL, then it is a good company to do business with."[26]

Prior to the joint venture with HP, the company had decided to work on UNIX and develop commercial applications based on the Singapore experience. Horizon1, HCL's first UNIX minicomputer, was introduced in 1984, followed by Horizon II with a Motorola 68010 chip and Berkclay's UNIX 4.2 version in 1985. The third computer in this series—Horizon III—deployed AT&T's Unix V.3. In 1987, HCL developed a symmetric multiprocessor based on Motorola's 68030 processor and fine-grained UNIX. It was done to overcome the U.S. embargo on higher-capacity chipsets. The symmetric processor system—called Magnum—became a roaring success in the Indian market.

Around 1988, McKenzie & Company did a report on the potential for HCL of doing business in the United States. Pointing to a mid-system gap in the U.S. markets, the report suggested that a system like Magnum could fill it. HCL acted fast and floated a subsidiary—HCL America Inc. in Sunnyvale, California—in November 1988 to market Magnum. HCL invested about $5 million in this venture. Pretty soon, it got a massive order from an original equipment manufacturer (OEM) for multiprocessor boxes worth $16.5 million. Bad news followed even before the company could begin to deliver. The order was canceled as the OEM supplier in question was taken over by SCI, which used to work with Intel and not Motorola chipsets; HCL's Magnum used Motorola chipsets. HCL decided to shut the hardware business and eventually to wind up its operations.

HCL America had a few engineers working with customers, mainly engaged in migrating databases from existing systems to multiprocessor systems, a few of which had been supplied to individual customers. U.S. customers, however, were reluctant to release Indian engineers and even made attractive offers to retain them. HCL engineers too did not want to leave because they had just relocated to America. To HCL management in Delhi, this appeared to be a strange situation. The billing rate of HCL engineers was high as they were rendering high-end services, yet customers wanted to retain them. The value U.S. customers attached to Indian engineers and their skills made HCL bosses reconsider. The decision to close down HCL America was reversed. The hardware business was terminated, but the subsidiary had discovered a new line of business—software services.

This was the time when UNIX had begun to be deployed in business environments and many users were starting to migrate to UNIX operating systems. This created a need for highly skilled programmers well versed with migration. For HCL America—with its set of UNIX-trained programmers and engineers—this presented a perfect opportunity. The services it offered included porting software from one existing system to another; writing software drivers to connect computer system components and networks; and conducting quality checks on software developed by clients. HCL America could now reposition itself as a software services firm focused on UNIX systems and database application software. Within five years the unit clocked revenues of $22 million and commanded a workforce of 300.[27]

HCL America gave its customers three options—they could get work done fully in their premises (called onsite work); the job could be handled in HCL offices in America (Sunnyvale and Connecticut); or work could be shipped to HCL offices in India where the labor cost was a fraction of that in the United States (called offshore work). In many projects, the work could be done through a mix of all three methods. Initially, the bulk of services was offered onsite. Once U.S. companies saw the advantage of HCL offerings and the company could get some recognition in technology circles, the proportion of offsite work increased gradually.[28] In addition to obvious cost advantages, outsourcing to HCL helped U.S. companies finish their projects much faster because HCL could afford to deploy far greater numbers of people skilled in different platforms and technologies than the U.S. companies could do themselves. Outsourcing also meant businesses could save the costs of hiring software programmers for short-term projects. HCL America was offering customized software programming and consulting services to American clients wherever they wanted. In fact, HCL America registered the term "offsourcing" as its trademark, shorter form of "service for offshore outsourcing". By the end of the 1990s, outsourcing had become a multibillion-dollar business for HCL and several other Indian companies.

From Vegetable Oils to Computers

In the late 1970s, several Indian companies including large industrial houses were trying to enter the computer business, owing to the initial success of companies like DCM and HCL, as well as the transition from mainframe- to microprocessor-based systems. Among them was a vegetable oil company called Western India Products Limited, based at Amalner, a small town in Western India. Mohamed Hasham Premji, who set this business up in 1945, sent his son Azim Hasham Premji to America for higher studies like most wealthy Indians of his era did. The young Premji, however, had to drop out of engineering studies at Stanford University when Premji Sr. died prematurely in 1966. Azim Premji was called back to take over the family business. After continuing with the traditional line of products for about a decade, Premji diversified into new areas like manufacturing of hydraulic cylinders in 1975 and ultimately into computers in 1980. As the company grew and diversified into new areas, its name was changed in 1979 to the modern-sounding Wipro, an acronym of the old name. The name also sounded like that of an "international" company because Indian firms of that period were not named this way.

For the computer business, Premji set up a new company named Wipro Information Technology Limited (WITL) in Bangalore in 1980. He wanted to make affordable minicomputers and microcomputers to fill the gap created by IBM's exit. Like most wannabe computer manufacturers of the period, Premji went looking for trained personnel from the government firm ECIL, which had a reservoir of talented professionals acquainted with computer design and fabrication. Premji hired Sridhar Mitta, an R&D engineer with a doctorate degree from Oklahoma State University. Convincing someone with a well-paying public sector job to join a little-known veg-etable oil manufacturer planning to start a computer business was difficult, but Premji succeeded. Mitta, in turn, poached on ECIL to get his core team of engineers.

The first task of the new venture was to get an industrial license. To bet-ter his prospects for securing one, Premji decided to locate the WITL unit in Mysore, a small town near Bangalore, categorized as an industrially back-ward region. The corporate office was situated in Bangalore. Premji sought the help of scientists in the Indian Institute of Science (IISc) in the city to make informed choices of the microprocessor and other technologies needed for fabricating a computer. A Swiss national, Serge Boada, working at the Centre for Electronics Design and Technology (CEDT) and N. J. Rao in the School of Automation handled the project at IISc. "We were asked if we could facilitate their effort of designing a PC. They did not specify which microprocessor they wanted to use. Ashok Narasimhan [a Wipro official] got literature from different companies. Three of us surveyed the market for products and microprocessors, and settled on the Intel 8086 processor because of its openness, despite the fact that several products based on TI 9900 were already in the market," Rao would later recall.[29] "You can say that Wipro was incubated in IISc." This was novel because at that time the concept of incubating start-ups or industrial projects in research and aca-demic institutions was absent in India.

Based on input from IISc experts, Wipro decided to build a 16-bit micro-processor-based system, instead of the 8-bit option that HCL and DCM were selling with Motorola and Rockwell processors. The idea was to design hardware, import components, and manufacture computers, instead of importing kits and assembling computers locally. A multiuser, multitasking operating system was licensed from Sentinel Computer Corporation in Cin-cinnati, Ohio.[30] The software had to be imported as "design and drawing" since software as such did not figure in schedules of products that could be imported into India.

The first product—Wipro 86—was designed using standard bus archi-tecture, which allowed different subsystems to be independent of each other. Other companies were designing hardware and software themselves in a serial fashion. This meant that hardware would be designed first and software would be developed next for this particular design. If it did not work, changes would have to be made in both hardware and software. Mitta would later explain his design strategy thus: "We bought a machine from the U.S. and gave it to the software team to develop software. They did not have to depend on [the] reliability of our hardware. And we used modular hardware. Ours was a multiuser machine and had [the] database built-in. The operating system was robust as it had been in use for ten years by then. Originally it was developed for mainframes and minicomputers. Other operating systems did not have this feature."[31]

The offering, unveiled at the annual convention of the Computer Society of India in February 1981, became a success. Though other firms also used the same chip from Intel, Wipro 86 was the first non-mainframe system to have multiple terminals and facility for multitasking. The minicomputer was targeted at heavy users and for core business applications like process control and production scheduling. Company officials would boast that Wipro was like a "mini IBM," giving customers hardware, software, peripherals, applications, training, and engineers to run their data centers.

Pricing was attractive too. Typically Wipro would approach a company having an ICL mainframe and tell them they could have a Wipro computer for a price equal to one year's rental but with twice the performance of an ICL system. Wipro 86 series systems were priced from $124,000 to $185,000. In the first year, Wipro sold machines worth $2.5 million and the second year saw sales turnover jump to about $10 million. The success followed several innovative products including a minicomputer with Intel's 32-bit processor, 80386 (popularly called 386), and UNIX soon after its launch in October 1985.

Intel shared with Wipro engineering samples of its new microprocessor despite Wipro being an unknown name outside India. "We could design a 386 minicomputer because of the decision taken in 1981 to go modular. All we did was to remove 286 CPU and replace it with 386. When we announced this product, Andy Grove sent us a letter congratulating us for designing the world's first minicomputer based on 386," Mitta recalled.[32] This boosted morale of the R&D group and perhaps gave an opportunity to Intel to gauge the potential of Indian engineering talent, paving the way for a long-term relationship between Wipro and Intel. The firm forged formal relationships such as licensing agreements with high-tech giants—Intel for microprocessors, IBM for UNIX, and SUN Microsystems for servers. Along with hardware, Wipro was working on software products through its subsidiary, Wipro Systems Limited. Wipro 456, a spreadsheet program similar to Lotus 1-2-3, was one of its first offerings.

As the Indian market opened its doors to imports as well as joint ventures with foreign companies, Indian firms with their own design and development teams like Wipro felt the heat. Instead of abandoning this activity, Wipro decided to look outward. Its R&D teams were already adept at assimilating technology from foreign collaborators and developing new products.

Mitta decided to convert this capability into a new business opportunity. He devised a concept called "Lab on Hire" to leverage competencies developed over one decade by providing R&D services to erstwhile technology partners like Intel, SUN, Motorola, and Cisco.[33] With the same base of R&D engineers, the company started developing subsystems, chips, and software for U.S. companies. Familiarity with technology platforms, networking, and design processes of U.S. technology companies helped Wipro offer them R&D services at a much lower cost.

The interest in UNIX for commercial applications among American vendors helped Indian companies like HCL and Wipro, who already had a reasonable experience in this system. Intel wanted its processors to run UNIX so that commercial software could be run on them. For this, it needed engineers well versed in UNIX applications. Initially, some Wipro engineers were sent to Intel for short assignments relating to UNIX. Based on this experience, Wipro then approached SUN and offered services in UNIX. Sun directed Wipro to its original equipment manufacturers. That's how the Lab on Hire business was seeded and ramped up. Over the next fifteen years, this business made Wipro into one of the largest independent R&D services provider in the world with over $600 million revenue in 2006. From one hundred engineers in 1990, the R&D division (renamed Products Engineering Services in 2005) had grown to become an organization of twelve thousand scientists and engineers in 2006.[34]

Indian Hardware Industry Evolves

The 1980s was a decade of transformation for the computer hardware industry in India. At the beginning of the decade, it was a small, low-demand, mostly R&D-driven industry. The technology gap between Indian and Western markets was large. Mainframe data processing dominated the market. At the end of the decade, in contrast, the industry was large, with several players in each segment, and demand for computers was high. The industry had become import-dependent, the technology gap had narrowed considerably, and microcomputers were the dominant type of computers sold in the market.

The shifting of focus away from state-controlled public enterprises to the import-led private sector was a landmark in India's economic history. New electronics and computer policies abolished limits on how much a company could produce, slashed import duties, and removed impediments to growth. The goal was to modernize the electronics, communication, and computer industries by opening up markets and allowing access to foreign technology, components, and systems. This approach helped India leap-frog from the era of mainframes to contemporary era of PCs, introduce a modern telecom system, and disseminate IT through applications in gover-nance, banking, and desktop publishing in Indian languages.

The restrictive policies of the 1970s had some unexpected fallout. Com-puter manufacturers were forced to invest in R&D as it was mandatory for them to invest 2 percent of their turnover on research. DCM DP developed design capabilities through induction of engineers from the IITs as well as professionals from IBM, ICL, and government manufacturing companies. Of the 550 employees in DCM DP in 1979, seventy were engaged in R&D. The import content in DCM's computers was said to be between 12 and 15 percent of the cost of the machine.[35] In HCL, fifty out of four hundred employees were engaged in R&D in the same year. Wipro and PSI too had an R&D focus and a strong design orientation.

Hardware prices fell due to slashing of duties on components, hard-disk drives, and floppy drives. Easy imports of completely knocked down (CKD) and semi knocked down (SKD) kits led to proliferation of IBM PC-compati-ble computers. Foreign-made computers came through other channels too. For instance, an Indian company imported Texas Instruments (TI) comput-ers from the United States at heavily discounted prices (after TI had folded up its home computer business) and sold them at inflated rates in India. Introduction of standard operating systems and application software pack-ages also forced prices down.

Indian companies introduced computers based on standard micropro-cessors from Intel and Motorola at almost the same time as was happen-ing in U.S. markets. Indian computers now featured several new hardware and software technologies with a time lag of just a few months, and in some cases there was no lag. Every major player in the market had a for-eign collaborator or partner. This virtually meant an end to indigenous research, design, and development in computer hardware and operating systems development. Companies like HCL, DCM, and Wipro, which had a large number of R&D engineers, had to either redeploy their workforce or retrench them. The R&D capabilities were utilized to some extent in tech-nology absorption and assimilation after the 1984 policy. They developed competence in systems integration. But there was no incentive to use this capability for new product development. So these companies began look-ing out for new business opportunities. In this manner, Wipro developed the concept of Lab on Hire, HCL entered the services export arena, and DCM began offering its hardware design services to other companies.

The state played a major role in creating demand for computers. Large programs for introducing computers into banks and schools boosted computer sales further. The Reserve Bank of India floated a tender for the purchase of 500 minicomputers. Indian Airlines also expanded its computerized ticket checking facilities to six cities. The National Informatics Centre began expanding its network to government offices up to the district level. All this created a huge demand for computers. In 1987–1988, India's computer industry crossed the turnover mark of five billion rupees. The development of local industry since IBM's exit was driven by technology and policy, while demand was mostly spurred by government-led projects.

The growth seen in the 1980s, however, could not be sustained. The growth rate progressively started to nosedive from over 30 percent in 1987, 1988, and 1989, to 10.7 percent in 1990 and 5.7 in 1991.[36] The reason for this was high prices—which in turn were a result of high import content, up to 95 percent, in Indian computers. The cut in customs duty implemented in 1984 was rolled back in the late 1980s. In the face of a difficult foreign exchange situation, the Reserve Bank of India enhanced the margin on importers from 50 to 133 percent between 1989 and 1991. The government also cut capital expenditure, which, in turn, meant reducing computer purchasing. All this hit India's hardware business because government and public sector companies accounted for a huge chunk of sales. The technological changes taking place in international markets—such as new operating system and hardware architecture—and sluggish domestic demand made Indian companies change direction. They started searching for deeper foreign collaborations and diversification into software services.

6 Software Dreams Take Flight

One way to reduce programming costs is to have all computer programming and systems analysis done in countries where technical labor is comparatively cheaper since this is a labor-intensive industry. A programmer in America earning Rupees 90,000 per year can be replaced by an Indian programmer working in India for Rupees 9,000 per year.

—A. K. Bahn, Universal Design Systems (India) Private Limited, March 1970[1]

The burst of activity in the Indian hardware market in mid-1980s onward that followed import liberalization led to some structural changes in the computer industry. The emergence of the software sector, as distinct from hardware business, was a major change. The PC—and not mainframes and minicomputers—were now the dominant systems in the market. The computer was not merely a tool of data processing in business, industry, and government but also had become a consumer product. The demand for applications to meet needs of existing and new users of computers in different sectors was high. Still the domestic market for software products was relatively small, and it was soon captured by pirated and illegal copies of standard software packages mainly due to lax regulations. Software firms that had developed products to serve the needs of the PC era could not withstand the onslaught of pirated versions of standard packages. Large Indian hardware manufacturers were trying to realign their operations by seeking to grab new opportunities in software services.

In the period dominated by IBM and ICL, software came bundled with hardware. Multinational corporations selling hardware did software writing in-house or some of it was subcontracted to outside agencies. Still, some Indian companies and entrepreneurs had begun carving out a place for themselves through software services. It was time to build upon those skills.

The Indian Institutes of Technology and other universities could offer fairly good Western-style engineering education to Indian students in a range of disciplines in the 1960s. Students thus trained, however, could not find suitable jobs either in private companies or academic institutions. This forced a majority of them head to the United States for higher education and possible employment. Elite engineering institutions became a stepping-stone for a bright future in America. Narendra Patni, son of a grain merchant from Agra, was one such ambitious young man who opted out of his family business to pursue higher studies in the United States after graduating from the engineering school at the University of Roorkee (which was later converted into an IIT).

With an engineering degree and a Grass Foundation scholarship in hand, Patni landed at MIT in 1964 to pursue a master's degree in electrical engineering and control systems. He was exposed to several new technologies including analog and digital computers, and use of computers in control systems and process simulation. After finishing his engineering degree, he continued at MIT to study management at the Sloan School of Management. Here he came in contact with digital computing pioneer Jay W. Forrester, who had made a career change to become a professor in management. Forrester focused on experimental studies of organizational policy and used computer simulations to analyze social systems—what came to be known as systems dynamics. In the 1970s, Forrester applied this model to global problems, concluding that industrialization was as big a problem as overpopulation in upsetting global equilibrium. This resulted in his most famous work *World Dynamics* in June 1971. Soon after he received his MBA in 1969, Patni started working part time with a new management consulting firm founded by Forrester.[2]

Data Conversion to Software

Working with Forrester Consulting, where he was in the company of high-profile academics and researchers, a young Patni developed an interest in publishing. He decided to diversify into publication of research-based academic books. Wright-Allen Press, a publishing house in Cambridge, Massachusetts, proved to be a perfect platform for Patni. He was involved in publishing about a dozen books, including the first edition of Forrester's *World Dynamics* by Wright-Allen. Printing was at the cusp of a technological change. Linotype machines were being replaced by high-speed photo typesetting machines driven by paper and magnetic tapes, which could be encoded on off-line keyboards. Encoding data on paper tapes was a laborious and demanding job. The process intrigued Patni, who had seen similar paper tapes coming out of telex machines back in India. "That's when this idea came to me that why this tape can't be punched overseas, and it started the whole thought process in me about trying to outsource data conversion work to India," he would recall later.[3] The business instinct in Patni was kindled; he sensed potential business opportunity in data conversion. He could hardly have realized that he was showing the way for a revolutionary way of doing business that would shake the world in the early twenty-first century.

The opportunity Patni recognized was converted into a real business proposition during a consulting assignment he handled for Arthur D. Little (ADL), a well-known consulting firm in Cambridge, Massachusetts. ADL was engaged in a project for Mead Data Central, which was developing LEXIS (Legal Exchange Information Service), a new online database for law firms, businesses, and libraries. It was to be the first commercial electronic database that allowed users to search legal records such as court judgments. The task involved putting almost five billion characters or keystrokes on disk storage for on-demand access for users. The cost of data conversion for such a huge database would have been very high in the United States, so Patni proposed that the work be outsourced to India. The data had to be encoded on paper or magnetic tapes with utmost accuracy because these were ad verbatim court proceedings and were to replace official court proceeding records in the legal search database. Accepting the challenge, Patni founded a new company called Data Conversion Inc. (DCI) in October 1972.

Before shipping tons of documents to India for conversion into tapes, Patni and his wife Poonam conducted an experiment to test the offshore model at their third-floor apartment on St. Paul Street, near Central Square in Cambridge. They designated the living room as the "United States" and the bedroom as "India." In one room, the couple wrote instructions for the conversion of data from paper documents to paper tapes. In the other room, a small team typed the data into a Flexowriter machine that sputtered paper tape as output. It was decided that there would be no oral communication between the people in "India" and the "United States"—simulating the on-the-ground reality of poor telephone links between the two countries. Only written communication was allowed between the two rooms, as Patni would recount three decades later. A team of two dozen data entry operators was then hired in Poona in Western India and the Patnis began sending documents from Cambridge to Poona.

DCI's business grew very fast, as many larger databases were getting converted from paper into magnetic disk storage to facilitate online access of information. Besides LEXIS, DCI's client list included the American Mathematical Society, American Film Institute, and publishers of Greek thesauruses. The work involved complicated typesetting operations such as triple stack integral calculus and similar typographically challenging scientific text. The work for the Film Institute, though, posed slightly different problems. Patni later recalled the nuances of the data conversion business: "The workers would get so engrossed with reading stories of Hollywood films that we had a hard time getting the required productivity and accuracy levels. . . . In fact, later on it was observed that Chinese workers had an advantage over Indians because they did not understand the meaning and typed blindly. Their accuracy was coming out much higher than that of Indians."[4]

At the peak of DCI's business, workers were punching something like five miles of paper tape every day at its unit in Poona. The operation was not without its hiccups. For instance, paper tape readers were not readily available in India for commercial use. The Indian Meteorological Department (IMD) in New Delhi had one in its data processing department. It took lot of convincing and a few visits to New Delhi by Patni before IMD would let his private firm use its facilities. Punched paper tapes were first flown to New Delhi and "read" at IMD before being shipped to the United States. The other problem was that when paper tapes were transported, they would get bent, or wet. "My wife had to iron crinkles out because you can't read a crooked paper tape," Patni recounted.[5]

A permanent solution was to typeset directly on computers and store data on magnetic media. Patni started looking for a suitable computer to buy. The first name that came to his mind was Digital Equipment Corporation (DEC), whose founders included Forrester. Patni was also acquainted with Kenneth Olsen who was a fellow researcher in the System Dynamics Group at MIT Sloan School of Management. But the commercial terms DEC offered were tough. Patni then approached Data General, another minicomputer maker founded by ex-DEC employees. Data General agreed to sell its minicomputer but said it won't be able to provide support in India. Patni had solution for this too—he offered to become a distributor for Data General computers in India and create the necessary base for it to grow there. Data General saw in Patni's proposal an opportunity to enter a promising market. A new company, Patni Computer Systems (PCS) was incorporated in 1976 with Narendra Patni's brother Gajendra and Ashoka—both engineering graduates from IIT Delhi—as cofounders.

A Data General M1 computer was installed at the headquarters of a cement company, Associated Cement Companies (ACC), in Bombay for management of its inventory. PCS used spare computer time on this machine for writing software for Data General's other clients in India and

overseas. This helped PCS generate some foreign exchange in or(
the mandatory "export obligation" against which the import of
was allowed in the first place. Data General's business grew in india
other orders coming in for its minicomputers.

Maintenance of minicomputer software and hardware was relatively
simple compared to that of mainframes. Companies could install such
computers in-house rather than rent computer time at an external data
center. However, every user had to develop its own applications. Data General helped them do so. Like the computer at ACC, other imported systems
were used to write application software for clients. Though PCS started as
a reseller for Data General minicomputers, it soon engaged in writing software solutions for customers of Data General in a big way. The hardware
business was morphing into software work. Software creators still worked
under severe constraints, as direct communication links for transmission of
codes between Data General and PCS did not exist. Software requirements
of Data General were sent in "a pouch" to India on a commercial flight,
development work was done in India, and codes were sent back the same
way, according to an account given by Jagdish Dalal, who was director of
Management Information Systems at Data General.[6]

As this new line of business grew, Patni felt the need for a dedicated team
of programmers. PCS expanded its operations by recruiting different teams
for its software, hardware, and marketing divisions in August 1977. Patni
hired N. R. Narayana Murthy, an M.Tech from IIT Kanpur, to write software. Murthy was sent to the United States for training for a few months
before he became full-time head of the PCS software group in February
1978. His previous experience included stints as programmer at the Indian
Institute of Management at Ahmedabad and at a French firm that designed
the cargo-handling system for the Charles de Gaulle Airport.

Murthy actually handled three tasks at PCS—selling Data General mini-
computers to Indian customers, managing a data center, and handling soft-
ware export projects. As his workload increased, Murthy recruited a team of
programmers including Nandan Mohan Nilekani (electrical engineer from
IIT, Bombay), S. Gopalakrishnan (M.Tech in computer science from IIT
Madras), S. D. Shibulal (MSc in physics from the University of Kerala), and
K. Dinesh (postgraduate in mathematics from Bangalore University). Soon
Nadathur S. Raghavan and Ashok Arora also joined the team.

With a full-fledged team of developers in the saddle and good experience
in developing applications, Patni was in a position to solicit work beyond
Data General and its customers. In 1979, PCS signed one of the largest offshore software deals in India till then, valued at $0.5 million, for developing

some components of a software package, Comprehensive Apparel Manufac-turer's Package (CAMP), and customizing it to be run on 16-bit computers of Data General. The product was owned by a third-party vendor in New York—Data Basics Corporation (DBC). It was a breakthrough deal for PCS, opening up a new way of doing business for the nascent Indian software industry. Instead of working for large minicomputer firms as dedicated soft-ware developers or looking for customers on their own, Indian firms could work for third-party vendors who had greater access to the U.S. market.

In less than a decade, Patni had successfully demonstrated the frame-work of an offshore model of business—first for data conversion and then for software writing. He had the advantage of combining his knowledge of the demand side (in the United States) and the supply side (India) to deliver services and products to American customers. This showed the way to many software companies founded in the 1980s and later. The model underwent several modifications over the next decades as labor-intensive processes like data conversion faded away with the onset of new technologies.

Infosys Takes Root

DBC's project with PCS made the American firm see the value of Indian programmers. This is reflected in comments DBC President Donn Liles made in 1989: "When I first went to India to hire people for a project, I was surprised by the caliber of job applicants, people with PhDs, people I could never afford to hire in the US, people who work very hard and still never forget to smile."[7] In fact, DBC project made PCS programmers realize their worth, and they began toying with the idea of starting their own software firm. The domestic market for software, in any case, was tiny.

In a near replay of Shiv Nadar walking away from DCM a few years ago, Murthy resigned from PCS in December 1980 with the programmers fol-lowing suit. The sudden departure of its entire software team was a bolt out of the blue for PCS. A sizeable chunk of its business vanished overnight. Murthy, however, stayed on for some more months in order to fulfill con-tracts PCS had with two Indian customers. The episode left a bitter taste in the mouth of Narendra Patni, who considered Murthy's act "unethical."[8] Murthy and colleagues incorporated a new firm, Infosys Consultants, in July 1981.

What further embittered Patni about the software team's departure was the fact that DBC, originally a PCS customer, became the first customer of Infosys. Murthy, however, did not feel it was unethical or wrong for Info-sys to have worked with DBC. According to him, DBC had set up its own subsidiary in the Santa Cruz Electronics Export Processing Zone (SEEPZ) in Bombay after severing links with PCS. When Infosys was in the making, Murthy claimed to have approached Liles and told him that he could do business with Infosys rather than go through the hassles of recruiting programmers on his own and dealing with Indian bureaucracy. "He (Donn Liles) realized this and he closed down the company in Bombay and signed a contract with Infosys," Murthy asserted.[9] By the time Murthy approached DBC with this offer, he said it had been nearly six months since he had resigned from PCS.[10] The fact that Murthy and his team had worked with DBC while they were employed at PCS and that they were familiar with the software needs of DBC must have convinced the U.S. firm to go with a start-up.

Infosys had modest beginnings. It was an entrepreneurial venture. Murthy and his colleagues had no family money or savings and all of them came from middle-class families. Murthy's wife Sudha, who was working as a systems programmer with the Tata Engineering and Locomotives Company in Poona, contributed the equivalent in rupees of $1,200 from her savings (figure 6.1).

While at PCS, Murthy's team of programmers had gained the experience of working on software package CAMP. The DBC contract with Infosys was to expand the functionality of CAMP and ready it for re-hosting on Data General's 32-bit Eclipse MV/8000. But Infosys did not have a Data General computer to work with. It had no money to buy one or necessary office space to install such a system. In addition, importing the system could take several months. Infosys did not even have a landline telephone connection. As a way out, DBC suggested that Infosys execute the project at its U.S. office. All Infosys founders, except Murthy, went over to New York to work on DBC computers—in the phenomenon mentioned in chapter 4 dubbed "body shopping," which was to emerge as a dominant model of software exports. Infosys dabbled in hardware too, through its little known subsidiary Infosys Digital Systems, but soon gave up to focus on its core strength—programming. The DBC deal lasted six years. After Infosys, DBC outsourced software services from other Indian firms like Mafatlal Consultancy Services, part of the Arvind Mafatlal group in Bombay, which specialized in developing software for the textile industry.

A few years later, claims relating to CAMP became a point of dispute between Infosys and DBC. In August 1988, DBC countered the claims Infosys made in a trade magazine that it had "developed" CAMP for the U.S. apparel industry. DBC clarified that CAMP was its registered trademark and copyrighted product and that Infosys had only provided support services to

Figure 6.1
Infosys cofounders (left to right): K. Dinesh, Nandan Nilekani, N. S. Raghavan, and
N. R. Narayana Murthy; two others—Kris Gopalakrishnan and S. D. Shibulal—are not
in this undated picture. All the founders of Infosys earlier worked for Patni Computer
Systems, which was initially a reseller for minicomputers of Data General and later
got into writing software solutions for Data General customers in India. Courtesy:
Infosys Limited

customers of DBC for CAMP under contract with DBC.[11] It also claimed that
it had advanced money in 1981 to help fund Infosys and for several years it
was the only customer of Infosys. DBC accounted for nearly 60 percent of
Infosys's revenue even in 1988. It was under the contract signed with DBC
that Infosys was hired to provide technical services to Reebok and Jockey.
Infosys admitted that the copyright of CAMP as well as the related software
developed for garment makers belonged to DBC, but it denied that DBC
had helped Infosys with capital funding in 1981.

When Infosys signed up its first major customer in the domestic market,
Motor Industries Company Limited (MICO) in Bangalore, it decided to shift
its base from Poona to Bangalore in 1983. Infosys acquired its first computer—the Data General MV/8000—in February 1984 and installed it at
MICO. The computer was used for MICO data processing and for software
development for other customers of Infosys. The data processing ensured a

steady flow of revenue. Banks had refused Infosys a loan to buy this computer. It was a chance meeting between Murthy and K. S. N. Murthy of the Karnataka State Industrial Investment and Development Corporation that resulted in the corporation sanctioning a loan.[12] Once again, a state agency became the source of capital for a private firm, in a striking parallel to HCL, which got its capital from a state corporation.

The successful execution of the software services for DBC apparel manufacturing software product prompted Infosys to scout for more such deals in America. In this quest, it entered into a partnership with the Atlanta-based Kurt Salmon Associates (KSA), a consultant for apparel manufacturers. The idea was to develop software packages for this sector by pooling domain knowledge of KSA and technical experience of Infosys. The two formed a 60–40 joint venture firm, KSA/Infosys in 1987. The same year, Infosys set up its first overseas sales office in Boston. The joint venture with KSA helped Infosys build credibility in a market in which it was a relative newcomer and gave it access to a number of opportunities it would not have otherwise had, as S. Gopalakrishnan would later recall.[13] Around the same time, Infosys got it first direct customer—Digital Equipment Corporation—for which it developed fleet handling software.

At the end of the decade, Infosys had about one hundred employees engaged in both onsite and offshore projects. During 1989–1990, its turnover was still small—about $1.4 million—and it ranked No. 10 in the Dataquest Top 20 list. TCS, with a turnover of $26 million, was the top exporter.[14] Despite its initial breakthrough in American markets, Infosys appeared to be struggling for survival in 1990. It entered the European market in 1991 with a contract from the Milan-based Labinf group. Reebok—which was introduced to Infosys by DBC in 1987—hired Infosys to develop a Distribution Management Application Package (DMAP) for its French operations. The system was later implemented in Reebok's UK operations as well. Infosys then used this package to create a standard application package. Interestingly, outsourcing helped the two struggling firms. While Reebok gave Infosys its first major business contract, Infosys helped Reebok launch its European operations with automated software.[15] The Reebok deal introduced Infosys to European markets at a time when most Indian companies were seeking to court U.S. customers.

The computerization initiative launched by the Indian Banks Association drew Infosys to the potential of India's domestic market. It began working on a "total banking automation" project in 1989 based on specifications defined by the IBA. The package, BANCS 2000, was delivered only in 1994. It was a modular package that could be customized for different banks. The package became a success in India and other developing countries in Asia and Africa with the addition of features like multicurrency operations.

The new industrial and trade policies announced in July 1991 helped fledgling software firms like Infosys in many ways. With foreign exchange restrictions eased, companies could send their executives on marketing trips without the sword of stringent foreign exchange law hanging over their heads. Tapping the equity market was also simplified, with the abolition of the office of the Controller of Capital Issues (CCI), which earlier used to fix initial public offering (IPO) prices. Infosys, short of capital for further expansion, decided to raise equity from the market. It was converted into a public limited company—Infosys Technologies Limited—in June 1992.

After raising about $4.4 million from the capital market, Infosys Limited took a number of steps to reorganize its operations. It set up strategic business units, announced a quality charter, launched an employee stock options scheme, unveiled a corporate governance plan, and hired a PR firm. Its new, fully equipped, modern-looking campus became functional in the Electronics City set up by the Karnataka State Electronics Development Corporation in Bangalore. Five acres of land for the campus was given on long-term, rent-free lease by the Karnataka government. Each of these steps was an attempt to make Infosys a Silicon Valley-like firm—both in looks and in substance.

The model of body shopping tested in the 1980s was subject to vagaries of Indo-U.S. relations, particularly to the contentious issue of visas to Indian workers. Infosys experimented with a new model—shifting more work offshore to its offices in Bangalore through its dedicated offshore software development center (OSDC) for major clients. The first such center was established for General Electric, which was already doing business in India. A sixty-four kbps data link was established between Infosys's Boston office and its Bangalore headquarters to connect the OSDC to the United States. Though this deal lasted only till 1995, it served as "proof of concept" for other American companies looking at India. The availability of high-speed data links at the government-promoted Software Technology Park facilitated the transition from body shopping to offshore development to software firms—a significant development detailed in chapter 7.

Over the next five years after its IPO and opening of the Bangalore campus, Infosys focused on setting up the quality process at all the levels, diversifying its client base, attaching value to its human capital (the first Indian company to assess value of its intangible assets—its employees—and print it in annual reports), and developing project management capabilities. A significant contributor to its growth was the offshore development model it developed—servicing customers from multiple sites by making optimal use of human resources. The offshore delivery model of Infosys, says cofounder Nandan Nilekani, was "cheaper, faster and better" and made customers switch to Infosys.[16] All these efforts, coupled with external factors, like the shortage of technical workers in the West to feed the so-called dot-com boom and "the millennium bug"–related work (also known as the Y2K problem), helped Infosys grow at consistently higher rates. Its revenue reached $100 million in 1999–eighteen years after it was founded, making it the fourth largest Indian software exporter. The same year the company became the first Indian firm to be listed on the NASDAQ Stock Exchange in New York. In March 1999, Infosys raised $70 million through issue of 2.07 million American Depository Shares.

After this, the company's growth was dramatic. In another five years, its revenue jumped from $100 million to $1 billion in 2004; and it doubled to $2 billion in just two years (in 2006). This is how Nilekani explained the post-2000 growth trajectory of Infosys: "The combination of Y2K, dotcom boom and telecom boom all worked. . . . The supply of technical talent in the US was far short of demand so that the boom was demand driven. By 2001 the demand driven by supply scarcity had created enough of a brand name and reputation for us so that when the market shifted from supply scarcity to 'value for money,' we were there to take advantage."[17] In 2013, Infosys revenues touched $8 billion and market capitalization was $33 billion.

TCS: Birth of a Giant

When Narendra Patni was pursuing his master's degree in engineering at MIT, another young Indian engineer from Bombay, Lalit Surajmal Kanodia, was studying management at MIT after having graduated from IIT Bombay in 1963.

It was while working on his doctoral thesis in management that Kanodia got interested in computing. This was the time when MIT was deeply involved in a pioneering program called Project MAC (multiple access computing), having developed the concept of "time sharing" for networked computers. Kanodia was a member of team engaged in developing a multiuser operating system—Multiplexed Information and Computing Service or Multicis.[18] While still writing his doctoral thesis, Kanodia took up a consulting project with the Tata Group during a visit to Bombay in 1965. He wrote three project papers for the group—one of which suggested that the group set up a computer center to take care of data processing requirements of all group companies. The Tata Group was already toying with the idea of pooling its data processing work under one business unit because of the high cost of renting IBM and ICL data processing equipment.

When Kanodia returned to MIT to finish his academic work, the Tata Group decided to set up a computer center based on his report as well as work done by Yashpal Sahni, a statistician who was hired in 1962 to supervise data processing work. Upon his return to India in 1967, Kanodia along with two of his colleagues from MIT—Nitin Patel and Ashok Malhotra—joined the Tata group and set up a data processing unit called Tata Computer Centre. Initially it was under the administrative control of Tata Electric Companies. Most Tata companies, however, did not want to hand over their data processing work to the new unit, except shareholder accounting, which was quite cumbersome. This means the new unit had to seek work outside the Tata Group.[19] Within a year, the center was spun off as a separate unit and renamed Tata Consultancy Services (TCS) so that it offer consultancy services to companies and customers outside the group to generate additional revenues for the holding company, Tata Sons. Two IBM 1401s were leased and one ICL 1903 system was purchased to kickstart data processing operations of TCS. The first set of TCS employees had some twenty PhDs including Kanodia.

Among the first non-Tata customers of TCS were commercial banks located in Bombay, which is considered India's financial hub. "We identified that branch reconciliation was a good application," recalled Sahni. "Trade unions were opposed to computers, but nobody objected to this as it was considered dirty work. Almost all nationalized banks became our customers. This made the data centre very large. We had 400 workers engaged only in capturing the data. This was necessary for survival."[20]

It is not clear why Kanodia parted ways with TCS in its early days but he did and was replaced by another MIT alumnus, Faqir Chand Kohli, who was already a senior executive in Tata Electric Companies. Kanodia founded Datamatics, which provided software support and services for customers of Wang Labs in the United States and other markets globally. Kohli, a graduate of electrical engineering from MIT, had a penchant for new technologies and had introduced digital computers for control and dispatch functions in the power company. Contemporary utilities elsewhere were still on analog systems. With this experience, Kohli actively started scouting for business for TCS. One of the first projects TCS executed in 1971 was publication of the telephone directory and yellow pages for Bombay Telephones, despite constraints of time and technology.

Software programming was yet to develop as a distinct business activity because mainframe and minicomputer systems from firms like IBM, ICL, and DEC came bundled with proprietary software—both operating and application. TCS realized that it would have to work around this system to break into the market. Since IBM was already a dominant player in India, it decided to explore other avenues. Kohli—who was then a member of the board of the International Institute of Electrical and Electronics Engineers (IEEE)—visited the United States as many as nine times between 1972 and 1974, building networks and contacts with the academic, research, and commercial worlds.[21] It was during these meetings that Kohli came in touch with senior managers of Burroughs and the idea of a partnership germinated in 1973.[22] TCS got its first breakthrough in the United States— Burroughs awarded it a contract to develop the operating system for a new computer series.

TCS did not have a Burroughs computer to work on. And importing one would have meant a delay of at least two years. Its programmers started writing software in ALGOL language on an ICL 1903 computer the company owned. This software had to be made compatible for the Burroughs platform. For this, ingenious engineers of TCS developed a software filter that could make ICL software work on a Burroughs system. This piece of software was written in Bombay. The code, along with the filter, was then sent to the United States, tested on a Burroughs computer, and it worked. This opened the eyes of Burroughs' top brass—they not only had an operating system for their new series, but also a tool by which they could convince existing users of other platforms to migrate to a Burroughs machine. In this way they won many ICL customers in the UK, who were looking to upgrade to a higher platform.

The first independent software contract of TCS came from the Detroit Police Department in 1974 through a Burroughs reference. Development work was split between Bombay and Detroit. Soon other projects followed from the City of Detroit, the State University of New York, and some banks. Most involved tasks like coding and testing, acceptance testing, and implementation—normally considered lower value-added development services.

Burroughs was already selling its computers in India through TCS. Now, with its experience with TCS in programming and applications, the next logical step was setting up a joint venture in India. An interesting deal was worked out—Tata would help Burroughs sell and support its mainframes in India, while Burroughs would use Tata engineers to develop software for these systems as well as for customers in foreign markets. Such an arrangement helped both partners—Burroughs could avoid the kind of legal problems IBM and ICL were facing, while TCS could generate revenues through software-related work to fund import of computers. The manufacturing activity of the joint venture would be restricted to peripherals. This was the model that IBM too had suggested before making an exit, and several U.S. hardware companies followed it.

Burroughs' decision to come to India was also influenced by hardening of the Indian government's position on IBM and ICL. A top official of the Department of Electronics visited Burroughs headquarters in Detroit in 1973 and met Chairman Ray McDonald. He insisted that any collaborative venture of Burroughs in India should include a manufacturing component, in addition to software exports proposed by it.[23] Such high-level lobbying resulted in Burroughs floating a joint venture with the Tata at SEEPZ in October 1975. The facility did not manufacture computers but only peripherals—serial dot-matrix printers and handlers used in Burroughs systems.

The government decision to make the state-owned Computer Maintenance Corporation (CMC) a monopoly in maintenance prevented Burroughs from providing maintenance services for computers imported by it. Burroughs was also denied foreign exchange entitlement similar to that enjoyed by IBM. The intention of the DoE was to prevent a situation wherein Burroughs effectively replaced IBM in India. Burroughs understood the situation and agreed to the government terms. The joint venture—Tata Burroughs Limited (TBL)—became operational in October 1977. Burroughs's entry into India with a leading industrial house like the Tata Group made other computer companies look at India seriously despite problems being faced by IBM and ICL on account of ownership.

With the new joint venture, the Tata Group had two units in the computer business because TCS retained a separate identity. It even became a competitor of TBL in software business. The initial software work with Burroughs had given TCS experience and confidence to explore the market on its own and pursue software development as an independent line of business. All it needed was high-quality human capital. But the going for the company was tough, given the central role played by the government in development of the computer industry. The only exception was SEEPZ, where electronics production units meant for exports could be set up. Importing computer platforms needed to develop software was still subject to red tape. It took the firm three years to get a computer and by the time it was sanctioned, the manufacturer had stopped making it. A floppy-drive-manufacturing unit of Tandon Magnetics Corporation, a disk drive manufacturer founded in 1976, was also located in SEEPZ and is one of first instances of offshore manufacturing.

As the environment within India was hostile to computers as well as to large industrial houses like the Tata Group, TCS thought it prudent to address the export market aggressively. It opened an office in New York in 1979 and appointed as head one of its experienced engineers, Subramaniam Ramadorai, a postgraduate in electronics and telecommunications from IISc. TCS's familiarity with the Burroughs systems helped it get work from the Institutional Group and Information Company, which was actually the data center for a group of ten banks in the Northeast United States. The work involved maintenance as well as migration of software from Burroughs to IBM mainframes. Migration services performed at the client's site became a major source of the company's export earnings by the mid-1980s. Gradually, TCS assumed project management responsibilities and emerged as a provider of customized solutions in the late 1980s.[24] In the domestic market, it focused on the banking sector. The early capabilities of TCS in finance and banking applications were a result of its association with Burroughs, which was very strong in this sector. The company would further develop its expertise in the sector over the coming decades.

TCS and TBL emerged as top software exporters in India, accounting for 63 percent of $4 million worth exports by twenty-one firms reported in 1980.[25] TCS remained on top as hardware technology changed from mainframes to workstations and software changed from proprietary operating systems to UNIX platforms in the first half of the 1980s. These changes made it possible for companies like TCS to do more work offshore, because they could afford to have UNIX workstations to work on (instead of the costly mainframes of the 1970s).

This shift to new hardware and software platforms generated greater business—migration work—for software services firms such as TCS. "We brought automation into the migration exercise," Ramadorai would point out later. "This made us a clear differentiator, because we had created the tools for automating the conversion from one platform to another, from one language to another."[26] The company leveraged this shift in global markets and began scaling up its offshore work. It developed project management tools that allowed it to manage software projects offshore. This line of business was further boosted as import of computers for software to be exported was liberalized. By 1988, about 10 percent of all work was being done onsite. The figure kept growing progressively. Under the global delivery model of TCS, projects were jointly handled by its programmers based in overseas subsidiaries and offices in India. It helped the company optimize the use of a workforce with different skill sets, depending on requirements of a particular project.

TCS changed its course once again in the post-liberalization era of the 1990s.[27] It started setting up dedicated software factories for large American and European clients. This was a further progression from the offshore and global delivery model. By now, many leading multinationals had set up their own software development facilities in India; the confidence levels of U.S. clients in Indian software companies had improved. American firms like IBM, EDS, and Accenture had set up huge operations, taking advantage of the cheap labor that Indian companies were exploiting so far.

In the late 1990s, another opportunity opened up for Indian companies—the Y2K problem—allowing them to scale up their operations. They could target customers who were not yet outsourcing. In the 2000s, TCS took to the acquisition route for further expansion into new geographies as well as new segments of the market. It acquired a controlling stake in the state-owned CMC Limited in India and several firms in the United States, Europe, Australia, and Latin America. TCS became the first Indian software firm to cross annual revenues of $1 billion (in 2003) and to reach the $10 billion mark in 2012.

Catering to Local Markets

In the late 1970s, the domestic hardware market in India had finally begun to grow with entry of private firms like DCM Data Products, Processors Systems India (PSI), and ORG Systems (an offshoot of the market research firm Operations Research Group based in Baroda) with their microprocessor-based systems, in addition to systems sold by state-owned ECIL. All such systems required operating system software and applications as standard products had not yet been developed. Early movers in the software business like TCS and PCS focused on customers in India and the United States who were migrating from mainframes to minicomputers. This created an opportunity in the Indian market for entrepreneurs who could cater to the software requirements of microcomputer users. Diwakar Nigam, a postgraduate in computer science from IIT Madras who worked with HCL, sensed this opportunity. He was part of the team that wrote operating system, compiler, and application software for the microprocessor-based systems HCL marketed in its initial phase.

Nigam noticed that hardware companies were finding it difficult to spend on developing their own software because of the high costs involved. He thought these costs could be brought down drastically if an independent firm developed and sold packages to hardware manufacturers. This way development costs could be spread over multiple companies. Nigam, along with three other engineers, left HCL and launched a software firm, Softek Limited, in February 1979. It was India's first software product company and one that was focused on the domestic market, much before standard packages from Microsoft became available. Softek developed operating systems, compilers, and basic utilities for microcomputers.

The first Softek product was a compiler, PLS, which doubled as an operating system and an application builder. It was mostly sold to users of ECIL's 8085 processor in scientific, academic, and research institutions. The hardware firm ORG then hired Softek to develop a simulator for IBM's 1401 system. Instead of a simulator, Nigam convinced the company to go in for a COBOL compiler. "It was a big deal at that time trying to build a compiler for COBOL because nobody till then had done so for a business language," explained Nigam.[28] This feature made all hardware companies—HCL, ECIL, Wipro, and others—buy the compiler for their respective systems. COBOL was used for business applications and FORTRAN for scientific applications. Softek wrote compilers in COBOL and FORTRAN, as well as BASIC.

For microcomputers, Softek developed operating systems, compilers, database and data entry programs, word processors, utilities, and multilingual interfaces for microprocessor-based systems. It worked on customized solutions for manufacturing, banking, and financial sectors as well. Its spreadsheet package called softCALC was compatible with Lotus 1-2-3, while its word processing package softWORD was similar to WordStar (of MicroPro) and could be used in DOS as well as UNIX. The company sold over twenty thousand packages of Softek OFFICE—a suite of softWORD, softBASE, and softCALC. It also launched word processor and desktop publishing packages in Hindi language.

The firm's fortunes, however, dipped with the arrival of PCs in India. The 1984 computer policy opened the floodgates for import of SKD and CKD kits. Along with hardware kits came pirated versions of software by Microsoft, Oracle, and other U.S. companies. Since it was focused on domestic markets, Softek struggled hard to remain afloat.[29] It was very difficult to export software products since marketing costs were too prohibitive. Unlike hardware, the government was not a big buyer of software.

Entrepreneurs like Nigam were attracted to the software business because of low entry barriers. Unlike the hardware industry, this business needed little capital and physical infrastructure to begin with. Ashank Desai, a design engineer at Godrej & Boyce Manufacturing Company, joined the PG Diploma in Business Management at the Indian Institute of Management, Ahmedabad in 1978. Along with some of his classmates, he toyed with the idea of starting an information technology company primarily because it did not require much capital. The team of first-generation entrepreneurs Desai, K. Sundar, and Ketan Mehta regrouped after about two years and founded Mastek (combination of management and software technology) in 1982. The fourth founder—Sudhakar Ram—joined in 1983.

Like Murthy of Infosys, Desai and his two cofounders had about $1,400 to start their software venture. They incorporated it in a two-bedroom flat in a Bombay suburb. Mastek's first project was developing a comprehensive production planning system for a healthcare company, Lyka Labs. Assignments from Hindustan Lever and Citi Bank followed soon. The domestic market was very tough to crack at the time, as hardware vendors bundled free software with machines and awareness of computers running management tasks was low. Mastek had no landline phone of its own, and no computer of its own until four years after it was started. Until then, it worked on customer's computers, and in this sense was engaged in onsite development work within the country.

The focus on the domestic market proved to be rewarding. In 1989, Mastek, with a turnover of about $275,000 could figure in the top ten domestic software firms, a reflection of the fact that software was a small market. In order to grow, Mastek soon was forced to target foreign markets. Its breakthrough in exports came in the form of an order from Singapore for development work on an IBM platform. Mastek did not have any people familiar with IBM but could still win the contract. Desai explained how this happened: "our programmers were so good that within a fortnight they could learn everything about the IBM platform. And this customer said, 'you have good experience in IBM,' whereas we did not have any. That is the strength of Indian programmers—they can read the manual at the airport and become experts."[30] Subsequently Mastek won orders from the United States and the UK, including software work relating to the congestion charging project for London where motorists have to pay a fee for driving a vehicle in specified congestion zones. Mastek engineers wrote the software for the payment process, imaging system database and backroom operations of the congestion charging system.

In Madras, another software programmer, K. V. Ramani, founded Future Software in 1985. His decade-long experience with the data processing department of liquor maker Shaw Wallace had exposed him to the worker shortage for software work in Europe. Shaw Wallace was using the spare capacity of its computer for software development for overseas customers. Ramani left the liquor company and launched his own firm, but found the going difficult despite winds of change blowing with the New Computer Policy announced in 1984. He wanted to focus on niche areas of communication and networking, embedded software, and systems software.

Future Software got its first export order from Denmark. The order was part of a large contract a Danish firm had won for replacing the multiple networks of American Airlines with a single one. The airline had separate networks for passenger reservations, cargo booking, and weather forecasting based on IBM proprietary hardware and software. The new contract involved changing communication subsystems of hardware and software to create an integrated network based on the X.25 protocol. Future Software was asked to develop a software emulator of the control unit of the IBM computer in use in the legacy network. The software emulator helped the Danish firm replace the IBM unit with its own proprietary hardware without any disruption in the network. Informal contacts helped fledgling software firms establish links with global customers during their early years of operation.

Startups like Future Software continued to face problems in importing computers for software export projects, despite a liberal policy and favorable political climate for technology promotion. The import-export policy of 1985 had allowed duty-free import of hardware for specific projects, provided it was paid for by the overseas customer and was sent back after two years. Making use of this provision, Future Software imported a system from Denmark and the consignment arrived at the Madras airport in early 1986. Much work relating to design and coding of the airport networking project had been finished. The imported system was crucial for software testing. Customs officials refused to release the computer, saying capital equipment could not be imported duty free under the Customs Act. When Ramani met the Customs Collector, he was told to go to New Delhi.

On his arrival at the capital, Ramani was refused entry into Udyog Bhavan, headquarters of the commerce and industry ministries. He found an innovative way to invade "the government fortress." In his words: "Officials had completely insulated themselves because they could not solve the problem. There was no way you could penetrate the fortress. I played a trick. I discovered that the Commerce Minister used another gate to enter the building. I went to my hotel, put on my best European dress, hired a posh car and told the driver to take me straight to the minister's gate. As soon as I got down, the guards saluted me. I entered the building without an entry pass and went straight to the officer who was avoiding seeing me."[31] That is how Future Software imported the duty-free computer for its first offshore project. The episode demonstrates that while the new government policy favored software exports, lower-level bureaucracy was still to change its ways.

Another important customer of Future Software during this period was Hughes Network Systems (HNS), a subsidiary of the Hughes Electronics Corporation. Future Software executed three projects for Hughes—LAN protocol concentration design; voice conferencing over VSAT networks; and fax and telex subsystems for the Inmarsat-C Land Earth Station (LES). This convinced Hughes of Indian software talent and it established a unit—Hughes Software Services (HSS)—in India for developing software for its vast array of communication and networking projects. Ramani had a 10 percent stake in this company. As was the trend, very soon HSS started serving non-HNS customers as well and became a specialist company in telecom software, licensing products globally. Many of the networking technologies that powered the mobile, Internet, and broadband booms in the 2000s were developed at HSS in India.[32]

By the mid-1980s, the country had a talent pool of experienced software professionals ready to become entrepreneurs. Saurabh Srivastava, for example, a graduate of IIT Kanpur, had worked with IBM, ICIM, and Tata Unisys Limited (TUL, the new name for TBL after Burroughs merged with Sperry to form Unisys). Srivastava launched International Informatics Solutions (later renamed IIS Infotech Limited) in New Delhi in 1989. Like Ramani, he too bumped into red tape while starting an export unit in 1989 but he decided to break all the rules. As soon as he got an export order, he started executing it without waiting for formal approval. Srivastava recalled: "We had to violate every rule in the book to get into business. There was no other way. You just had to use your personal standing in the industry to get good people to start with. The environment was about as unfriendly as it can be. It is surprising that any industry came out at all."[33]

Having worked in IBM and TUL, Srivastava was aware that it would not be possible for his start-up to compete with them in size and branding. So he decided to focus on offshore development rather than body shopping. Srivastava thought Western customers would not trust firms like IIS unless they were assured of good quality work through an internationally certified quality process. IIS worked to get the ISO 9001/TickIT assessment, a certification system for software processes published in 1991 by the United Kingdom Accreditation Service. Within a year, IIS became the first Indian company to get this certification, which, in turn, helped it attract overseas customers.

Another constraint in handling offshore projects was lack of IBM or ICL mainframe platforms. IIS could not afford to buy and maintain such large computers. One of its customers offered to loan one, but IIS could not even afford the costs associated with the needed premises, false flooring, and air conditioning for the system. That's when Srivastava made virtue out of the necessity and suggested that his U.S. client to let him use its platform through leased lines from India.

In a strategy designed to attract more and more Indian corporations to the use of information technology, the New Delhi firm NIIT, which initially started with computer education, diversified into a niche area called information system planning. NIIT was an offshoot of HCL. It developed a methodology to guide corporations in planning their information systems. Its Critical Information Systems Planning or CRISPAN was largely influenced by contemporary Western academic work in management theories. NIIT propagated the idea that information technology resources that focused only on critical areas would give high returns on investment.

With CRISPAN, NIIT approached large public-sector and private corporations in 1984 and signed up dozens of top two hundred blue chip companies in India. Having such a large customer base helped NIIT develop capability in IT consulting and planning. It also opened up new business avenues for NIIT. "We would do an IT or IS plan, and the chairman or CEO would immediately respond and say, 'Okay, you have told us the plan for five years with budgets, etc. Now, help us implement it.' That's how we got involved in building turnkey solutions for companies," Rajendra Pawar, NIIT founder, would recall.[34]

In early 1990s, the company put its experience in new technologies and skills in consulting to address the Southeast Asian markets with turnkey offerings. In Singapore, NIIT won the contract for creating digital filing of tax returns and financial systems for the Ministry of Defense. Another NIIT innovation was setting up software factories for international clients in India. The idea was to try and emulate as closely as possible the customer's physical environment (hardware and software), software tools, and development methodologies. NIIT went to the extent of even matching the color schemes of software factories with those of their customers. The idea was to build confidence among Western customers. The factory concept then evolved into the Offshore Development Centre model, later adapted by other companies for offshore exports. British Airways was among the early customers for whom NIIT set up software factories. NIIT also pioneered computer training in the private sector and spread it fast through franchises.

First Pieces of Jigsaw Puzzle in Place

Over the years Indians acquired early software development capability and skills through a variety of means—academic training in India and the United States, interaction with multinational companies operating in

India, and linkages with American minicomputer firms and state-funded R&D programs.

The software writing skills developed in parallel with hardware design innovation. In the mainframe era, software came bundled with hardware. Application software had to be written specifically for each computer. Since all commercial computers came from multinationals, software-writing skills also developed on their platforms with the help of foreign firms. This made IBM and ICL pools of experienced programmers. When TIFR acquired the large mainframe from CDC, it had its scientists trained in programming at CDC. Subsequently, these skills spread to other institutions across the country through training and hands-on experience.

Faculty members and students at IITs were exposed to software programming through their interaction with suppliers of large systems and faculty from collaborating foreign—mainly American—universities. Both IBM and ICL operated data centers where customers could hire computer time and get customized applications developed for their use. A number of data processing personnel in large corporations cut their teeth in software writing at these centers. Till the early 1970s, most of the Indian programming professionals owed their skills and experience to IBM, ICL, and, to some extent, CDC.

In the mid-1970s, a number of minicomputer companies started selling through Indian companies. PCS sold Data General's products and later formed a joint venture with it. Datamatics partnered with Wang Laboratories, Hinditron had a joint venture with Digital Equipment Corporation called Digital Equipment India Limited, and CDC later teamed up with DCM Data Products. IDM, which inherited IBM's data center business, became a reseller for Prime Computers. Similarly, ORG Systems had a marketing arrangement with Sperry.

All these U.S. minicomputer firms entered the Indian market hoping to fill the void created by IBM's exit but found the market sluggish and small. They did not see large enough margins to justify offering their full suite of products and services. In order to maintain economically viable operations, these firms began using local talent to write software for computers sold locally. This exposed them to something unexpected—they realized that not only were Indian engineers cheaper but the quality of software they wrote was very good. This made multinationals use Indian programmers for customers back home.

In the early 1970s F. C. Kohli persuaded Burroughs to farm out some software development work to TCS. Kohli said: "The main thing is that you needed somebody to test you out, and they (Burroughs) could test us out."[35]

The arrangement of using local software developers also helped computer firms compensate for the comparatively low revenues from hardware business in India. The Indian partners, in turn were exposed to standard practices in programming, marketing, and customer care. For instance, Burroughs was a leader in the basics of microprogramming, software architecture, and software engineering. In this process of give and take, Indian engineers could not only grasp technical skills but also decipher the basics of software business, and some of them eventually branched off as entrepreneurs. The seeds of an Indian software industry were thus sown in the late 1970s and early 1980s.

Pioneers like TCS learned a lot from technical journals, professional societies like IEEE, and through interaction with leading American universities. For instance, TCS benefited from the migration and conversion tools developed at the Carnegie Mellon University.

In the same way as multinationals discovered Indian software talent, Indian companies partnering with them realized that they could operate on their own in the area of software development. PCS is a good example of this trend. "When we started selling Data General machines here and began talking with them closely for a joint venture to manufacture computers, they saw the pros of India. There was a lot of business exchange, and we started doing software work for them including operating systems. That's how our software stream started," Narendra Patni commented on the initial phase of partnership with Data General.[36]

ORG Systems took up distributorship of the mainframe computers of Sperry Systems (which merged with Unisys in 1988) after the exit of IBM. "We developed P1024 protocol, which Sperry used in its mainframes worldwide. We also developed several systems software products for them," recalled K. R. Trilokekar, who worked with ORG Systems in the 1970s.[37]

While large industrial houses like the Tata Group had the necessary capital to fund their software ventures, entrepreneurs like Murthy, Nigam, Desai, and Ramani had to depend solely on human capital. For many such entrepreneurs, software writing was a "paper and pencil" activity, for they could not afford to buy a computer system. They all used to work on their clients' computers in initial years.

Since the domestic IT market was small, Indian companies had to look to export markets for survival and growth, right from the beginning through their dealings with minicomputer vendors. After the advent of the PC, demand for commercial software packages and applications rose in the United States as the market moved toward standard hardware and software from proprietary systems. So Indian companies also did not want to remain tied to hardware vendors and started seeking independent customers.

Taking up export assignments, however, was not easy. Indian companies did not have the necessary hardware and software tools as well as the basic infrastructure to take up any meaningful work. So the best way to leverage it was to go to the customer site and work using its computers. TCS and PCS had been doing this in the 1970s and this became a dominant way of doing software business in the 1980s. The industry gave this model the name "body shopping." Software firms had to hire the right people, train them for a brief while, and send them to American clients to execute projects, and then they would come back. This was a high-margin business. Two Tata companies—TCS and Tata Burroughs (which became Tata Unysis in 1986)—accounted for nearly 70 percent of exports through body shopping.

In body shopping or workforce contracts, customers would typically buy "hours" and not a total project or product with the associated management and value-added technical services. The contracts mostly related to routine tasks of coding, debugging, data conversion, and migration rather than higher-skill tasks of design, analysis, and project management. These contracts were short-term (six to eighteen months), and low in risk, value addition, and investment; yet they made up for 70–80 percent of export revenues. This, as a World Bank study pointed out in 1994, did not lead to the expansion of the domestic knowledge pool; training costs were high as programmers would opt to remain abroad; those who returned lacked experience in large-scale project management.[38]

The market conditions somewhat changed with the new computer and software policies announced in 1984 and 1986, respectively. Imports of hardware and software were liberalized, though the actual import of hardware still took time. New software packages and tools started becoming available when software was brought under the Open General License (OGL). Companies began exploring offsite development, or remote software development as it was called, as opposed to onsite development work and body shopping. But still there were impediments, such as high telecom costs. In this post-1986 phase, software companies set up links with American clients, got hooked to their large systems, and began working from India. U.S. companies went the other way round—they came to India and set up software development facilities, taking advantage of high-level skills and low labor costs. The number of software companies in the market also grew, mostly looking at exports, because of low entry barriers. The number of companies with sales exceeding $1 million grew from fifteen in 1990 to forty-four in 1992. And twenty-seven of them exported over $1 million each in 1992.[39]

Software exports rose from about 100 million to 1 billion rupees by 1991, which was still a minuscule percent of the global software market. During the decade of 1980–1990, the Indian software industry took shape and exports to the United States and Europe began in a modest manner. We have seen how software companies were founded, then picked up skills and business through interaction with foreign collaborations and joint ventures. In the wake of size constraints and import restrictions, these companies introduced an innovative method of exports: body shopping and onsite services. The real breakthrough in software exports came in the post-1991 period, which is examined in detail in the next chapter.

7 The Transition to Offshore

When a foreign company wants to set up an oil refinery, it goes to the Middle East. But when it wants to set up a software development center, it comes to India.
—Anil Sharma, President and Managing Director, Hughes Software Systems, May 1994[1]

A single government scheme—for Software Technology Parks (STPs), which envisaged the use of satellite data links for exporting software—is often credited with the rise of Indian software industry in the post-liberalization period of the 1990s. But this journey began much earlier.

Anecdotal stories and press reports about good and relatively cheaper software talent available in India had begun surfacing in business circles internationally by the mid-1980s. The new computer policy and economic liberalization under a young prime minister had attracted attention in the Western world. In September 1985, the widely read trade magazine *Electronics* featured policy changes in India under the caption "India Strives to Join the High-Tech World." Technology journalists wrote articles on the emergence of the Indian software industry after visiting the country. David Bunnell, publisher of *PC World* and *Mac World* magazines observed after visiting India: "Today India is finding an important niche in the global marketplace as a software exporter. This is due mainly to recent government policies liberalizing India's computer industry as well as to the high volume of well-trained programmers whose talents are available for less than half the going international wage." *Business Week* also noted "the availability in India of the world's third largest pool of engineers and skilled technicians, most of whom can communicate well in English work for a relative pittance."[2]

While Indian software firms were trying to link up with American customers and seeking to use data links for offshore development jobs, a few American companies began to try the reverse—come to India and use Indian engineers for development work. A new segment of the business opened up when Citibank decided to float a fully owned subsidiary in India to develop software for its internal software requirements. Up to this point Indian firms were developing software for American clients mostly at customer locations in the United States. Some multinational customers having operations in India also sourced software from Indian firms, besides a handful of third-party developers. Citibank was the first instance of a major end user setting up a fully owned unit in India to cater to its in-house software needs.

The bank previously had the experience of working with several local software firms and had been considering to establish a dedicated unit in India for some time.[3] It chose the duty-free enclave, the Santa Cruz Electronics Export Processing Zone (SEEPZ) in Bombay, to locate its software unit. Besides duty concessions on imported equipment, companies in this zone benefited from relaxed labor and statute requirements. A few software units were already functional in a mini cluster in the zone in 1985. At the opening ceremony of its new unit, named the Citicorp Overseas Software Limited (COSL), bank officials stated that Citibank hoped COSL would develop a large chunk of the $250 million worth of software the bank sourced every year for its global operations.[4]

In its formative years, COSL exclusively developed software for internal use in the United States and other regions. A few years into the operation, officials determined that some of the packages developed in Bombay could well be marketed to other banks without much modification. MicroBanker, a package developed on Citi's mainframe platform, was one such product that could easily be sold to banks in Asia and Africa, which used similar platforms. Within five years, software exported by COSL to Citibank units globally and to other banks made it India's third-largest software exporter, following TCS and TUL.[5] A PC version of MicroBanker was also developed covering branch banking functions like front office automation, funds transfer, electronic delivery system, accounting, and trade and investment tasks. The Local Area Network (LAN) version was priced at $120,000 for ten terminals and $200,000 for twenty terminals.[6]

COSL lost interest in MicroBanker in the early 1990s despite its success. This prompted Rajesh Hukku, an enterprising employee, to persuade the bank to spin off MicroBanker-related business into a separate company. Hukku thought the spin-off could be profitable if the product was aggressively marketed. He roped in Citicorp Venture Capital to invest $400,000 into the venture and also absorbed about 150 employees from COSL. The new firm, Citicorp Information Technology Industries Limited (CITIL), initially marketed MicroBanker and then developed a new suite of products under the Flexcube series. These products were sold to a large number of banks in the Middle Eastern and African markets. The prefix "Citi" helped open many doors, though Citibank itself was not a major customer. Oracle eventually bought CITIL in 2006 in one of the biggest deals of the period.[7]

Around the same time as COSL, another U.S. firm was attracted to SEEPZ. Prabhakar Goel, an alumnus of IIT Kanpur, had turned entrepreneur after working in IBM in the United States for close to ten years. With $50,000 he received on winning the IBM Corporate Award for Innovation in 1979, Goel launched Gateway Design Automation (GDA) in 1982 to develop and market chip-testing tools. GDA products like TestScan became a huge success, with customers including Texas Instruments and Raytheon signing up.

GDA's most famous product was an electronic design automation (EDA) tool, Verilog, which was granted Golden Simulator status by Motorola. While working on Verilog, Goel felt the need for developing "libraries"— fundamental building blocks of electronics design. This was labor-intensive work and GDA could not have afforded a large workforce in the United States to do this.[8] Goel decided to move this work to India, taking advantage of low labor costs and availability of skilled engineers. He first set up a unit in SEEPZ, but soon moved over to a similar export processing zone (EPZ) in Noida near New Delhi in early 1985. This was the first baby step in India's journey toward becoming a chip design destination by the turn of the century. In 1989, GDA had clocked about $25 million in revenue and was "half way through" to an IPO, when San Jose–based Cadence Design Systems acquired GDA including the Indian unit. The deal, thus, facilitated an automatic early presence of Cadence in India. Within a decade, Noida, along with Bangalore, would emerge as a hub for silicon design firms.

SEEPZ was home to top software firms like TCS, Tata Burroughs, and COSL, though the export zone was primarily meant for hardware manufacturers. It was not completely free of bureaucratic red tape, but industrial units in the zone were offered subsidized land, a five-year tax holiday, duty-free import of hardware, and clearance within a week. The four software firms operating in the zone had together exported software worth about $1 million during 1982–1983.

Private and State-Supported Software Enclaves

The idea of boosting software exports through a special zone was first proposed to Prime Minister Indira Gandhi during her visit to the United States in July 1982, by Sharad Madhav Marathe, a young Indian engineer settled in America. Indira Gandhi was paying an official visit during which she signed a science and technology pact with President Ronald Reagan, signaling the beginning of a new phase of technology cooperation. It was a significant move coming in the wake of the infamous exit from India of two of the most visible signs of U.S. capitalism—Coca-Cola and IBM.

At an informal meeting with a group of expatriate Indians, Marathe argued that India should leverage its intellectual labor to enter global export markets since it lacked the necessary infrastructure to compete in manufacturing like Taiwan or Singapore. Inspired by the Research Triangle Park in North Carolina, he proposed privately managed technology parks as a platform to begin knowledge-based exports. Probably because of her familiarity with government-run electronics export processing zones like SEEPZ and the need to take a new path to economic growth, Indira Gandhi could appreciate Marathe's idea of similar parks in the private sector. She invited Marathe to India to talk with the Department of Electronics and gave her an "in principle" go-ahead for the proposal.

Marathe would later recall a meeting he had with Gandhi in December 1982: "She asked me where the difficulties would lie. And I mentioned to her that two key departments/ministries would be customs and communications. When I requested her for guidance, she told me not to worry. She said, 'Go for it, but don't make me answer in Parliament!' and smiled."[9] Clearly, Indira Gandhi was giving in to forces of economic liberalization, yet wanted to maintain her public image of a socialist leader for political reasons. As with the 1984 New Computer Policy, she played midwife at key times. Most software industry analysts eulogize Prime Minister P. V. Narasimha Rao and economic reforms introduced by his Finance Minister Manmohan Singh in 1991, unaware of the key links in the chain forged during Gandhi's last term in office.

Indira Gandhi's ready acceptance of a radical idea such as duty-free, privately managed technology parks was indicative of her changed stance on private capital and the need to dismantle socialistic controls over the economy. She was also keen to shrug off the image of India being anti-multinational or anti-American business—an image created due to the departure of IBM and Coca-Cola during the previous regime. Following her 1982 visit to the United States, a large trade mission of the Overseas Private Investment Corporation (OPIC) visited India. It was said to be the first official American investment mission to India since 1964.

Technology firms like CDC, Rockwell, and 3CI International were part of this mission. Of the twenty-eight U.S. companies that came to India as part of the exploratory visit, twenty-six were negotiating joint ventures and fourteen projects were finalized by September 1983.[10] It was indicated that the Indian government would waive the 40 percent ceiling on foreign holding—a clause that led to the exit of IBM in 1977–1978—in areas of high technology. Indira Gandhi rationalized the shift in policy toward foreign investment by saying, "If it helps our exports, or it does not endanger our self reliance, or come in the way of development of Indian industry, then we may allow multinationals in."[11] In addition to the traditional emphasis on self-reliance, the willingness to boost exports was now part of government policies.

Independent of the idea of a privately managed technology park for export promotion, some proactive officials in the government were exploring state-led efforts to promote software exports. N. Seshagiri, who took over as director (Computers section) in the Department of Electronics in January 1982, initiated a dialogue with software firms to discuss ways to remove hurdles so that software exports could take off. Exasperated with having to deal with multiple government agencies, industry representatives suggested there should be a single agency to act as liaison between small Indian firms and foreign software buyers. The result of this interaction with industry was a new body called the Software Development Agency.

Participation in international deliberations on satellite communication and the New Information Order—a UNESCO initiative to promote more equitable flow of information to developing countries—had familiarized Seshagiri with the potential to deploy new communication technologies in developing countries. He thought intracity data networks in developing countries could be modeled on the lines of the ALOHA Network established in the University of Hawaii in 1970. But satellite communication had to become cost effective in order to be useful for developing countries to access databases in the developed world.[12]

In an experiment conducted in 1979, a bibliographic database at Frescati, Italy, was connected with TIFR in Bombay via a satellite link. The cost, however, was exorbitant—ranging between $30 and $70 per query and retrieval—compared with a similar service between Frescati and locations in Europe.[13] This demonstrated the technical feasibility of using satellite communication for software and database transactions between India and America or Europe, but it was highly uneconomical. As part of another exercise on data communication in 1981, UNESCO asked Seshagiri to prepare a report on the establishment of a regional informatics network for South and Central Asia. In this report, he proposed use of external gateways of satellite-based networks for import and export of databases on a semicommercial basis to avoid duplication of large international databases.[14] This is perhaps the first reference to use of nontelex data communication for import-export of databases between two locations—a model that would be followed for commercial software exports just a few years hence. The report suggested "focal points" in each country to act as secured custom bonded units for taking up semi-commercial import-export double funneling (IEDF)—a system for controlled two-way flow of data between countries.

The idea of deploying satellite-based data communication for software exports to developed countries was further crystallized in a report the Indian official authored for the United Nations Centre on Transnational Corporations (UNCTC) in April 1984. India at that time had seven operational data networks including those run by Air India, Bombay Stock Exchange, PanAm, and Dunlop. The state-run National Informatics Centre (NIC) had just applied for membership in Tymnet, the San Jose-based international data communication network. The existence of these networks and the government's promotional schemes, however, had not resulted in "giving the desired impetus to software exports."

Data links were crucial as Indian software companies found it difficult to develop software for U.S. computer firms, which were unwilling to let Indian companies have their hardware prototypes for developing systems software. American firms feared that information about hardware architecture and other techno-commercial details would get leaked if they sent prototypes or newly introduced systems to Indian software firms for development of firmware, microprogramming, and application software. As a possible solution, the UNCTC report on transborder dataflow (TBDF) suggested external gateways to link up overseas firms with software developers so that "by stationing their manpower in India itself, software export houses can maximize the advantage of low labor costs in India. This will also help the manufacturer abroad to minimize his cost on the development of system and utility software."[15] For instance, it noted, Indian software firms could access CAD (computer-aided design) software available on computers in developed countries for further development, while the cheap intellectual workforce in developing countries could also be used for the creation of databases in the West.

The report, which was like a blueprint for promoting knowledge-based exports from developing countries such as India, evoked interest among transnational corporations. Within months of its publication in May 1984, the Department of Electronics got some inquiries from U.S. and European firms for software exports or for database transactions with their offices or partners in India. Texas Instruments, Westinghouse, Dunlop, Society for Worldwide Financial Telecommunications (SWIFT), Societe Internationale Telecommunications Aeronautiques (SITA), PanAm, Reuters, and the National Library of Medicine were among those who showed interest.

In India, the report was circulated among different government ministries and Seshagiri was asked to include the idea of software exports via transborder data flows in the computer policy that was in the making. The empowered Cabinet Committee on Economics Affairs (CCEA), presided over by Indira Gandhi, approved the Foreign Trade Policy for 1985–1988 on September 6, 1984, with specific clause that "software exports shall also be permitted through satellite based data links with overseas computers." This was a landmark decision that would change the contours of India's nascent computer and software industry over the next decade. Once again, Gandhi became a facilitator in India's quest for knowledge-based exports in general and software exports in particular.

Meanwhile, Marathe incorporated a firm called Indo-American Capital and Technology Corporation (ICAT) and on October 27, 1984, ICAT applied for a license to set up a technology park as a 100 percent Export Oriented Unit (EOU) using satellite links for data communication. Three days later, Indira Gandhi was assassinated by her bodyguards at her residence in New Delhi. She did not live to see the results of her government's most radical export promotion measure yet. The New Computer Policy with a provision for software exports through satellite links (approved by the Cabinet chaired by Indira Gandhi) was announced by the new Cabinet headed by her son, Rajiv Gandhi, on November 19, 1984. Software Export Technology Parks were conceived as mini export processing zones.

A Pennsylvania-based firm Indus Technologies and Texas Instruments also applied for licenses under the new policy. All the proposals were approved as 100 percent EOUs on December 16, 1984, by the Board of Approvals in the Ministry of Industry and Company Affairs. With a view to cut bureaucratic red tape, a Standing Committee on Software Export Technology Parks with Seshagiri as chairman was set up to act as a single-point approval mechanism. Subsequently, the program name was shortened to Software Technology Parks.

Still the Ministry of Communications, which controlled external communication gateways, was unwilling to give up its authority over external communication. It suggested that private companies could set up satellite earth stations but they would be owned and operated by the Overseas Communication Service (OCS) of the government. Investments to be made by private companies for procurement of earth stations were to be adjusted against annual rental charges to be paid by the technology park to OCS. Similarly, the Ministry of Home Affairs raised security concerns and wanted all earth stations to maintain "a recording facility at the cost of the technology park to record all messages transmitted and received on magnetic media and hard copies for technical inspection."[16]

Texas Instruments Comes to Bangalore

While a privately managed technology park conceived by Marathe—ICAT—did not take off due to various problems including opposition by government agencies, the project of another licensee, Texas Instruments (TI), did succeed. A key difference was that TI wished to use the satellite link for its in-house data transmission, while ICAT and Indus had proposed to establish and manage STPs with communication links and other infrastructure needed for software export so that smaller software firms could be located in such parks.

TI had begun showing interest in India following the OPIC mission in 1982. The technology market in the United States was highly competitive and TI's bid to enter the home computer market had failed miserably. It announced plans to lay off two thousand workers in January 1985, citing "continued weakening of the worldwide semiconductor market."[17] The company was plunged into a deep crisis in 1985, with profits sliding in the first two quarters and the third quarter ending in huge losses. In the course of one year, TI had laid off more than seven thousand workers and decided to close down two of its major semiconductor manufacturing plants—one in El Salvador and another in Houston.[18]

While facing rough weather at home, TI was constantly exploring new ways to expand its business and remain afloat. A senior vice president of Indian origin, G. Ram Mohan Rao, was keeping a close tab on the changing policy environment in India. He was instrumental in making TI Chairman Mark Shepherd Jr. consider India as a possible location for software development and design facility in Asia Pacific, which was fast emerging as a market for TI products. Many Indians like Rao himself were employed by TI in America, providing evidence of Indian engineering talent. Asia was not new to TI as it had its semiconductor fabrication and testing centers in Singapore, Malaysia, Taiwan, Korea, and Japan. In fact, India too had been on TI's radar for a long time. Shepherd's predecessor, Patrick E. Haggerty, had visited India in the early 1970s and proposed a plan to set up a manufacturing and research facility for integrated circuits in India. But the proposal was not accepted by the government.[19]

Unlike Haggerty, Shepherd was given a warm reception in 1985. India of the 1980s was vastly different from India of the 1970s. He met Prime Minister Rajiv Gandhi and a few officials, besides visiting major cities hunting for a possible location for TI's new venture in India. Bangalore was not a natural or first choice for the location of the TI design center as it was yet to be recognized as India's foremost technology hub.

TI wanted to link up its Bangalore center with Dallas via a live data communication link using a satellite. Such a service was not commercially available in India, so TI decided to establish its own earth station (figure 7.1). However, a direct satellite link from Bangalore to the United States was not feasible, so TI India initially linked up with its office in Singapore and then Bedford, UK, for exporting software to Dallas. The link allowed TI's Bangalore office to use electronic mail over TI's global network. The Bangalore center was connected to an earth station of British Telecom at Goon Hilly in the UK, from where it was connected to the TI unit at Bedford near London. As per the security clause in the license, all data sent out had to be monitored for security reasons and a Department of Telecommunications (DoT) official was posted at the earth station for this purpose. Ostensibly the Home Ministry wanted to ensure that no state secrets or sensitive information was transmitted to the United States, though the official posted to monitor could make no sense of what was being sent. All that he could see were 0s and 1s in printouts.

Figure 7.1
Texas Instruments was the first company to set up a dedicated satellite link to directly connect its Bangalore software development center to its offices in the UK and the United States in 1985. The same model was then deployed in Software Technology Parks promoted by the Indian government to connect small Indian software firms with customers in the United States. Courtesy: Texas Instruments India

Early TI employees attribute the company decision to come to India to the shortage of design talent in the United States and not cost cutting alone. "TI was seeing India as a strategic place for long- term talent," said Srini Rajam, one of TI's first recruits in India, who would rise to become managing director of India operations.[20] It was the same reason why Citibank had set up its software operations in India in 1985. Krishna Landa, director of TI India in 1987, had echoed similar sentiments then: "With the reputation that TI enjoys worldwide, its strategic move to expand operations in India would have a snowballing effect, and we could see many other companies applying for similar facilities."[21]

TI presented an operational model for offshore software development for U.S. multinationals as well as Indian software companies. Officials of a number of companies including Wipro and Infosys visited the facility to gain firsthand view of how the model worked. For three years, TI was the sole user of the satellite link. In 1989, HP, Motorola, and IBM began exploring the possibility of setting up software operations in India. They also expressed an interest in using the satellite link of TI. The first Indian company to use a satellite link for commercial software exports between an Indian firm and an American customer was Bombay-based Datamatics, which linked up with AT&T Bell Labs in 1989.

Winds of change also started blowing in the corridors of the DoE. For the first time, senior officials were talking of facilitation, rather than regulation or control. Some of them also realized that policy alone would not bring in the desired change. India would have to actively market itself for software services, particularly in the largest market—the United States. The result of this new thinking was "Software India" conferences in the United States. Seshagiri led a delegation of sixteen select Indian companies for a series of seminars during October and November 1987. These seminars were held in Palo Alto, Seattle, Dallas, Chicago, Boston, and Washington, DC. In the Dallas meeting, representative of TI India presented a case study of the newly set up Bangalore operation. Representatives of Atari, National Semiconductor, Intel, HP, IBM, Xerox, and Excelan, among others, attended the meeting in Palo Alto cosponsored by the American Electronics Association.

Executives from DEC and Data General shared their experience of working with Indian firms and professionals, speaking highly of Indian software capabilities. In the Washington meeting, an official of Miami's municipal government presented a case study of the work done for the city by an Indian software firm.[22] At the same time, U.S. participants expressed concern about the poor state of communication facilities and data protection. These meetings provided a forum for Indian companies to make contacts with participating technology firms. Many of the U.S. firms that participated ended up doing business in India over the next decade or so.

The DoE signed a Memorandum of Agreement with the Commonwealth of Massachusetts for setting up a data link between Boston and Pune for "double funneling" of software and databases. The project was designed to encourage joint ventures between Indian and American companies, R&D deals, and technical collaboration. A Boston-Pune software network was developed for which the Massachusetts Office of International Trade and Investment committed $2 million while the DoE's Software Development Agency contributed about $1.5 million. This was the first state-sponsored effort that provided an opportunity to software firms to link up with companies in one of America's best-known high-technology clusters, Route 128 in the Boston area. For Americans, it provided a platform to explore a new and promising information technology market. Officials of the Massachusetts Office of International Trade noted that "India has just embarked on its own information age and this presents Massachusetts' software producers, keen to participate in the development of this strategic area, with an extremely promising and lucrative area."[23]

Building up an image for the Indian software industry among prospective customers in the United States was crucial. Industry representatives recall that it was difficult to sell India as a destination for technology business, as the country had a poor image abroad. "We had political instability after the term of Rajiv Gandhi's government ended in 1989, the foreign exchange situation was very bad, and India had no high-tech industry to show off," recalled Saurabh Srivasatava, former IBM and TUL engineer who turned to entrepreneurship in 1989.[24]

In 1989, the DoE participated in the CeBit fair at Hannover, where the theme was "Business with India." Software seminars were held in Amsterdam, Zurich, Paris, and London the same year with help from the Commission of European Communities, now commonly known as European Commission. A similar exposition was held in Moscow, where seven Indian companies participated. Fifteen Indian software firms participated in COMDEX '89 in Las Vegas. All this gave Indian software firms—a small number of them, though—much needed exposure to export markets. Sharad Marathe of ICAT arranged for a visit of government officials from Maharashtra state to familiarize them with the kind of infrastructure needed to boost software exports from India.

The "Software India" conferences held in the United States also provided Indian companies an opportunity to network and know each other better. During one such seminar in Boston in November 1987, a small group of entrepreneurs discussed the idea of forming an industry association that could lobby the government. The bonding eventually gave birth to the National Association of Software and Services Companies, known by the acronym NASSCOM. Over the next few years, NASSCOM successfully changed the software industry's relationship with the government. This helped influence decision-making processes in the government, resulting in far-reaching policy changes. The industry body was also able to engineer a change in government officials' perception of the industry. This attitude of mutual mistrust—a remnant of the old economy era—gave way to one of cooperation and coordination.

Game Changer STPs

While sufficient interest was generated among Western companies through direct marketing efforts as well as media reports highlighting early movers like TI, the situation on the ground remained difficult for smaller Indian software firms. Emulating the software export model demonstrated by TI was beyond their reach due to high costs of privately owned earth stations and satellite links. The original idea of an export zone where several software units could operate using shared communication links and other facilities remained on paper even at the end of the 1980s.

In addition, tentative liberalization introduced in 1985 by Rajiv Gandhi was beginning to falter due to political uncertainty and a precarious foreign exchange reserve. Many progressive steps were rolled back. The duty on software was hiked from 60 to 65 percent in 1988 and to 107 percent in 1989. A new 15 percent tax was introduced on foreign exchange spent on travel, adversely hitting firms engaged in onsite services and body shopping.

Whatever little liberalization had taken place, it yielded decent results. Software exports grew from $3.5 million in 1980 to $96 million in 1990. However, 80 percent of it was accounted for by body shopping or onsite work.[25] Offshore activity was restricted to operations of companies like TI and Citibank. Though the 1986 policy permitted data communication links using satellites, Indian software firms lacked necessary capital to fund such links. The domestic market was still small and software piracy was rampant. Entrepreneurial firms started at the beginning of the decade were either considering selling off or closing down their operations. It was necessary to make the STP scheme useful for Indian companies. A formula was proposed to simplify calculation of export obligations, and the need for custom bonding for software export firms was done away with. Software exporters were also permitted to sell in the domestic market. However, clauses relating to ownership of earth stations by the government and security monitoring were not liberalized.

In view of aborted takeoff of private STPs like ICAT licensed in 1985 and the inability of Indian firms to invest in satellite links like TI, the DoE decided to promote state-sponsored STPs, where several Indian companies could set up their units. The idea was to provide software units a common location where they could share core computing facilities, data communication links, and other infrastructure. Units located in such parks could also enjoy benefits given to exporters of commodities and goods. In order to give functional autonomy and ensure speedy clearances, STPs were to be given the status of an autonomous entity within the DoE.

In June 1990, a leadership change occurred at the DoE with the appointment of Nagarajan Vittal as its secretary (the topmost civil servant in a government department). He had earlier served as head of an export processing zone at Kandla in Western India. K. Roy Paul, another civil servant working in the Ministry of Commerce, was posted as joint secretary in charge of the electronics industry. Pronab Sen, an economist who headed the Economic Research Unit in the Steel Ministry, was appointed economic advisor. It was the combination of these three individuals that changed the outlook of the DoE. The trio ensured that the DoE shed its scientific department image to become an industry- and business-oriented ministry. This also reflected a change in the government's outlook because traditionally the post of secretary in the DoE was occupied by a scientist and not a generalist civil servant.

Within a week in office, Vittal summoned representatives of hardware and software industries and gave them a sympathetic hearing. The industry wanted high-speed data communication links to facilitate software exports and government help to overcome the lack of venture capital funding. In addition, software companies wanted the concessions and tax holidays enjoyed by other export-led activities to be extended to the software sector. Vittal presented all of these demands at the Committee of Secretaries, the next level of decision making in the government, at its meeting on August 20, 1990.

Vittal wrote of this meeting in 1993: "The Finance Secretary (Bimal Jalan) asked me, 'If we give all these concessions, can you promise $500 million exports by next year?' I said this much was not possible, but we could try for $300 million. As a compromise, a target of $400 million was agreed."[26] Within a week, the government formally announced a package of incentives including the much sought-after tax holiday on profits earned through software exports. In return, Vittal wanted the industry to achieve the target of $400 million exports, which many in the industry thought was unrealistic. The change in the attitude of bureaucracy in commerce and finance ministers had a lot to do with the professional approach of software entrepreneurs. Most software companies were run by highly educated, skilled, first-generation entrepreneurs, unlike old-style industrialists who believed in lobbying the government for gaining access to licenses, permits, and other favors.

Vittal pushed the idea of state-operated STPs and decided to set up these parks as autonomous bodies under the DoE. An umbrella body called Software Technology Parks of India (STPI) was incorporated to oversee seven parks, located in Pune, Bangalore, Bhubaneswar, Gandhinagar, Noida, Thiruvananthapuram, and Hyderabad. Each park had its own management board that included industry representatives—again, a departure from the past. Decision making was decentralized. Directors of these parks were given the power to approve new units.

The state-run STPs acted like oxygen for the gasping software industry. The STPs virtually freed them from governmental controls. Now they did not need a license to import computers. Any software export unit located in an STP could import computers just based on an "import certificate" issued by the DoE. All imports into software parks were made duty-free. The export obligation was to be calculated based on factors like the cost of imported equipment and the annual wage bill of the unit. Equipment bought from the domestic market was also made tax-free. Very soon, STP units were permitted to sell up to 25 percent of their export value in the domestic market. In STP units, foreign equity up to 100 percent was permitted and firms were allowed to repatriate profit after paying requisite taxes. In the 1991 annual budget, software exporting firms were granted a tax holiday on their export earnings.

Availability of affordable satellite links, however, was still a bottleneck. For units in the Bangalore STP, it was suggested that idle capacity of the Texas Instruments gateway could be used by other software exporters since TI was using less than 10 percent of its capacity. But TI was located in downtown Bangalore, far away from the STP in the Electronics City. The units in STP could not use the TI links, but Motorola, IBM, and MICO Bosch, which were located in the vicinity, could do so. Commercial 64 kbps links provided by state-run Videsh Sanchar Nigam Limited (VSNL) were overpriced. For example, a 64 kbps link in 1991 would cost $180,000 annually for a half-circuit, compared to the international rate of $84,000 per annum.[27] Moreover, the link was unsuitable for high-bandwidth data-grade traffic. The government corporation showed no willingness to upgrade to facilitate data communication.

In 1992, just a handful of such links were in use. A Hyderabad-based start-up, Satyam Computer Services, got a Madras-Chicago link to execute a reengineering contract worth $1 million for John Deere Corporation by remotely working on Deere's IBM mainframes located in Moline, Illinois.[28] The time difference between India and the United States allowed the Satyam development crew to access mainframes in Moline in the dead of the night when Deere's computers were far more accessible than during day. The same year, another link was established from New Delhi to Toronto for the software unit of Bell Canada. Datamatics, which first got connected to AT&T Bell in 1989, set up dedicated offshore development centers for Singapore Airlines and Itochu Corporation. The annual tariff of about $36,000 for a low-speed data link was too high for software firms; 550 out of 700 software firms in 1991 reported their turnover to be less than this amount.[29]

High-speed telecom links were vital not just for exports. They could help smaller firms overcome the lack of computer infrastructure locally and bring down costs associated with body shopping. They had no option but to send their employees to work at clients' sites, which added to the cost of companies and also severely restricted the nature of contracts they could undertake. Since they could not afford to send large teams to America to work for a single client, Indian firms were restricted to relatively small jobs or they acted as subcontractors in large projects. This led to a gross underutilization of Indian talent. Since there was a restriction on the number of people who could be sent, Indian engineers not only did systems design but also had to write code, which was labor intensive, required a lower level of skills, and was not highly remunerative. Though the average salary of an Indian software professional was only 15 percent of his American counterpart, his productivity was probably no more than 30 percent.[30] This meant the practice of body shopping did not really offer any significant cost advantage to Indian firms.

At the same time, some in the industry argue that body shopping was the right strategy given the situation in the 1980s. It was an innovative way to overcome the shortage of finance and venture capital to fund infrastructure, training costs, and high-speed data links. All that start-ups needed was to recruit engineers and buy one-way tickets for them to the United States. Once the project got going, monthly cash flow would help the company sustain itself. In retrospect, this activity had positive fallout though unintended. Many software engineers opted to remain in America either with companies where they had onsite contracts or with software companies. This created a pool of Indian professionals in various American technology firms. And when these engineers climbed up the ladder and took up executive positions they ended up contracting more work to Indian companies or returned to India as heads of Indian subsidiaries.

When pressured by Vittal and the software industry, the DoT agreed to provide high-speed data links at STPs through satellite earth stations. But it put forth a condition—software units would have to pay the annual charges in advance while applying for a high-speed leased line, citing this as the standard procedure. Software firms were in no position to do this, as they had no idea of their bandwidth requirement, nor did most of them have the money to pay up front. Even when some of them were ready to pay, the DoT was not willing to give a time frame as to when data links would become available. Vittal took a bold step. He said the DoE would book data links and pay the advance fee to the DoT.

The first link became operational at the Bangalore STP in April 1993. In the first week of June 1993, a video conference was held with a company located in Washington, DC. Vittal and representatives of software firms, including Infosys Limited, Wipro Infotech, and BFL Software, participated. The facility was soon made available to software units in the park to enable them to hold remote meetings with their overseas clients.

The monopolistic attitude of telecom agencies made the DoE explore further alternative means of data communication. The opportunity came in the form of a bilateral agreement with France, under which equipment could be bought from French companies. The DoE used this offer to import communication equipment from the French firm CGR, and set up satellite data links at STPs parallel to the earth stations controlled and operated by VSNL. High-speed data circuits were offered to exporters at rates lower than those offered by VSNL. The DoE offered the links at $60,500 per annum compared to VSNL/DoT's $250,000. This saw companies shifting to Satcom—a new entity set up with French financial aid—eventually forcing VSNL to bring down its rates to $68,000. As a result of this competition, the number of high-speed links used by software companies in the country rose to two hundred by October 1994 compared to just three in 1992. Of these, ninety links were on DoE-sponsored earth stations.[31] A major battle was thus won.

Full-scale opening up of the telecom sector—including basic, mobile telephony, and Internet services—had to wait a few more years.

Liberalization Injects Growth

Besides its open mind and friendly relations with the nascent industry, the DoE bureaucracy could have its way because the policy environment in the 1990s was vastly different from the one prevailing in the 1980s.

The Congress Party, voted back in power in June 1991, was forced to unleash economic reforms under pressure from the World Bank and the International Monetary Fund in order to overcome an adverse foreign exchange situation of the country. The "license-permit Raj" came to an end on July 24, 1991. Industrial licensing was abolished for all projects except health and environment. Public sector monopoly was ended in all sectors barring strategic- and security-related areas. The 40 percent cap on foreign equity investment was done away with and entry restrictions on firms covered under the Monopolies and Restrictive Trade Practices Act were scrapped. Foreign equity up to 51 percent was allowed, and rules relating to foreign technology agreements, hiring of foreign technicians, and release of foreign exchange for business travel were all relaxed.

Industrial liberalization was accompanied by liberalization of external trade. Import licensing on virtually all intermediate inputs and capital goods was done away with. With the removal of licensing, existing high tariff rates acted as barriers to imports. So a gradual lowering of import duties followed. The top rate fell to 85 percent in 1993–1994 and to 50 percent in 1995–1996. Importers were authorized to purchase foreign exchange in the open market at a higher price, effectively ending the exchange control.

The opening up of the economy had a major impact on computer hardware and software industries. Hardware manufacturers, facing tough times following the import of kits allowed earlier, suffered further as import duties started falling. Importing finished products became cheaper than importing components and manufactured parts. Local manufacturing gradually faded away. The Indian manufacturers formed alliances with foreign firms—Wipro with Acer, HCL with HP, the Tata Group with IBM, and so on—for manufacturing computers.

On the software side, too, foreign firms entered the market. All major information technology companies—IBM, SUN, Oracle, Microsoft, Cisco, Novell, SAP, and so on—began doing business in India through a variety of arrangements (fully owned subsidiaries, offshore development centers, joint ventures, marketing and distribution partnerships, expansion of existing operations, etc.). Indian engineers working in Silicon Valley firms played a catalytic role in forging most such alliances. Several of those, who migrated to the United States in the 1970s and 1980s for lack of professional challenges in the Indian industry then, had reached top positions in Silicon Valley by now. The list of high-profile nonresident Indians who became champions of Indian IT industry in the United States included Vinod Khosla (cofounder of SUN Microsystems), Vinod Dham (designer of Pentium at Intel), Raj Reddy (Carnegie Mellon), Kanwal Rekhi (cofounder,

Excelan), Arun Netravali (AT&T), Pradman Kaul (Hughes Network), Suhas Patil (founder of Cirrus Logic), Umang Gupta (founder of Gupta Corporation), Gururaj Desh Deshpande (cofounder of Sycamore Networks), C. K. N. Patel (Bell Labs), and so on. The U.S. Agency for International Development and the Silicon Valley Indian Professionals' Association (SIPA) helped promote networking among Indians there as well as spurring Indo-American joint ventures back home. As a senior Hewlett Packard executive of Indian origin remarked, "A lot of companies that have been successful in setting up shop in India have a champion within the company in the U.S. For India, they tend to be Indians."[32]

The Indus Entrepreneurs (TIE), founded in 1992 by a group of entrepreneurs of South Asian origin based in Silicon Valley to mentor young entrepreneurs, acted like a bridge between Indians there and India. The role played by the Indian diaspora in the making of Indian software industry is remarkable in many ways.

The entry of foreign firms did not affect local software firms directly, as very few made competing products. The alliances Indian firms forged with Western corporations helped them acquire domain-related expertise in areas like telecom and networking as well as technological capabilities to meet global standards in software development. Indian firms, however, faced the heat in other ways. Foreign companies started targeting the same talent pool as Indian companies. Now local firms had to take additional steps to hire and retain engineers and programmers. This led Indian firms to adapt innovative HR practices and schemes like employee stock options.

Reforms also facilitated access to capital for software firms. Entrepreneurs had started companies using their measly savings and other similar resources. Banks did not finance software companies, for they had no formidable assets to be offered as collateral. At the most, they would advance loans for buying computers. Venture capital was not viable till then. The two existing technology venture capital funds—Technology Development and Investment Company of India and Risk Capital and Technology Finance Corporation—tended to advance only against the security of fixed assets, much like nationalized banks. Software companies had a low fixed-assets base and were heavily based on intangibles such as human skills and intellectual property. The concept of "sweat equity"—a norm in Silicon Valley in the United States—was yet to be recognized in India.

The option of going public was available, but the pricing mechanism was regimented with the Controller of Capital Issues (CCI) fixing a premium on the public offering. As a result, many of software and technology firms shied away from going public. In any case, the cost of going public was also too high for them. The office of CCI was abolished and companies were permitted to fix the price of their initial public offering premium in consultation with their investment bankers. This opened up the equity route for software companies to raise funds from the market.

Yet another move was to relax foreign exchange regulations for certain purposes like hiring foreign consultants for marketing, quality, and production; for setting up sales offices abroad; and for buying companies abroad. All these measures, though a part of the overall reforms process, helped the software sector a great deal. For instance, IIS acquired companies in Singapore, the United Kingdom, and the United States within a short period. Leading firms like NIIT, Infosys, and Mastek went public to raise funds for new projects.

In 1992, the World Bank sponsored a study of India's software industry to gauge its potential in the world markets.[33] This was the first formal SWOT (strengths, weaknesses, opportunities, and threats) analysis that examined various aspects of the software sector. It analyzed the relative strengths and weaknesses of eight competing countries in this emerging area—Singapore, Israel, the Philippines, Mexico, Hungary, Ireland, India, and China—and put India in second place, Ireland being on the top. The report pointed to six potential markets—Italy, the United Kingdom, France, Germany, Japan, and the United States—that accounted for 80 percent of all global information-technology spending. In 1991, India's software services exports were worth $164 million, which was 11.7 percent of what the report called "total foreign opportunity." It said that this figure could rise to $640 million in the next five years in a "business as usual" scenario. And it could reach $1 billion by 1996 with necessary policy and industry interventions.

Indian software services, the report said, had the lowest labor costs after China, had one of the largest pools of labor supply, and enjoyed the advantage of English-speaking workers. But compared with competitors, India had the disadvantage of poor telecom infrastructure, lacked specialized education and training, and had not exploited the domestic market potential. The areas that needed policy and industry action were the removal of import restrictions and tariff walls, ending procedural delays for importing hardware and software tools and upgrading of skills. The report said firms needed to strengthen their marketing capabilities to get greater access to international expertise and information on potential markets. But Indian companies had low marketing budgets and were not doing any strategic marketing due to foreign exchange restrictions. They mostly relied on "word of mouth" publicity.

The World Bank report was used by the DoE as well as industry to improve the prospects of the industry both within the country and abroad. As one former DoE official observed: "It helped us project India, and the World Bank tag helped. It was a useful report to flaunt." Industry leaders felt that this report gave the industry some amount of respectability and hope of reaching the magical figure of $1 billion from $100 million in 1990.

Addressing Quality Concerns

The opening up of the economy posed new challenges for the Indian software industry. There were gaps in quantity and quality of the IT workforce to serve both export and domestic demands, as observed in another World Bank study in 1994.[34] The country had a good number of programmers or code writers, but software engineering and project management skills were in short supply. Another factor was the limited output and low quality of IT graduates from most public institutions. The quality of private training institutes was uneven. Software firms also lacked access to software productivity tools and technology platforms as well as access to international expertise and information about overseas markets.

Indian software firms also realized that cost alone could not be their advantage going forward. Competition within the country was also growing. In body shopping, just the quality of programmers mattered. This was not so in the offshore model, in which quality processes was a prerequisite to win export orders. Customers had to be convinced that their projects would be handled professionally and delivered on time. The attrition rates also forced companies to document knowledge as projects progressed, so that the quality was retained and projects were delivered on time even if some employees left midway. The World Bank study pointed out that India must transit from the "low cost, low quality" quadrant to the "low cost, high quality" quadrant in order to achieve $1 billion in software exports by 1996.

Seeking to attain international quality certification was the way to go. In 1992, International Informatics Solutions (IIS) became the first Indian software company to get the ISO 9000 certification, the European standard designed to ensure consistent and orderly execution of customer orders.[35] The industry body NASSCOM addressed quality on a priority basis while the government gave incentives. Software exporters awarded ISO 9000 or equivalent certification were made eligible for the grant of Special Import Licenses by the Director General of Foreign Trade. The Export Import Bank of India announced a scheme to subsidize up to 50 percent of the cost of obtaining quality certification. By December 1998, 109 Indian software firms had this certification or an equivalent, internationally recognized quality certification.

The next wave of quality certification came with the Capability Maturity Model for Software (CMM) scheme of the Software Engineering Institute (SEI) of Carnegie Mellon University. Poor quality of software was a major problem facing large U.S. corporations as well as the U.S. defense establishment in the 1980s. In a study of seventeen major system contracts given to top suppliers, the U.S. Air Force found that every project had cost and budget overrun. On an average, a four-year contract took seven years. And in every case, the source of the problem was software.[36] The Air Force referred the problem to SEI asking it to develop a method to evaluate software vendors. SEI asked Watts Humphrey, a former director of IBM's Systems Research Institute, to work on this problem along with a team at defense supplier Mitre Corporation. Over the next five years, Humphrey's work at SEI led to the development of a new benchmark for software industry—the Capability Maturity Model for Software.

The first version of the Capability Maturity Model for Software (SW-CMM) was published in August 1991. It was a five-level framework that described key elements of an effective software process, and achieving each level signified adopting a particular component in the software process—planning, engineering, and managing software development and maintenance. The objective was to improve the ability of software firms to meet the goals for cost, timely delivery, functionality, and overall product quality.

India's involvement with CMM began soon after it was unveiled. Like all its contemporaries, Motorola too faced problems of poor-quality software. When it was planning to establish a software development unit in India, Motorola thought of building in quality principles from day one. Motorola India Electronics Limited (MIEL, later renamed Global Software Group India) established a fully documented software process and a detailed metrics program to achieve CMM Level 5 in 1991. In November 1993, it reached the Level 5 status to become the world's first commercial organization to do so.[37]

India thus became a testing laboratory for a global technology giant. The reason for Motorola gaining such high rating so quickly, according to Michael Cusumano (consultant to Motorola and later a professor at MIT's Sloan School of Management), was the fact that MIEL was designed to be a

Level 5 facility from scratch.[38] Since the quality process is highly demanding in terms of documentation and tracking accountability for each step in the process, it faces resistance from managers. But introducing the right practices from the beginning helps a new entity achieve high levels of CMM fast. Motorola then imported these high-quality practices back to its development centers in the United States and elsewhere.

After Motorola, Wipro Infotech Group was the second Indian firm to have reached Level 5 of CMM in 1998. The number of Indian software firms with Level 5 CMM has been growing steadily since then. In February 2000, India had fourteen companies with Level 4 and ten companies with Level 5 maturity levels. Indian companies took advantage of CMM not just as a marketing ploy to win over American customers, but also as a productivity tool. The adoption of Humphrey's new process methods in 1996 by U.S. companies had doubled profits and reduced defects by 98 percent or 0.05 bugs per one thousand lines of code.[39]

Humphrey believed that software process improvement requires a concerted effort at three distinct levels—the organization, the team, and the individual. While CMM addressed the organization-level for quality, he developed Team Software Process (TSP) and Personal Software Process (PSP) to address the other two levels. A small software firm founded by an Indian, Girish Seshagiri, in Peoria, Illinois, became the first one to adopt PSP. The company, Advanced Information Systems (AIS), had just thirty-five engineers when it began implementing quality processes. Quality became a passion with Seshagiri, who in 2000 founded the Watts Humphrey Software Quality Institute in Chennai, where AIS has a subsidiary.

The Millennium Bug

In the mid-1990s, a chance factor hit the software industry in the form of the Year 2000 or Y2K problem. The origins of this problem go back to 1959 when Grace Murray Hopper and Robert Berner created COBOL, one of the oldest programming languages in use until the 1990s. The language was designed for large mainframe computers that had very limited memory. In order to economize on memory and keep the language simple, standardized dates with two digits each for the day, month, and year were built in. For instance, 052185 would be written for May 21, 1985. However, this could also mean May 21, 1785 or 2085. Berner himself had discovered this problem when he was involved in a project to create a genealogical database—spanning over centuries—in Salt Lake City. He created a "picture clause" in COBOL that allowed years to be written with four digits. However, when companies like IBM and Burroughs adapted COBOL, they ignored u.. continued to use the two-digit-year formula in their systems.

Indian programmers, too, continued to write programs with only two digits for the year field. Sharad Godbole, who began his career as a programmer with the Mafatlal group in 1969, wrote nearly four hundred applications using COBOL over two decades. All these programs were Y2K noncompliant. He recollects that Indian programmers used two digits for the year and one digit for the month.[40] They used digits zero to nine to denote January to October, punching special signs at the top of the card for November and December. The program was written to recognize these signs. This way they could store more records in fewer cards. The cost savings for cards as well as card punching, verification, and processing were enormous.

This COBOL date field glitch continued for years; only in the 1990s did computer users globally begin to realize that their systems would stop working on January 1, 2000, when all old programs would show "00" in the year field. Bank and credit card companies dealing with medium- and long-term loans detected the problem in the mid-1990s. The problem was enormous and the cost of fixing it was estimated at several hundred billion dollars. It was a labor-intensive process to identify date fields in various programs and then rewrite them. The technical workforce available in the United States and European countries was not sufficient to handle such large volumes of work. Western countries, therefore, started looking elsewhere to outsource this work. India appeared to be a good choice as programmers here were familiar with mainframe and other legacy software needing repair. The cost was also low.

The government once again stepped in to let the private sector take advantage of the Y2K opportunity. The DoE published a comprehensive report on the subject and encouraged STPs to offer short-term courses in COBOL and the Y2K bug. Units in STPs were permitted to use their computing facilities for commercial training. Subcontracting of work from one STP to another similar unit was also allowed. The DoE teamed up with NASSCOM to hold road shows in the United States during October 1997 to interact with American firms as well as the Information Technology Association of America. Similar meetings were held in Japan and Europe. India's Export Promotion Board offered special incentives like a subsidized telecom tariff and provision of radio links for the "last mile" problem to software companies working on overseas assignments to address Y2K. NASSCOM set up a Special Interest Group on Solutions to the Year 2000 Problem in July 1996 to promote India as a destination for Y2K solutions.

Large and medium-sized software firms—grabbed the opportunity. Infosys, Wipro, Satyam, and TCS used the chance to ramp up their applications-maintenance capabilities. HCL formed a joint venture with Fairfax-based James Martin & Co in April 1996 to provide Y2K fixes globally. Over 23 percent of Infosys's revenue in 1998 and 20 percent in 1999 came from Y2K-related work.[41] Cognizant Technology Solutions earned 30 percent of its revenue during 1997–1998 from the Y2K solution. Satyam Computer Services set up a subsidiary, Dr. Millennium Inc., to offer web-based Y2K solutions in North America. Of its $100 million in revenues during 1998–1999, Y2K accounted for 28 percent.[42]

TCS set up a Y2K factory in Chennai housing nearly a thousand programmers capable of churning out two million lines of code every day. The company invested one billion rupees for the facility, which had two large IBM mainframes and 512 kbps satellite links to New York and London. TCS used proprietary as well as commercially available analysis, conversion, and testing tools to execute eighty Y2K projects for clients in the United States, Canada, the UK, Europe, Australia, New Zealand, Singapore, and Malaysia.[43] The volume of work involved was so huge that TCS had to contract out work to seven smaller software firms.

Overall, Indian software companies earned revenues worth $2.3 billion from Y2K-related exports and services rendered to U.S. and European corporations between 1996 and 1999. During one year alone (1998–1999), Indian firms clocked revenues of $560 million from Y2K software solutions.[44]

For the Indian software industry, the Y2K proved to be more than just an opportunity to scale up operations and revenues (figure 7.2). It helped them increase their exposure to new export customers and spread their reputation for quality, timely delivery, and cost effectiveness. The investments large players had made were clearly aimed at business potential beyond the Millennium Bug, as a TCS official had articulated then: "TCS offers value addition to the Y2K conversion process and could convert OS/VS/COBOL II and help isolate or indent unused segments of the code. In addition, we can capture the systems details into a repository, which can not only be used for the conversion itself, but also become useful for future re-engineering and maintenance requirements."[45]

The Birth of a Software Giant

A strong information technology industry emerged in India at the end of the 1990s due to the combined effect of overall economic liberalization, promotional schemes of the government, and factors like telecom

Figure 7.2
Infosys campuses across India are famous for the innovative and futuristic architecture of their office buildings. The eighty-acre campus in Bangalore's Electronics City is designed to resemble a college campus. Over twenty thousand employees work in fifty buildings on this campus. Courtesy: Infosys Limited

liberalization. The bulk of the Indian software exports were in "professional services" or "projects" categories till 1995. This was a period of significant change for the Indian software industry—it shifted away from body shopping and onsite services to offshore development and services. In 1999, onsite development came down to 59 percent of total exports from about 80 percent at the beginning of the decade. The establishment of STPs, a fall in telecom tariffs, and emergence of the Internet played a key role in this transformation. External factors like Y2K, euro conversion, and emergence of electronic commerce helped the Indian industry ramp up its operations and garner new customers in North America and Europe.

The launching of the Software Technology Parks of India on June 5, 1991, was a unique effort. For the first time, a government scheme focused on a single product or industry and exclusively targeted export markets. It integrated features of earlier export promotion schemes such as 100 percent Export Oriented Units (EOUs) and export processing zones of the Indian government as well as the science and technology parks operating elsewhere in the world. As expected, this effort boosted software exports. Software units operating from STPs have emerged as major contributors to software exports from India. Total software exports from India rose from $164 million for 1991–1992 to $6.2 billion in 2001–2002—the bulk of which came

Figure 7.3
This building houses Software Development Block 3 at the Infosys campus in Pune in Western India. Courtesy: Infosys Limited

from units located in STPs (figure 7.3). No other government scheme in independent India has given this level of return in terms of export revenues in such a short span.

Within a decade, the STP scheme made software exports a major contributor to India's export earnings and the software industry a significant contributor to the country's GDP. The success of STPs was mainly due to the single-point contact provided to software units and the ease of cost-effective satellite links to customers in North America and Europe. The lure of tax breaks and duty-free imports provided were the major attractions for companies, as was evident from the large number of units registered in March 2000. The STPs' success was, however, limited when it came to the other objectives of providing incubation, training, marketing, and venture capital facilities to entrepreneurial and small software firms.

The provision of high-speed data links via satellites at affordable rates greatly boosted the shift toward offshore development. The links were used not just to transmit the software developed in India to customers abroad, but also to develop a new model for working with clients. These links allowed Indian programmers to access computers located anywhere in the world on a real-time and online basis. This helped customers of Indian companies as well. Even if a client was situated ten thousand miles away, he or she could still monitor software development on a minute-by-minute basis, ensure quality checks, communicate with the programmers as if they were just next door, and still get efficient software developed. All this, as an industry report noted, meant immense savings of both time and costs. An average twelve-hour time difference with India means that a high-speed data link could connect Indian firms with American customers through a virtual twenty-four-hour office environment.[46]

The STP scheme symbolized a new partnership between industry and the state. It was the first such scheme in which the private sector participated in decision making and it was run by an autonomous society and not a government ministry. In the 1990s, the DoE transformed itself from being a regulator to a facilitator. Mutual mistrust gave way to a sense of partnership. The "deal" of $400 million in exports that DoE Secretary Vittal struck with the software industry is a rare example of a bureaucrat playing the role of an industry promoter. In his view, "secretaries of government departments must act as champions for their sector to improve India's competitiveness in that sector. The Secretary as a champion of an idea has to argue his case, persuade his colleagues, and make compromises if necessary, so that the basic objective of the proposal is finally approved by the process of consensus."[47] It was this thinking that prompted Vittal to push the STP scheme vigorously and get income tax exemption for software exports as well as set up affordable satellite data links. This was in total contrast to the vision of "government entrepreneurship" pursued by the DoE in the 1970s.

The new thinking in the DoE did not amount to a diminishing role of the state in the post-liberalization era. In fact, the state's role was amplified: it played a greater role in making available to private firms infrastructure, capital, technology, skill development, marketing assistance, training, and a legal framework, besides stepping up diplomatic efforts in the United States to issue a higher number of H1B visas. The DoE and other government departments implemented several policies and programs specifically to boost the software export industry in the first half of the 1990s. The government provided concessions and subsidies to software firms for land, power, water, and rentals, in addition to exemptions on income tax, sales tax, excise tax, and import duties. The Copyright Act was amended to provide copyright protection to software.

When the United States tightened visa rules in the mid-1990s, government help extended to the industry in its exploration of European markets was a good example of state intervention to find new market opportunities for the software industry. In December 1994, the Commerce Ministry partnered with the Commission of European Communities and launched a one-year project to identify joint ventures in software; within a few months it catalyzed software export contracts worth one billion rupees for Indian firms. This was followed by the DoE and the European Commission establishing Software Services Support and Education Limited in Bangalore specifically to promote the Indian software industry in Europe. Factors like economic recession in many countries in Europe, opportunities arising out of the unification of Germany, and the shortage of skilled personnel to take up low-end, migration-related work also helped Indian companies enter the European markets.

Another dose of state benevolence came in the form of recommendations of the National Task Force on Information Technology and Software Development in 1998. Electronics and information technology were classified as the "infrastructure facility" under the Income Tax Act, showering on this sector several additional fiscal incentives. The income tax concessions were further broadened to include profits of overseas branches, data conversion activity, and work done by subcontractors. Software units were also exempted from service tax. The task force suggested setting up a state-sponsored IT Venture Capital Fund as well as offering concessions to Indian and foreign venture capital funds. The Companies Act was amended to allow for "sweat equity." The Finance Ministry allowed the Dollar Stock Option Scheme for employees of software companies floating American Depository Receipts and Global Depository Receipts. Procedures for mergers, acquisitions, buyouts, and overseas listing were also liberalized. Software companies were allowed access to the India Brand Equity Fund, operated by the Ministry of Commerce. A large-scale program for promotion of electronic governance and IT in rural areas was adopted to boost the demand for computer hardware and software.

In addition to supportive and preferential policies for the information technology sector adopted by the Indian state in the 1990s, several external as well as internal factors helped boost exports from India, making it a major player in customized software development. Such factors include the shortage of technical workers in the West, low labor costs in India, firm-level changes such as quality certification, transfer of knowledge and capability through linkages with U.S. and European firms, linkages with the Indian diaspora, and the emergence of opportunities such as Y2K and euro conversion. With all these developments, India was able to forge ahead in global technology markets despite the handicap of having a small domestic market and low penetration of technology at home. India's example also disproves conventional wisdom that countries can't succeed in export markets without possessing a large enough technology market at home. It may still be true with software products but certainly not so in information, software, and engineering *services* where India emerged a formidable player at the beginning of the twenty-first century.

8 Turning Geography into History

I think it's fair to say that companies come to India for the cost; they stay for the quality and they invest for the innovation.
—Dan Scheinman, Senior Vice President of Corporate Development, Cisco, 2005

An Indian accountant sitting in Pune is preparing tax returns of a consultant in New York. A customer executive of an American bank in New Delhi is helping customers in London place a request for a demand draft. A help-desk executive in Gurgaon is assisting a British customer change his travel plans on a European airline. A stock market researcher in Bangalore is doing equity research for a brokerage firm on the Wall Street. A fresh commerce graduate in Jaipur is processing the mortgage application of a nurse in Connecticut. A lawyer in Mysore is preparing a case brief for a Hollywood studio caught in a copyright row with an online store. A doctorate in biotechnology in New Delhi is scurrying through databases to prepare a patent profile for a new cancer drug developed by a Nordic drug company. Another group in the same company is developing an innovative investment product for a large bank in Hong Kong. A group of young Indian scientists in Chennai is working on a new drug delivery system for an American pharmaceutical firm. Mechanical and aviation engineers working together in Noida are designing doors of the next-generation wide-bodied aircraft and writing software for its flight control. Yet another firm in Bangalore is working on a video phone and a gaming console that would hit the market three years hence.

That description gives a taste of how Indian firms are participating in the outsourcing that has become a multibillion-dollar industry in the twenty-first century. The range of outsourcing services Indian companies offer is phenomenal—from taking customer calls and enlisting new customers for credit cards to developing prototypes of next-generation entertainment products, coding software for the next Boeing or Airbus and safety systems for the next Ferrari or Lexus. Strictly speaking, all of this is not software or information technology services outsourcing or exports as discussed in this book. This is outsourcing of various business processes of corporations and functions relating to technology development, research and development, testing, new product development, patent filing, and so on. The outsourcing industry is serving mainline business functions of Western corporations and helping them deliver services and products faster and ahead of competitors. In this sense, outsourcing of this kind is not exactly an extension of the software industry. However, since outsourcing is enabled by a combination of software, IT, and communication technologies, it has been dubbed IT-enabled services (ITES). A more appropriate description of this activity would be business process outsourcing (BPO) as specific business processes are outsourced.

The outsourcing industry has broadly developed in four streams—BPO or ITES, R&D, engineering services outsourcing (ESO), and knowledge process outsourcing (KPO). Most of these activities were seeded between 1995 and 2000, though the first venture to outsource business processes from India was set up as early as 1992. Since then the industry has grown phenomenally. The BPO segment was estimated to have clocked export revenues of over $16.5 billion during financial year 2011–2012. The software services and BPO sectors together had employed 2.8 million at the end of 2011–2012.[1]

Airlines, Banks Showed the Way

Swissair was the first foreign company to have set up an operation in India to outsource its backroom processes in October 1992, within a year of economic liberalization taking off. The Zurich-based airline, now defunct, floated Airline Financial Support Services (AFS) as a joint venture with TCS to handle its revenue accounting operations at SEEPZ. The unit employed about thirty workers and Swissair held the majority stake of 75.1 percent in it.

AFS soon grew to include sales accounting, processing of coupons for passengers, interline invoicing and accounting, and cargo and mail accounting. Connected with computers in Zurich via satellite link, AFS also handled functions related to maintenance of time schedules.[2] Other functions such as the frequent flyer program were added subsequently. AFS started as a Swissair subsidiary only to serve in-house service requirements of the airline. Such units in outsourcing parlance are referred to as captive units. AFS began offering services to other airlines and customers in the hospitality industry by the late 1990s, mainly to boost revenues. The unit handled finance functions including traffic and cargo revenue accounting, passenger interline billing, in addition to navigation and hardware support. Tyroclean Airlines, Sabena, Austrian STET, Lauda Air, Malmoe Aviation, Loyalty Gate, and Unit Pool were among its nonSwissair customers. After Swissair was liquidated in October 2001 in the wake of the financial crisis following 9/11, the fate of AFS hung in the balance for some time. TCS bought over the Swissair stake in May 2003, merging AFS with its other outsourcing operations. The unit then had four hundred workers on its rolls.

This is how a new industry—executing backroom functions or business processes at a remote location—was founded by a European airline in partnership with an Indian software firm with the twin objective of cutting costs and improving turnaround time.

Another European airline, British Airways (BA), established a unit in Bombay in 1996 to handle customer relations and revenue accounting functions of its global operations, as part of cost-cutting drive initiated the year before. The airline wished to shift part of its backroom processes—with a low skill requirement but high volume—to an inexpensive location. In 1995, a number of countries were screened as possible locations for setting up such a unit. India scored high on factors such as the existence of a reasonably good IT infrastructure, availability of young, English-speaking talent, government incentives to foreign investors, and low salaries and rents. The time difference between the UK and India would have helped to get the work done before BA offices in the UK opened in the morning.

The Mumbai unit was named World Network Services (WNS) and placed under the administrative control of Speedwing, a BA subsidiary. The presence in India of other multinational firms, particularly a European airline, doing similar work was a major factor. Recalled BA General Manager Roy Marshall, who was involved in planning the unit: "Airlines are bitter rivals in marketing and sales sectors but [the] rest of the divisions work closely with their counterparts in other airlines around the world. This gave the BA and WNS transition team a chance to see what Swissair and AFS were up to."[3]

According to Shaunne Shaw, head of accounting operations for BA, the decision to set up a unit in India was driven by the urge to "achieve results cheaper, better, faster." In addition to cost reductions of up to 60 percent, the airlines selected processes that could be done faster and better. Faster turnaround was achieved by round-the-clock operations. The availability of infrastructure and a young, educated workforce were cited as prime drivers for the selection of Mumbai by Speedwing officials in media interviews. The unit's revenue reached $8.05 million by 1999, and it opened another center in Pune.[4]

Like AFS, the operation of WNS too was modest initially, with just a dozen workers. The numbers were scaled up gradually. In 1999, WNS opened a second center in Pune and increased the number of processes handled to over a hundred. The operation became an additional revenue stream for British Airways and, WNS began offering accounting and other services to as many as fourteen other airlines. In 2002, the Mumbai center of WNS handled sixty projects for BA, while the Pune facility serviced as many as thirty-two other airlines.[5]

Over the years, the effort resulted in annual savings of up to 60 percent in the costs for certain processes. For every 1,000 jobs relocated to India, BA saved $23 million a year.[6] For every forty Indian workers deployed to WNS, savings for the airline worked out to £1 million. The savings were not solely due to the lower costs of Indian workers but also to the type of processes they handled, like refund and recovery. For instance, a scanned copy of each of the thirty-five million tickets the airline sold were sent to India, where workers reconciled the tickets with billing information sent by travel agents. A team of eighty people engaged in refund work were thus able to recover £6.6 million from travel agents in 2001.[7] BA's decision to move some of its functions to India attracted criticism at home and the company had to defend its decision to hire Indian workers. "The Indian workers are more hard-working than their British counterparts and excel at handling processes," Shaw told critics in 2003. "They start work later but carry on until 9 or 10 at night."[8]

The aviation crisis in wake of 9/11 forced BA to sell off its majority stake in WNS to private equity investor Warburg Pincus in April 2002. From subsidiary of an airline handling in-house jobs, WNS emerged as one of the largest BPO companies in India with a total strength of about 1,600 workers in Mumbai and Pune by the end of 2002, catering to outsourcing needs of corporations other than its parent. For some time, BA continued to be its largest client. But this soon changed as WNS began providing offshore services to other airlines as well as companies in other sectors—insurance, pharmaceuticals, and market research. The outsourced services included revenue accounting, customer relationship management, loyalty program support, account payables and receivables, and management data analysis and reporting.

Economic liberalization in the early 1990s triggered expansion in operations of foreign banks like Citibank and American Express in India. In June 1993, American Express launched its rupee-billed personal card as part of this expansion. As the volume of work in the card division grew in complexity and numbers in a few months, senior managers of the bank noticed that the cost per transaction in India was almost 40–50 percent lower than in the United States while execution efficiency was higher. They decided to watch the trend over a period of time and John McDonald, the bank's comptroller, wanted to leverage lower cost and better efficiency to other regions.[9]

Around this time, the bank was in the process of reorganizing its backroom functions at three operational centers. Phoenix, Arizona, was selected for the Americas, while a site at Burgess Hill near Brighton, UK, was chosen for Europe. The third center was to be located in Asia to serve Asia Pacific and Australia. McDonald set up a team—with some managers from India—to suggest a suitable location for the third center. After screening different Asian cities for factors like government policies, telecom infrastructure, and availability of workers, the choice fell on New Delhi. The three centers were developed to act as branches of one virtual finance center rather than three independent regional operations. The objective was to enable seamless movement of work and people among the three centers.

Raman Roy, a chartered accountant working with the bank in India, was given the task of setting up the new unit called Finance Center-East in New Delhi. The unit was registered as a 100 percent Export Oriented Unit (EOU) in December 1993. Despite hiccups like the lack of adequate bandwidth or a continuous power supply, the bank leadership was very happy. The reason was the quality of workers the bank could employ. For the cost of an associate in the United States, it could hire a qualified chartered accountant in India. Roy would recall later: "We brought down costs dramatically, as we brought down the turnaround time in the payment of invoices where there were incremental discounts that American Express could get (for prompt settlement). . . . I just took the incremental discounts . . . and compared that with the salary bill of the unit that I used to run for American Express. I told the company, 'You have got us for free, because the incremental discounts that we got alone were more than the salary bill in India.'"[10]

The operation expanded with the bank setting up a global service center to provide voice- and data-based processing support for its card, financial, and travel-related businesses in the United States and other countries. The subsidiary also started performing risk and credit analytics for several American Express credit card divisions worldwide. The success of the American Express operations caught the attention of other U.S. multinationals. One of them was General Electric, which was already working with several Indian software companies. GE hired Roy to set up a backroom operation for GE Capital in 1996. A new subsidiary called GE Capital International Services (GECIS) was launched in Gurgaon near New Delhi. The early success of the operation prompted faster scaleup. Within two years of the Gurgaon another was opened in Hyderabad, followed by one at Dallian in Roy, in the face of stiff resistance from GE managers, was also able to introduce voice-based services for the first time from Indian customer centers.[11] This marked the beginning of the much-talked-about call center business—which would soon emerge as the public face of outsourcing in the Western world.

GECIS grew to include five centers in India and one each in Mexico, China, and Hungary by 2005. Indian centers were handling 800 processes covering actuarial support, data modeling, risk management, loan processing, underwriting, and claims processing, and had resulted in cost savings estimated at $1 billion by 2002.[12] For GE Chairman Jack Welch, the results from Indian centers were simply sensational. "The global customer centers run from India have had better quality, lower costs, better collection rates and greater customer acceptance than our comparable operations in the United States and Europe," Welch later said.[13]

The work Raman Roy did for American Express and GE made him gauge the potential market for third-party service providers who could serve anyone who was interested and not just one parent company. He launched an independent outsourcing firm, Spectramind, in March 2000, to offer services to a number of clients. Other entrepreneurs had already entered this arena. Krishnan Ganesh, a hardware engineer who had worked with HCL in the 1980s, founded CustomerAsset in 2000. Sanjeev Agarwal, who had helped Motorola set up backroom operations in India for its Asia-wide financial systems, launched Daksh in 1999. Jaithirth Rao, who headed several business units of Citibank in the United States, Europe, and Asia, joined forces with Jeroen Tas, who was head of the bank's technology subsidiary, to float MphasiS in Santa Monica, California, in 1998.

The year 2002 saw a wave of mergers and acquisitions in this nascent industry. Wipro marked its entry into the BPO segment by acquiring Roy's Spectramind for $88 million in July 2002. ICICI Bank purchased CustomerAsset for over $19 million in May 2002 and renamed it ICICI OneSource. Around the same time, Infosys launched its BPO operations under a separate company called Progeon. In April 2004, IBM bought Daksh in a deal worth $180 million. Hewlett Packard acquired Digital Globalsoft and renamed it Global Delivery Indian Center.

In 2004, GE decided to sell 60 percent of its outsourcing business unit for $500 million to two U.S. investment companies—General Atlantic Partners and Oak Hill Capital Partners. This transformed GECIS from an in-house outsourcing unit of GE to a third-party service provider that could serve other global companies. Up to this point, 95 percent of the backroom business in the company came from the parent. The company was then renamed Genpact. In December 2013, it had over 63,000 employees across a network of delivery centers spread across twenty-five countries globally (including India, China, Mexico, and the United States) and reported annual revenues of $2.1 billion.[14]

The BPO industry, which began in a small way with in-house or captive units of multinational banks and airlines in the mid-1990s, had matured into a multibillion-dollar industry acquiring its own character by 2006. In the first stage of this transformation, dedicated units like those of British Airways and WNS opened their doors to customers other than their respective parent companies. The second phase saw mushrooming of start-ups founded by entrepreneurs who had worked with American firms like American Express, Citibank, and GE. In the next phase, established Indian IT services companies entered the BPO segment—Wipro with Spectramind, Satyam with Nipuna, Infosys with Progeon. In 2008, TCS bought over Citibank's backroom operation called Citigroup Global Services for over $0.5 billion. Around the same time, another set of players made their entry—large international BPO firms like Convergys and Sykes, setting up fully owned subsidiaries in India to take advantage of low-cost Indian labor. Convergys set up India operations in 2001 and soon had call centers in Bangalore, Gurgaon, Mumbai, Pune, and Thane. Within five years, it had a workforce of 10,000 in India compared to 65,000 globally. Large consulting and service companies such as Accenture and IBM too joined in the BPO bandwagon either though their own subsidiaries or by acquiring Indian companies. In June 2006, Texas-based outsourcing giant EDS acquired a controlling stake in MphasiS for $380 million. Soon big players like EDS commanded the largest number of workers in the Indian outsourcing market.

In a span of just fifteen years, the BPO industry matured from captive units to large broad-based service companies with revenue growing from just a few million dollars in 1995 to $16 billion in 2012. Yet the Indian BPO market would be just a fraction of the global market, which was estimated to be worth $300 billion in 2008.

The R&D Gold Rush

The wave of outsourcing that started around 1996 and turned into a tsunami in 2000 was not limited to the IT industry. It embraced a variety of segments—healthcare, banking, financial services, aviation, pharmaceuticals, automobiles, manufacturing, and so on. Also, the type of services being outsourced was wide ranging—from medical transcription to product development and testing. In the late 1990s, research and development (R&D) emerged as an important segment of the outsourcing industry.

Though R&D outsourcing gained momentum only in the late 1990s, pioneers had moved to India in the 1970s. The Hoechst Center for Basic Research, founded in 1972, was the first instance of a multinational setting up an R&D unit in India for its global operations. Another European pharmaceutical giant, Astra AB, set up Astra Research Centre India (ARCI) in 1985 in the vicinity of the Indian Institute of Science in Bangalore. Although it was fully funded by the Scandinavian firm, the unit had to function as a nonprofit society as per prevailing government norms. It was only in the post-liberalization period in the 1990s that the center could set up a wholly owned subsidiary—Astra Biochemicals Private Limited—to commercialize technologies it developed. Eventually it became a part of AstraZeneca India Private Limited following the global merger of Astra AB and Zeneca PLC in June 1999.

The primary aim behind this unique R&D venture, according to the company, was to recruit high-caliber Indian scientific personnel for research in view of the shortage of R&D personnel in Sweden. In addition, the company was also able to exploit lower costs of R&D in India.[15] It was these two factors—availability of high-class talent and lower costs—that were tapped by Fortune 500 companies in the late 1990s and the post-2000 period, creating a virtual R&D boom in India. A number of multinational companies sent their officials to ARCI to study its model for outsourced R&D and networking with Indian institutions and companies. The model demonstrated that a corporate R&D culture could be introduced and nurtured in a developing country like India with a pool of qualified workers trained in scientific research.[16]

The trend of multinational firms offshoring R&D to India—even those not having any manufacturing or marketing presence in the country—got more pronounced in the 1990s. From 1991 onward a number of such units were opened across several sectors—General Motors, Bell Labs, DuPont, Unilever, Volvo, Fujitsu, Philips International, Merck, AVL, Gulf Oil, LG, Ford Motors, Delphi, and so on. Most were independent research subsidiaries linked to the parent's R&D set-up. Daimler-Benz Research Center India, established in 1996, is a typical example. It acted as "a link between the country's famed universities, software industry and research establishments" and benefited from the cost advantages of performing R&D in India while catering to the needs of Daimler-Benz's business units in Asia.[17] Some of these firms setting up full-fledged R&D centers have had opportunities to experience the potential of India's scientific competence through their engagements with national laboratories. DuPont, for example, had a contract research deal with the Pune-based National Chemical Laboratory (NCL) in early 1990.

A number of global IT and software firms also opened their research and product development centers post-1991 making sizeable investments. IBM Research Laboratory—founded in July 1997—in the campus of IIT Delhi was one such. IBM decided to open a research center in India at a time when it was losing researchers in America to the dot-com boom. In 1997, IBM committed investment of $25 million over the next five years to develop the laboratory and another $10 million in grants and equipment to support independent university research projects.[18] The lab worked with other R&D centers and business units of IBM globally to provide research services and products in e-commerce, supply chain management, speech recognition, wired and wireless networking software, media mining, and systems management.

General Electric (GE) is another American giant to have set up a large research center in India. Its engagement with India began in September 1989 when Chairman and CEO Jack Welch visited India at the insistence of Senior Vice President Paolo Fresco, in charge of GE's international operations. The visit was a turning point for GE. "After that trip, I became the champion for India," Welch recalled.[19] He wanted to bet on India, because "it had a strong legal system, a potential market and an enormous number of people with great technical skills." In his opinion, India was highly developed from an intellectual standpoint, but an underdeveloped country from an infrastructure perspective.

In 1992, Welch identified India, along with Mexico and China, as a priority country for GE. He was particularly struck with the "terrific scientific, engineering and administrative talent" the country possessed. It was this love for India's skilled and talented workforce that led to GE Capital getting into business process outsourcing, as already discussed, and into doing research out of India toward the end of the 1990s.

In June 1999, GE set up a research unit for its plastics business at the International Technology Park in Bangalore. When Welch visited the center and saw the work of Indian engineers and scientists, he declared that the Indian center should cater to all business units as well as GE Research. In September 2000, the center moved to its own fifty-acre facility named John F. Welch Technology Centre (JFWTC) at Whitefield near Bangalore. It was GE's first and largest integrated, multidisciplinary R&D center outside the United States. It started with 275 scientists and engineers, which grew to

4,000 by 2012. About 60 percent of them were engineering or science post-graduates and doctorates. In comparison, the Shanghai research center of GE had 1,300 researchers and Munich about 150. GE invested $80 million in 1999 in the Bangalore center.

The R&D center has teams developing technologies for different business units—infrastructure (rail, energy, and aircraft), industrial business (plastics and silicon), consumer and industrial appliances, medical equipment, and corporate R&D, which works on innovative and futuristic technologies. Of all personnel, about five hundred scientists work in corporate R&D. JFWTC also houses an Engineering Analysis Center of Excellence, which provides engineering analysis and develops analytical tools for the design of new commercial aircraft engines. The infrastructure group is working on aircraft engines that will be quieter and more energy efficient. JFWTC developed about 30 percent of the design as well as 80 percent of the engineering analysis of the nX engine that would power the Boeing 787. Similarly, specially designed locomotives, which GE delivered to China for its Tibet rail project, had their crucial variable injection technology developed in Bangalore. Variable injection of air and fuel, depending on the altitudes, prevents turbochargers in locomotives from getting stalled at high altitude.

Starting with small contract research assignments given to government research laboratories in the early 1990s, multinationals had set up large captive R&D units in India by the turn of the decade. Between 1999 and 2004, as many as seventy-seven multinational companies had set up their R&D units as direct subsidiaries involving an investment of $1 billion, while several others had formed R&D alliances with local firms or research labs, as noted in a study by Evalueserve.[20] Another study sponsored by the Technology Information, Forecasting and Assessment Council (TIFAC) of the Ministry of Science and Technology put the number of multinational corporations (MNCs) having R&D units in India at over 135, involving an investment of $1.13 billion during 1998–2003. These companies employed close to 23,000 scientists and engineers and accounted for R&D exports worth $2.3 billion a year, the study noted.[21] The number of foreign R&D units operational in India rose to 700 by 2010.[22]

The reasons for this boom are not hard to find: availability of a large pool of professional workers, cost savings, access to a well-developed R&D infrastructure, faster development of products and processes, reduced "time-to-market" and the lure of a potentially large local market. With over 250 universities and 10,000 higher education institutions in 2004, India churned out 5,000 PhDs, 200,000 engineering graduates, and 300,000 technically trained graduates.[23] Competitive pressure in global markets has led technology companies to look for innovative ways to do R&D in global markets. A 2012 survey of foreign R&D units in India revealed that development of new technologies for global and regional markets is more important for these centers than modifying or adapting technologies for local market needs or manufacturing requirements.[24] The study also confirmed that the availability of quality scientists and engineers at considerably reduced compensation levels compared to their home countries is a key determinant of the foreign R&D units' location in India.

The case of the networking firm Cisco proves the point. Cisco set up its business operations in India in 1995. Within three years it established R&D facilities in Bangalore, as an extension of its global R&D efforts based in San Jose, California, and not as a separate entity. The Indian center since then has been involved in core product R&D and engineering across Cisco's entire product family. It is the company's largest development center outside the United States. In October 2005, the company laid the foundation for a $50-million campus to house its R&D center and customer support operations in Bangalore with a capacity to house 3,000 people. It also announced an investment of $750 million over the next three years for its R&D activities in India—at that time the largest commitment of that kind ever made by any multinational firm in India. The funds were meant for training, development, and staffing as well as engagement with partner Indian companies.

Dan Scheinman, senior vice president of corporate development, succinctly described Cisco's journey in India: "I think it's fair to say that companies come to India for the cost; they stay for the quality and they invest for the innovation. That's certainly true for Cisco."[25]

Data compiled by the Indian Institute of Management, Ahmedabad, shows that the investments U.S. giants are making in R&D in India have begun to pay off when measured in terms of the intellectual property generated.[26] By 2012, the John F. Welch Research Center of GE in Bangalore had been granted 400 international patents since its inception. IBM had been granted 250 U.S. patents between 2006 and 2010, while Texas Instruments Bangalore got 211 patents from the U.S. Patent Office. In all, nearly 2,000 U.S. patents had been granted to fifty-nine foreign R&D units during 2006–2010. The share of patents from India-based research and development units in the portfolio of American companies is also rising. For some like Symantec, U.S. patents obtained by Indian R&D units made up as much as 22 percent of their patent portfolio. A number of foreign R&D units are also filing with the Indian patent office. This further points to the capability of Indian scientists and engineers to generate intellectual capital, provided they get the right kind of environment and challenging opportunities.

Spurt in Engineering and Design Services

The origin of Indian companies offering engineering design-related services to multinationals can be traced back to early data conversion work done by Indian companies in the 1980s. It involved scanning engineering drawings to convert them into digital files as well as preliminary computer-aided design (CAD) work. This kind of work was shipped to India primarily because it was high volume and could be done at lower costs. The situation changed after 1991. A number of American and European engineering companies began looking at the Indian market to expand their businesses. In the process, some of them discovered the virtues of using the low-cost technical workforce available in India for their processes globally. This activity was not linked directly to their business prospects in India. One such company was Bechtel Corporation, which came to India in 1992 as an equipment supplier to the Dabhol Power Project (India's first private-sector power project with Enron as foreign partner, which subsequently failed).

Within a couple of years' exposure, Bechtel discovered India's engineering and design talent and decided to set up a multidisciplinary unit to support its projects globally. Bechtel India began operating from a New Delhi hotel room in April 1994 with just a handful of personnel. By the end of 1996, it had 270 employees working on several projects such as the Millennium power project in Massachusetts, Rocksavage power plant in the UK, the Comisión Federal de Eletricidad's Samalayuca II power plant in Mexico, and expansion of Dubai International Airport.[27] By 2005, Indian engineers had worked on engineering designs of nearly two dozen power plants in the UK, Mexico, Turkey, Australia, and the United States. The total number of engineers working had risen to six hundred by 2006. Engineers in Gurgaon used three-dimensional computer modeling, collaborative software, and a high-speed communication network to work with Bechtel's engineering and design teams spread all over the world.

Bechtel's engineering design work in India was followed by similar activity by other multinational engineering and automotive firms such as Caterpillar, Flour Daniel, General Motors, Ford, Daimler Chrysler, Emerson, and many others. Cummins Research and Technology India Limited was started in 2003 in Pune to provide mechanical engineering design and analysis for Cummins technical centers. This way engineering services outsourcing (ESO) started as captive units of parent companies.

In the second phase of ESO, beginning around 2000, large domestic software service firms entered the arena, looking to leverage their strength in software development as well as management of outsourcing projects. The rapid expansion of Wipro's Product Engineering Solutions (PES) group is an example. In 2011, the group had close to 18,000 engineers working in different areas such as telecommunications, aerospace, automobiles, medical devices, industrial automation, and semiconductor design. About 13.8 percent of Wipro's revenues came from PES during 2010–2011. Market research firm Zinnov Management Consultancy named Wipro the world's topmost third-party R&D service provider in semiconductors, peripherals and storage, cloud computing, telecom, and communication stack and automotive segments.[28] There were thirty offshore development centers operational for specific clients, running over 550 projects. Most of these projects related to devices such as smartphones, tablets, television and cable set-top boxes, home entertainment devices, and consumer durables. For instance, company engineers in 2012 were designing the spray arm of the world's smallest dishwasher for emerging markets. The brief was to ensure effective performance with low usage of water and low noise levels.

HCL Technologies, which entered the engineering services arena in 2000, has emerged as a leading player having signed up more than two hundred customers, including fifty Fortune 500 companies, in diverse sectors—telecom and networking, medical devices, consumer electronics, semiconductors, manufacturing, aerospace and automobiles. It employs nearly 17,500 engineers for ESO work in Bangalore, Chennai, Noida, Pune, Rochester, Redmond, and Welwyn Garden, UK. Nearly 20 percent of its $3.9 billion revenue in 2011 came from engineering and R&D services.[29] Its customers include component vendors, original equipment manufacturers, original design manufacturers, and independent software vendors in North America, Europe, and Japan. For instance, it works for over two dozen aerospace clients, including Boeing and Airbus. The company has worked on subsystems, components, software, and avionics of twenty-five fixed and rotor wing aircraft. Similarly, in the automobile sector, all leading manufacturers like Ford, BMW, and Ferrari are its clients. The company claims that the electronic products it develops have been installed in every major European brand of cars and commercial vehicles.

Design and development of medical devices is another niche area of HCL. It is registered as a medical devices design house with the U.S. Federal Drug Agency and is working on several Class I, II, and III medical devices and equipment for American and European device makers. Its services cover concept, design, manufacturing, certification, and support; and result in up to 60 percent cost reduction and 70 percent reduction in time-to-market. The company has invested in a $5-million-dollar product testing and certification facility. Several medical devices that HCL developed have been commercialized. Some of them are in the pipeline, like an implantable drug delivery device, which could release a drug as and when required via remote control. Since such a device would remain inside a patient's body for a long time, it would have extremely low power consumption. A battery that would run for thirty years is being developed for this device.

In addition to IT companies, a host of non-IT firms have been active in engineering and R&D services. These include both Indian and foreign companies such as Tata Technologies, TVS Electronics, Infotech Enterprises, Neilsoft, Sierra Atlantic, Geometric, QuEST, and Plexion. The Pune-based Tata Technologies, with a team of about 1,500 engineers, counts GM, Ford, Daimler Chrysler, Toyota, Volkswagen, and Honda among its major clients. U.S. firms focused on engineering services and product developments for home markets in America too have opened captive units in India. The Michigan-based Altair Engineering is one such. It started its India office in 2003 to provide support services to its U.S. operation. By 2007, it had 300 staff members in Bangalore working for its core areas—product design, engineering software, and grid computing.

The Indian ESO industry had four major segments in 2012—captive units of multinational companies, Indian IT majors with large ESO units, niche Indian and foreign engineering players, and dedicated units of American ESO firms.

The size of the global R&D industry was estimated at around 1.1 trillion in 2012. Of this, about $100 billion was being offshored mostly to Canada, China, Mexico, and countries in Eastern Europe. India, with ESO worth between $13 billion, accounted for 13 percent of this offshored market, a market research report projected in 2012.[30] This figure could jump to $45–$50 billion by 2020 if the country could build up capacities, capabilities, infrastructure, and a reputation for engineering services. The nature of work being done by Indian ESO units is gradually progressing from low-end and relatively generic engineering design processes to higher-complexity projects. For instance, the rising demand for automotive products in emerging markets like India and China is pushing the transition of engineering tasks to these very markets.[31] While capitalizing on low labor costs, new models and variants of cars are being customized and developed locally to meet specific local needs.

India has the largest engineering talent pool among the low-cost countries competing for the emerging ESO pie, but the quality and skills of this pool need to be improved a great deal. Also, the manufacturing infrastructure—a prerequisite for engineering services—needs to be built up to match the requirements of ESO.

The Knowledge Business

International consulting firms such as McKinsey and Company and Price-waterhouseCoopers (PwC) began engaging with Indian companies in the post-liberalization era. These firms were also the early ones to see the potential benefits of doing some of their global consulting operations out of India. The availability of highly qualified workers, consultants, and managers was the prime driver behind this. PwC started outsourcing from India in 1995 through one of its operating entities—Lovelock and Lewes Services Private Limited based in Bangalore. Its first client was a multinational bank that wanted to outsource the entire back-end processing of its credit card operations. Over the next few years, PwC had outsourcing centers in over a dozen cities in India, servicing clients like HSBC, Standard Chartered, and ABN Amro. In 2003, this operation was sold off to iSmart BPO.

McKinsey also started its outsourcing work from India in 1995. One of the studies the firm did in this period examined the digital economy's impact on services. It concluded that the rapid fall in telecom rates, coupled with the spread of the Internet, would lead to the creation of "remote services" making it possible for providers in locations like India and China to work for customers in the United States. McKinsey decided to test this out for itself and set up a Knowledge Center in New Delhi as a back-end service to its consultants worldwide. The Knowledge Center soon became a model outsourcing operation that McKinsey could showcase to clients. "We were the first to legitimize the early thinking," Anil Kumar, who led the study, commented in 2003.[32]

The center hired MBAs and engineers to offer business and market research services to McKinsey's consultants worldwide. Since then, the Knowledge Center has emerged as "the largest hub of knowledge management professionals" for McKinsey globally. Marc Vollenweider, a Swiss national who had joined McKinsey in 1989 was sent on a three-year assignment to oversee the Knowledge Center in New Delhi in 1999. A year into his new assignment in India, he began toying with the idea of quitting McKinsey and offering research services as a third-party provider since McKinsey operated the New Delhi unit as captive center and could not serve third parties.[33]

Similar thoughts were crossing the mind of Alok Aggarwal, founding director of the IBM Research Laboratory. The lab, by now, had begun filing patents for invention disclosures. But Aggarwal discovered that it was difficult to find patent attorneys in India who could write applications for filing with the U.S. Patent Office. Sending these invention disclosures to be written up by U.S. lawyers meant an expenditure of $10,000 per application in 1998. This was almost equivalent to what someone holding a good master's degree in computer science earned in a whole year at the research lab. Recalls Aggarwal: "Since we were located inside IIT Delhi, I started thinking that someone should take 50–100 IITians and train them to become patent application drafters and IP specialists. By January 2000, this idea had completely germinated and I was planning to quit IBM in July 2000 and start a small company that would only provide research and analytics related to intellectual property."[34]

A chance meeting between Aggarwal and Vollenweider at a birthday party gave them an opportunity to exchange notes. Both of them found that they were talking about two sides of the same coin—providing high-end research and analytics services. That's how the idea to float a company jointly was born. Vollenweider named the venture Evalueserve—short for evaluation services because this is what the two wanted to do: collect internal or external data; cleanse it; analyze and synthesize the data, and produce an appropriate report. The company coined the term "knowledge process outsourcing" (KPO) in an effort to differentiate its services from those offered by BPO firms.[35] KPO has since come to refer to those outsourcing activities that require significant domain expertise like market research, business research, investment research, and data mining.

Since its inception in December 2000, Evalueserve has grown to become the largest third-party KPO provider in the world with 2,600 employees at Gurgaon (India), Shanghai (China), Santiago-Valparaiso (Chile), and Cluj-Napoca (Romania). In addition, it has marketing, sales, and business development offices all over the world. The company has over a thousand clients in the United States, Latin America, China, and Japan. "We are working in areas where nobody is willing to work in the West. So it has as much to do with cost as with talent availability," a senior company official pointed out.[36]

Following in the footsteps of PwC and McKinsey, a host of consulting, management, market research, and audit firms set up captive units in India to handle their research and analysis work for global operations. They include Bain and Company, Monitor Group, Everest Group, Ernst and Young, Anderson Consulting, Boston Consulting Group, Avalon Consulting, and Deloitte Consulting. Frost and Sullivan is a Silicon Valley–based market research and consultancy firm that started with outsourcing back-room processing work to India in 1999, and eventually set up an analyst team at its Global Innovation Center in Chennai in 2000. A. T. Kearney also has a Global Research Center in India to undertake activities such as research, database search, report preparation, and editing and formatting for client reports and presentations.

In 2007, about 120 captive units of large multinational companies were providing these services to their offices in North America and Europe. The majority of the mid-sized and large IT and BPO companies in India have a KPO division, and there are at least 262 "niche" companies in India that are providing third-party KPO services.[37] Some such units soon transformed themselves into third-party service providers.

The revenue earned by the KPO industry globally was $1.2 billion in 2003–2004 and rose to $4.4 billion in 2006–0007, registering an annual growth rate of 54 percent, according to research by Evalueserve. The number of people employed in this sector totaled 106,000 in 2006–2007. A sizeable part of the growth is coming from India. KPO revenues in India grew from $260 million in 2000–2001 to $3.05 billion in 2006–2007.[38] A subsequent study found that many captive units had begun to stagnate in size after an initial phase of intense growth due to factors like high attrition rates resulting from "uninteresting work" and limited career opportunities and hidden costs (management time and travel).

A variety of services can be handled by knowledge outsourcing units.[39] GE became the first foreign company in 2001 to offshore its in-house legal work to India. The GE Plastics' Gurgaon unit employed lawyers to write and review contracts with vendors. In the very first year of operation, the unit saved $500,000. This encouraged the company to float a subsidiary comprising thirty lawyers, who supported all critical legal services of GE's units worldwide, resulting in annual savings worth $2 million. Corporate legal departments of Oracle, Sun Microsystems, Microsoft, Cisco, and DuPont followed GE's example and began doing legal work in India either through captive units or third-party vendors.

Education services such as curriculum design, academic pedagogy, and content development as well as actual delivery of lessons to students form another area of the KPO industry. Firms like Career Launcher, Educomp Datamatics, and tutorvista.com are offering these services from India. They use proprietary software for two-way voice and chat interaction between the tutor and the student. While it is a one-on-one session for the student, the tutor usually attends to three students simultaneously on different links. Indian tutors are trained in U.S. accents, teaching methods, and other skills. The teaching subjects usually are in science and mathematics.

Writing, content development, and design layouts for the publishing industry are also being handled offshore in India. PureTech, established in Pondicherry in 1988, is believed to have pioneered this segment. Now large third-party players like TechBooks, OfficeTiger, Datamatics Technologies, and Integra Software dominate this space. TechBooks has over 2,300 employees.

The global executive search company Heidrick & Struggles runs a sixty-strong team in New Delhi that services its offices in the Americas, Europe, and Asia. The WNS market research team includes analysts with master's degrees in statistics, mathematics, and computer science and most of them have worked previously with market research agencies in India. In 2005, the firm won a three-year research contract from the media conglomerate WPP for market research. This involved questionnaire design, survey programming, conducting the survey, data cleansing, data processing and analysis, and preparation of the final presentation. The essence of market research was shifting from information capture to its transformation into knowledge, notes a report on the KPO industry by PwC.[40]

Large corporations handle a lot of data. Reviewing and analyzing large volumes of data is important for drawing future strategies and operations and the knowledge thus generated is considered a source of competitive advantage. But the process of reviewing and analyzing data is both time- and labor-intensive. Therefore, companies began outsourcing this work. For instance, the Gurgaon-based marketRx specializes in providing sales and marketing analytic services to the pharmaceutical industry. Cognizant Technology Solutions acquired marketRx for $135 million in 2007. The analytics Center of Excellence of GE has a team of 700 statisticians, MBAs, and PhDs. Another U.S. firm, Symphony, set up units in Bangalore, Mumbai, and Pune with a total of 1,000 employees. It offers data analytics for the telecommunications, manufacturing, and retailing sectors.

All major international accounting firms have established captive units in India for the preparation of tax returns of their global clients. The India office of Ernst & Young provides tax return preparation support to global offices, as does PwC. The cost savings are estimated to be up to 60 percent, mainly due to lower labor and infrastructure costs. It is due to these very advantages that a large number of foreign investment banks such as Goldman Sachs, JP Morgan, and Lehman Brothers have set up captive operations for financial research. At its Bangalore unit, Goldman Sachs handles tasks such as asset management, equity and treasury operations, investment banking, and corporate services. Morgan Stanley has a research division for equity and fixed-income research. JP Morgan, which started outsourcing with a call center in Mumbai, now does financial research as well. The Chennai-based OfficeTiger, which started by offering secretarial services to Wall Street firms merged with a leading third-party provider of financial research services before it was acquired by R. R. Donnelley & Sons for $250 million. European banks Credit Suisse and Deutsche Bank have also set up captive units for equity research and related services.

The Indian Advantage

Low workforce hiring costs and cheap infrastructure have been the most notable advantages India has offered in the outsourcing business. A typical customer relations call center in India charges its U.S. client between $1.50 and $2 to process a medium-to-complex query through e-mail and about $3 for troubleshooting over the phone. The task would cost about $3 for e-mail support and $9 for phone support in the United States. In India, the average annual labor "cost to company" per person is $7,500, against $19,000 in the United States, $22,000 in the UK, and $17,000 in Australia.[41]

According to analysis done by trade groups, the typical cost savings for backroom operations like transaction processing is between 25 and 40 percent; for call center services it is between 30 and 40 percent; and for finance and insurance-related work it is between 40 and 60 percent. The total loaded cost of one full-time employee engaged in ITES comes to $58,598 per annum, compared to $13,121 in India. This is 78 percent gross savings on the U.S. cost base. The loaded cost includes salary, telecom and IT infrastructure, office facilities, and other administrative costs.[42]

The cost difference is still higher in the case of KPO services such as market research, patent landscaping, and data mining. The rates in India vary from $25–$30 an hour compared to $200–$300 per hour in the United States and Europe.[43] Lawyers in India charge $30 to $90 per hour, compared to $200 to $700 an hour in the United States.[44] In the R&D sector a qualified scientist could be hired in India for $10,000 a year compared to $100,000 a year in the United States. The per hour rate for R&D personnel in Bangalore is estimated at $80, which is much lower than that in the United States and Europe.[45] In engineering services, India has one of the lowest labor costs compared to other competing destinations such as China, Malaysia, and Israel.[46]

One of the key reasons for India's low salaries are its favorable supply conditions. The country has a large pool of fresh graduates, with about one million of them entering the job market every year. In addition, a large number of professionals such as managers, chartered accountants, lawyers, researchers, architects, and engineers also become available every year. All of them speak and understand English. All of these supply factors help link the talent advantage to the cost advantage. However, as the outsourcing business has been growing, companies are realizing that they are not getting graduates and professionals with all of the right skills. They need to be retrained before they can handle the work of these companies. For instance, Indian accounting or commerce graduates have to be trained in American accounting systems and practices and Indian law graduates in American copyright laws before they are hired to serve U.S. clients.

India's major advantage is numbers, compared to other countries like the Philippines, Egypt, or members of the Commonwealth of Independent States (CIS). One of the reasons BA chose India in the early 1990s was that scaling up its operation would be easier. The logic still holds. Clearly, India has a demographic advantage. With about 60 percent of its population between the ages of fifteen and fifty-nine, and more than half below the age of twenty-five, India continues to have a large number of people in the productive age group in contrast to countries such as the United States, Europe, Japan, and China.

Though it emerged as a cost-saving tool, outsourcing has become an essential management process in the globalized economy. Corporations, under competitive pressures in a borderless economy, have been forced to resort to outsourcing to improve their performance. With the emergence of digital technology, companies need to reduce their time to market. For example, Microsoft was able to launch its gaming console, Xbox, ahead of a similar product from rival Sony because it had been outsourcing its quality testing to a technology firm in India.[47] There are several such examples. Outsourcing is helping companies to cut their R&D and new-product-development cycles drastically in sectors ranging from drugs to airplanes. Similarly, service companies are looking at improving their customer services and work efficiency. By outsourcing a number of processes, companies are able to focus on their core areas such as marketing, growth, and innovation. Reduced international trade barriers and falling costs of communication are fueling this trend.

Multinationals setting up R&D units or outsourcing product development and engineering services to Indian companies are also beginning to look at the potential of the vast Indian markets. Indian scientists and engineers engaged in local development units are developing products meant specifically for Indian markets. Mobile phones by Nokia, Motorola, and Qualcomm are examples of this. Indian-language handwriting recognition and other products under development at IBM and HP research centers also fall in this category. Some of these new products could find applications in other emerging markets—Russia, China, Mexico, and Brazil—that are being targeted by all multinationals.

How long can India ride the cost and talent advantage? Aren't other countries catching up? These questions are often posed in any discussion on the Indian outsourcing industry. By all indications, the cost advantage is eroding slowly as the industry grows. The difference has narrowed down in the upper end of the chain such as product development and semiconductor designing. In some sectors, companies are facing a talent shortage, though a large number of fresh graduates becomes available every year. This shortage is leading to higher attrition rates and escalating salaries. The only way out would be to improve the quality of education at all levels so that universities and colleges could produce employable graduates and postgraduates.

Though English is the medium of instruction, an average graduate has very poor communication skills in English. Such candidates need to be trained when they are hired for a call center job. In countries like the Philippines training costs are low because people have a neutral accent in English and are far more "Americanized," the country being a former U.S. colony. Similarly, the Indian college curriculum is not geared for the global economy. For instance, a commerce graduate is not taught about medical and life insurance or about the accounting and tax system in the United States—areas that he or she would end up dealing with in an outsourcing job. The education system needs to be transformed, teachers have to be trained in new skills, and teaching facilities need to be upgraded. Some companies and industry associations have taken the lead with academic alliances and programs for soft skill development. Without these measures sooner or later competing countries will catch up. Media reports in 2011 suggested that the Philippines has already surpassed India in terms of the number of call center agents deployed.

Another question often asked is: How is the outsourcing industry helping India? The obvious answer: by creating direct and indirect employment opportunities. Graduates who would find it difficult to get a white-collar job a decade ago have become employable. The IT and ITES industries have become the darlings of the Indian middle class and are raising expectations among the low-income and rural populations as well. Critics, however, argue that a vast section of the Indian populace steeped in poverty and illiteracy is still untouched by the IT industry. In fact, growing income and prosperity among one section of the population is increasing the wide socioeconomic gulf that exists between the have and have-nots. Farming communities have been directly hit as agricultural lands are diverted for the creation or expansion of software parks and enclaves for BPO companies in places like Bangalore, Hyderabad, and Gurgoan.

A significant outcome of the outsourcing industry has been the growth of the domestic service sector. More and more Indian companies engaged in the service industries are setting up call centers for their customers and outsourcing their work to other Indian vendors. The higher end of the outsourcing pyramid, too, is having a beneficial impact on the technology and innovation ecosystem in the country. The availability of high-skilled jobs in R&D, product development, chip designing, and consulting is attracting experienced nonresident Indians back to India. In some of the technology firms in Bangalore, Indian expatriates returning home constitute 10–25 percent of the workforce. Multinational captive units, in any case, send back their India-origin employees to head their Indian units or hold senior positions here.

The presence of so many multinationals is also boosting entrepreneurship. A number of managers and engineers have come to India from firms like GE, American Express, Citibank, Texas Instruments, McKinsey, and IBM—all of whom pioneered outsourcing in India in 1990s—and started successful ventures. The experience they gained in technology, management, and processes while working with these corporations helped them discover new niches in the market and build profitable businesses. All of this has led to the creation of a favorable ecosystem in the area of intellectual property, innovation, and technology. India's journey to the world of high technology has begun.

9 Conclusion: The Making of a Digital Nation

From a stage when scientists and policymakers in India thought the country needed just two computers to its positioning as a leading global technology outsourcing hub, India has traversed a great distance in a short span of time. In 1977 India had hardly one thousand computers of different sizes. In early 2014, the number of computers was estimated to be 100 million. The number of telephone lines in the country in 1982 was 2.30 million—all landlines. The waiting period to acquire a phone connection was forty-seven months. In early 2014, India had close to 900 million mobile phones, with 110 million connected to the Internet. And there is no waiting list. Millions of these mobile phones have put more computing power in the hands of ordinary Indians than the most powerful of the systems that a handful of labs and companies possessed in the 1960s and 1970s. This book has examined the factors that have caused this transformation over the past four decades.

The history of computing technology in India is not very long. Under the colonial rule spanning almost two centuries, India was economically exploited and it missed the industrial revolutions, though it contributed to the success of the British Industrial Revolution in several ways. An era of modernization and infrastructure building with the help of modern science and technology was heralded by India's first Prime Minister Jawaharlal Nehru only after the country gained independence from the British on August 15, 1947. Nehru was a man of science and firmly believed that science and technology could be used to overcome shortages of natural resources and skilled workers, and help uplift the masses from their poverty and deprivation. Such an approach was in contrast to the village-centric development model proposed by Mahatma Gandhi, the Father of the Nation. Surrounded by a group of like-minded scientists and engineers— most of whom were Western-educated and well networked with Western scientific elites—Nehru patronized science and technology development.

This explains the early investments India made in scientific research, particularly nuclear energy, space, aeronautics, and defense technologies as well as modern engineering education. Development and application of computer technology was an integral part of this effort.

The use of computers in India first started in scientific institutions like ISI, TIFR, and the IITs and universities as an aid to help solve scientific and statistical problems. Some of these "scientific problems" were strategic in nature, such as the development of nuclear reactors and rockets. Around the same time, commercial applications of data processing and computers in large private firms helped them automate tasks such as accounting, inventory management, process control, and so on. Large state utilities like the Indian Railways, commercial banks, insurance companies, and airlines used imported or refurbished data processing equipment in the 1960s. Academic institutions, supported either by funding from UN agencies or those from the United States, acquired new and near-contemporary computers that were used for both academic and commercial applications on a time-sharing basis.

Though the national planning process initiated after India won independence was influenced by the socialist ideology, India did not opt for a fully state-controlled Soviet-styled model of economic development. Instead it chose a mixed economy, in which certain sectors of industrial manufacturing were controlled by state or public enterprises while private companies could operate in the rest. Foreign capital and foreign technology was allowed in many sectors through joint ventures with public and private enterprises or foreign-controlled subsidiaries. The long-term goal, however, was to attain self-sufficiency and "import substitution." In the emerging area of electronics and computers too, the same approach was followed. Foreign companies like IBM and ICL were permitted to operate in the country, and at the same time, the government funded development of computer systems and later manufacturing units to make these systems.

The state's role in seeding, nurturing, and developing first the electronics and computer hardware industry, and then the IT industry at different points in time was pivotal. A large industrial infrastructure for electronics manufacturing was created in the public sector. The R&D activity received adequate support from the government. All this spurred development of skills and capabilities in computer software, hardware, and design in laboratories, academic institutions, and public-sector undertakings supported or funded by the state. A large number of such institutions received R&D grants for hardware- and software-related projects. The skills thus developed in the state sector spilled over to the private sector companies when they were permitted to enter computer manufacturing activity in the late 1970s. The transfer of skills happened through consultancy, training, internship, and direct hiring of personnel by private firms.

Political Economy Shaped Computer Policies

The government recognized the electronics and computer industry as a strategic sector in the backdrop of the 1960s wars and the emergence of IBM as a near-monopoly. Till this time the use of data processing equipment in the government spread in the absence of any policy on computerization. With the setting up of the DoE in 1970, the government took control of the sector and gave a predominant role to public sector enterprises such as ECIL so that it could cater to the computing needs of nuclear, defense, and space labs. The policy goal in the early 1970s was to end the monopoly of IBM and move toward self-reliance in the field of computer technology. The government began to control the size of the market for computers and other electronic equipment through its system of licensing and production capacities. Socialistic fears about automation and computers replacing human labor had to be balanced with the genuine needs for computers of scientists and commercial firms.

The first tenure of Prime Minister Indira Gandhi—from January 1966 to March 1977—was marked by restrictive economic policies that prevented Indian companies from entering electronics manufacturing. DCM Data Products' joint venture with Sony to assemble electronic calculators was rejected, while CDC backed out of a proposed joint venture with the Tata Group to manufacture ferrite-core memories for their computers in the United States, fearing red tape. Texas Instruments too came with a manufacturing proposal but it was rejected. Fairchild Semiconductors had suffered the same fate a few years earlier. This was the period when the U.S. electronics and computer industry leaders were exploring Asia to locate labor-intensive manufacturing of components and assemblies. Indira Gandhi did make an attempt at trade liberalization and export-led growth but rolled it back under pressure from left-wing elements inside and outside the Congress Party—which was then her main political support base.[1]

While India was rejecting applications from American firms to set up export-led manufacturing units, Hong Kong, Taiwan, Singapore, and Malaysia were formulating aggressive policies to facilitate foreign investment in high-technology manufacturing. Indian efforts in the form of an export processing zone set up at Kandla on the western coast in 1965 were half-hearted. The package of incentives and facilities was not attractive, zone authorities had limited powers, entrepreneurs had to obtain clearances from state and central government agencies individually, and custom procedures for bonding, bank guarantees, and movement of goods were too rigid.[2] This is perhaps one of the reasons why India missed the electronics or hardware bus.

Yet the state's grip over the electronics sector had positive fallout when private computer firms were allowed to begin manufacture of computers and peripherals in the mid-1970s. With restrictions on imports, Indians were forced to innovate hardware designs, improve old machines, and make them run novel applications. The availability of computing infrastructure in the form of mainframe computers in state-run institutions helped private companies and entrepreneurs at critical points. They also benefited from the talent pool and facilities in government institutions. For instance, Patni Computer Systems used mainframes at IIT Bombay for data conversion work; DCM Data Products hired design personnel from ITI and BEL; HCL worked on computers at the National Physical Laboratory to develop software for its first microcomputer; Wipro's first PC was incubated at IISc and its core R&D personnel were hired from ECIL; a large number of hardware design and software personnel from private industry were trained at CEDT and NCSTC. The state was also a major consumer of electronics and computers manufactured by private sector companies.

If the socialist policies of Indira Gandhi are to be blamed for India missing the hardware bus in the 1970s, strangely it is the same person who should be credited for opening the doors for a liberalized computer policy during her second tenure in office beginning January 1980. The thirty-three months she was out of power seem to have changed her thinking on economic matters. She abandoned the "statist and the nationalist" model of development of the Nehru era and shifted India's political economy in the direction of a "state and business alliance" for economic growth.[3] She downplayed redistributive concerns and gave priority to economic growth through alliances with private business. Factors responsible for Indira Gandhi changing her mind when she was out of power are yet to be fully understood.

The shift from left-leaning state intervention to the pro-private sector approach in post-1980 period was not dramatic but was executed in a subtle manner. It was camouflaged to maintain the public image of Indira Gandhi as a leader of poor masses with socialist credentials. She broke away from the set of Nehruvian economic advisers and readily received new ideas presented to her from outside this closed group. Gandhi gave her nod for preparing a liberalized computer policy early on and deregulated consumer electronic manufacturing on the advice of a technocrat-turned-industrialist friend of her elder son, Rajiv. She also took note of the blueprint prepared by an expatriate Indian technologist for development of a digital switch and modernization of the telecom network. Her support to the electronics sector was crucial in the post-1980 period. It was almost as if she was repenting for the excessive socialist policies unleashed under her rule in the 1970s. After her assassination in 1984, her son Rajiv completed the task that his mother had started in the post-1980 period.

The policy approach under Indira Gandhi became liberal in early 1980s but the control structure in the government remained intact. Doing business for electronics and software firms was still tough. Indira Gandhi sought to change this when she agreed to the radical concept of privately owned duty-free Software Technology Parks (STPs) for taking up knowledge-based exports, in the months preceding her assassination in October 1984. It took several more years to translate this idea into a functioning reality mainly due to inter-ministerial turf wars and bureaucratic bungling. But once STPs became functional, software exports witnessed exponential growth.

Software technology parks helped free software firms from two major stumbling blocks—bureaucratic delays and lack of physical infrastructure. Companies had to deal with a single point for all approvals. The STPs freed exports from going through the drudgery of ports and customs and gave software firms fiscal incentives in the form of tax holidays. This was the first export industry that did not depend on the physical infrastructure of roads, ports, and airports to earn dollars. Bits and bytes of information could simply be exported via computers connected through satellite data links. The parks brought Indian software companies closer to their customers in the United States and other countries through improved communication links and video conferencing. This was also the first export industry that did not employ unskilled or semiskilled labor, but instead depended on highly qualified technical personnel. It was a people-, not capital-, intensive export industry.

Besides a favorable domestic policy climate and a highly attractive export promotion scheme, a host of external factors were crucial for the growth of the software industry. The emergence of the Internet as a tool of communication accompanied by changes in the telecom industry brought down the cost of communication drastically and gave rise to a host of new communication products and services. And all this, in turn, fueled the demand for new software and services, as well as migration services (from old to new platforms). This led to a shortage of technical personnel in the U.S. market, forcing companies to come to destinations such as India, which had already proven their capabilities in terms of cost and quality. Several U.S. software firms set up Indian subsidiaries or signed deals with local vendors. Many Indian firms won contracts that involved sending their personnel to the United States as well as undertaking part of the development work locally.

The opportunities created by the Y2K problem and euro currency conversion brought a large number of U.S. and European corporations in direct contact with a host of large, medium and small software firms in India. These projects opened the door for Indian firms. First, the opening up of telecoms and Internet connectivity brought down the cost of communication for existing firms engaged in software exports, further enhancing their competitiveness. Second, it gave rise to another set of services—other than core software development and related services—known as business process outsourcing or IT-enabled services.

Domestic Technology Diffusion

Dependence on exports was necessary for the software industry's survival, as the domestic base was very small. That's the reason the Indian computing history is often only gauged through the prism of software service exports and outsourcing. Technology diffusion in the domestic market has progressed slowly. In the first phase, the use of computers spread in scientific, academic, and research institutions. Such diffusion helped ordinary Indians in indirect ways. For instance, deployment of the latest computing technologies in space and atomic energy programs resulted in Indian agencies launching weather, communication, and remote-sensing satellites and in designing nuclear power reactors. With the help of powerful supercomputers, the Indian Meteorological Department (IMD) could improve daily forecasting as well as monsoon prediction a great deal. This, in turn, has benefited millions of farmers who depend on monsoon rains for their livelihood as well as food production.

The second phase of IT application in India comprised of computerization of government services to improve their efficiency and cut transaction time for citizens. The computerized passenger reservation system of the Indian Railways and preparation of the UIDAI database are good examples. The banking and financial sector is another area to have successfully deployed information technology to significantly improve the quality of public services, given the fact that most of these services were poorly run under public sector management for a long time. In all these indirect ways, computers have touched the lives of millions of ordinary people in India, unlike developed countries where this technology reached people through personal computers. This phase of technology diffusion continues to unfold.

With the rapid decline in prices of computers and liberal imports began the third phase of technology adoption, which saw the rise in numbers of personal devices. Telecom privatization and availability of the Internet contributed to this growth. The numbers of computers, laptops, tablets, mobile phones, and other digital devices grew rapidly in the 2000s. Indians' consumption of digital technology continues to grow. As a result of all this, computers and other digital devices have become ubiquitous not only in scientific, academic, government institutions, and industry, but also in small businesses, schools, and homes of middle-class Indians. If the mobile phone—which has several functions of a computer—is included, the reach of digital technology in India is now quite deep. However, the full potential of its reach is yet to be realized, because not many useful applications in Indian languages that meet local needs have been developed yet. This is one of the challenges India faces.

Challenges to Sustaining Growth

Now that the domestic market is witnessing rapid growth, the demand for local software products and services is bound to grow. But product development has been a weak area for Indian IT industry, the bulk of which is focused on providing software services. It achieved high growth rates in the 1990s by catering to the demands for skilled personnel and services in Western markets. Indian companies kept hiring engineers to execute projects that involved labor-intensive work. Large U.S. outsourcing firms like IBM and Accenture also started emulating this model, and set up huge operations in India, employing local people. Thirty percent of services and outsourcing revenue in 2013 was estimated to be from multinationals working out of India. The competitive edge of Indian IT services firms was eroded on other counts as well. The productivity per employee of Indian companies is lower than their Western counterparts. For instance, Accenture earned revenue of six million rupees per employee—nearly three times that of Infosys and TCS in 2005–2006.[4]

U.S. consulting firms with their experience in strategic report making and complex technological deployments are giving Indian service companies stiff competition in consulting and IT infrastructure management. IBM and Accenture have won long-term IT management contracts from Indian corporations such as Bharti, Idea, and Dabur. All such deals involve transfer of existing IT employees to the U.S. vendors. In these instances, Indian firms could not compete with their Western counterparts despite being successful in customized software development and services. On the one hand, Western giants have started adding application support to their offerings, while Indian companies are moving into consulting. On the other hand, Indian IT firms are acquiring companies in the United States, Europe, and the Asia Pacific to expand their customer footprints. They are expanding operations in the United States by hiring local talent. Besides helping them better serve U.S. customers, it helps Indian companies ward off politically motivated criticism that they are taking away American jobs. Indian IT companies supported 280,000 jobs in the United States during 2011 and have invested over $5 billion in FDI through acquisitions and green-field projects.[5]

In addition, the entry of U.S. companies hungry for an Indian workforce has resulted in spiraling attrition rates and rising salary costs for local firms. In high-end areas of software development, silicon chip designing and R&D, the cost advantage has diminished significantly and may not be a competitive advantage any more. Realizing the need to improve per employee productivity and likely erosion of a cheap labor force, Indian companies have begun exploring avenues that yield higher revenue per employee such as consulting and product development. They are also exploring newer revenue models such as transaction-based payment and licensing of software.

It is well recognized that for the long-term sustainability, Indian firms will have to focus on innovation, product development, and high-end R&D services. Product development has been the Holy Grail of the Indian IT industry. Only a handful of Indian software products have become successful in domestic or international markets. The list includes the accounting software Tally and banking applications like Finacle from Infosys and Flexcube from I-flex Solutions. Unlike services that depend on people, product development is capital intensive, involves the risk of failure, requires domain knowledge, and needs a domestic market where products can be tested before being taken to international markets. It is too expensive to test products elsewhere. With the growing domestic IT markets, Indians firms have begun product development. Larger ones are taking the route of acquisition to access capabilities and customers in consulting and software products. The shift from customized software to consulting, IT infrastructure management, and products is likely to become more pronounced in the future.

Besides cost and overdependence on services, the shortage of high-quality, employment-ready workers in the future is another likely threat. India claims to possess a sizeable pool of engineers and technical personnel suitable for IT and related services, but only a small percentage of this workforce is industry-ready. The availability of a skilled workforce is a prerequisite for the growth of the IT industry, as human resources are its primary raw material. India entered the high-technology exports business with the advantages of a robust engineering and higher technical education system as well a large pool of skilled workers competent in the English language. Both these advantages are slowly eroding.

While the IIT alumni have contributed to the growth of industry in the early part of its trajectory, it was the addition of massive numbers of engineering and other graduates from lesser-known and unknown engineering colleges that helped in scaling up operations. The primary pool from which the industry draws its workforce is about 1,500 engineering colleges that turn out over 500,000 graduates and 30,000 postgraduates every year.[6] IITs contribute just 1 percent of the number of skilled workers in the engineering labor force. This would make one believe India has enough engineering graduates to feed the software industry. But it is not just the numbers but quality and skill sets that matter. Of late, the quality of technical education has emerged as a major challenge. Most of the engineers from Indian colleges beyond the top-tier centers are not considered employment-ready. Very few pursue higher education and only about a thousand engineering PhDs are produced every year. Poor quality is also reflected in global benchmarks such as the Times Higher Education World University Rankings where Indian institutions are not represented in top 100 to top 200 tiers, while Chinese universities are constantly moving up the rankings.

Serious concerns have been raised over declining interest in research at IITs and the trend of IIT graduates opting for nonengineering careers in investment banking, retail industry, and so forth. Experts believe that IITs must consider emphasizing postgraduate education and research and lower the rising barriers between science and engineering.[7] Some alumni have also expressed doubts about the caliber of students who make it into the IITs by undergoing rigorous coaching for the entrance test.[8] In the long run, such students may not be suitable for creative thinking and research. The situation in engineering colleges other than IITs is much worse due to their poor quality of faculty, outdated curriculum, and "chalk-and-talk" pedagogy. A test of computer programming skills among computer/IT engineering students in 2013 revealed that 30 percent of them did not know basic theoretical concepts used in computer programming.[9] Only 14.97 percent of those specializing in IT exhibited skills to write a simple program. Between 50 and 60 percent of engineers did not understand the subtleties of programming concepts, while more than 80 percent were unable to apply them to real-world situations.

The oft-cited Indian advantage of a workforce competent in English also seems to be losing its sheen. Performance of engineering students in the English Comprehension module of AMCAT (Aspiring Minds Computer Adaptive Test)—a standardized employability test—conducted in 2012 was shocking.[10] The sample size of this study was over 55,000 engineering students from 250 colleges across multiple Indian states. It was found that over 25 percent could not understand the elementary English necessary for them to comprehend the engineering curriculum. Only around 50 percent of engineering students demonstrated grammar competencies equivalent to those imparted in the seventh grade in Indian schools. This level of grammar is required to express oneself in a comprehensible manner and write error-free emails. Less than 48 percent of the students understood moderately sophisticated English words.

A Digital Future

The information technology industry with its focus on exports is seen as a wealth creator and job provider to millions of middle-class Indians. It is amazing how computer technology has raised the aspirations of an entire nation. Though the outsourcing industry remained cut off from domestic market needs for a long time, it has contributed to the growth and well-being of people in many direct and indirect ways.

The story of the computer revolution in India has now reached a critical stage, with technology touching the lives of ordinary citizens in myriad ways. Computers are no more the preserve of scientists, academicians, and businesses. They have become a part of the day-to-day lives of people, even in many rural areas, and among those who are not educated or literate. Mobile phones—loaded with software and processing power several times that of the million-dollar mainframe computers of the 1960s—are in the hands of millions of Indians. They are empowering citizens in many ways and even boosting the incomes of the poor. The use of computers is providing succor to Indians in these sectors in many ways—from enabling them to access agriculture-related information to supporting their fight against corruption in government departments.

The challenge before the Indian industry now is to rise up and cater to the demands of a growing domestic market. For Indian companies to remain competitive, the focus must shift to innovation, R&D, consulting business, and geographical expansion. The focus on innovation would encourage companies to design products and services for the Indian market. Such innovation would also help in accessing other emerging markets in Africa and elsewhere. In the global outsourcing market, several me-too players already are beginning to compete. Destinations like the Philippines have caught up with India in some parts of the business such as call centers, while the Chinese software industry is fast catching up despite rising labor costs in India.

As the ecosystem for innovation develops in IT hubs such as Bangalore, Noida, Gurgaon, Pune, and Hyderabad, entrepreneur-driven technology firms are preparing to lead the innovation and product race. They are seizing opportunities created by the growth of telecom, broadband, and media markets in India and elsewhere. This new wave of innovation is helped by the existence of trained Indian workers, the influx of experienced talent from the United States, the availability of venture capital funds, a good academic and research environment, and positive state policies. Many Silicon Valleys are waiting to be discovered and explored in India.

Notes

1   India's First Computers

1. Letter from H. J. Bhabha to Dr A. N. Khosla, Planning Commission, August 22, 1961, D-2004-01340, TIFR Archives.

2. David Arnold, "Nehruvian Science and Postcolonial India," *Isis* 104, no. 2 (June 2013): 360–370.

3. Sambit Mallick, E. Haribabu, and S. G. Kulkarni, "Debates on Science and Technology in India: Alliance Formation between the Scientific and Political Elite during the Inter-War Period," *Social Scientist* 33, no. 11/12 (November–December 2005): 49–75.

4. "Interview to Charles Petresch and Others," in *The Collected Works of Mahatma Gandhi: Vol. 48* (New Delhi: Publications Division, September 1931–July 1932), 245–247.

5. A. M. Zaidi and S. G. Zaidi, *The Encyclopedia of the Indian National Congress VIII [1921–24]* (New Delhi: S. Chand, 1980), 95–97.

6. Deepak Kumar, ed., *Science and Empire: Essays in Indian Context, 1700–1947* (New Delhi: Anamika Publishers and Distributors, 1991), 169.

7. Mallick, Haribabu, and Kulkarni, "Debates on Science and Technology in India," 49–75.

8. Deepak Kumar, "Reconstructing India: Disunity in the Science and Technology for Development Discourse, 1900–1947," *OSIRIS* 15 (2000): 241–257.

9. Ibid., 250.

10. Robert S. Anderson, *Nucleus and Nation: Scientists, International Networks, and Power in India* (New Delhi: Supernova Publishers and Distributors, 2011), 91.

11. For a comprehensive study of a history of modern science in pre-independence India, see Uma Dasgupta, ed., *Science and Modern India: An Institutional History, c.*

1784–1947: Project of History of Science, Philosophy and Culture in Indian Civilization (New Delhi: Pearson Education India, 2011).

12. Norma Clark and Ashok Parthasarathi, "Science-based Industrialization in a Developing Country: The Case of the Indian Scientific Instruments Industry 1947–1968," *Modern Asian Studies* 16, no. 4 (1982): 661–662.

13. Robert S. Anderson, "Empire's Setting Sun: Patrick Blackett and Military and Scientific Development of India," *Economic and Political Weekly* 36, no. 39 (September 29–October 5, 2001): 3707–3720.

14. Ashok Rudra, *Prasanta Chandra Mahalanobis: A Biography* (New Delhi: Oxford University Press, 1996), 276.

15. Memorandum of Article, Indian Calculating Machine and Scientific Instrument Research Society, September 28, 1943, Document number 511–185, ISI Archives.

16. From the film *History of Computers*, part of the course Computers in Office Management (New Delhi: Indira Gandhi National Open University, 1991).

17. S. K. Mitra, "Electrical Analog Computing Machine for Solving Linear Equations and Related Problems," *The Review of Scientific Instruments* (May 1955): 453–457.

18. See note 16.

19. *Indian Statistical Institute: History and Activities 1931–1959* (Kolkata, India: Indian Statistical Institute, November 1959).

20. Donald W. Davies, "Letters to the Editor," *Resurrection: The Bulletin of the Computer Conservation Society*, no. 24 (Autumn 2000): 29–30.

21. Paul Ceruzzi, *A History of Modern Computing* (Cambridge, MA: MIT Press, 2003), 27.

22. "Electronics Division," *Samvadadhvam* 3, no. 1 (July 1959): 42.

23. Anderson, *Nucleus and Nation*, 159.

24. Alan L. Mackay, "J. D. Bernal (1901–1971) in Perspective," *Journal of Biosciences* 28, no. 5 (September 2003): 539–546, 543.

25. Rudra, *Prasanta Chandra Mahalanobis*, 277.

26. Mohi Mukherjee, "The Electronic Brain," *Samvadadhvam* 1, no. 1 (July 1956): 24–27, 27.

27. Former ISI scientist D. Datta Majumder, interview with the author, Kolkata, April 2007.

28. *Indian Statistical Institute: History and Activities 1931–1959*, 20.

29. "Soviet Electronic Computer—URAL," *Samvadadhvam* 2, no. 4 (July–September 1958): 22–23.

30. Majumder, interview with the author.

31. "Soviet-American Cooperation at the Institute," *Samvadadhvam* 1, no. 3 (March 1957): 48.

32. B. Nag, "Computer Design and Development in India," in *Computer Education in India: Past, Present and Future*, ed. Utpal Banerjee (New Delhi: Concept Publishing Company, 1996), 21–25.

33. Majumder, interview with the author.

34. "Electronics Division," *Samvadadhvam* 5, no. 1 (1961–1962): 53–54.

35. Ramachandra Guha, *India after Gandhi* (New Delhi: Picador, 2007), 208–209.

36. Letter from Homi J. Bhabha to Sir Sorab Saklatvala, March 12, 1944, TIFR Archives.

37. Indira Chowdhury and Ananya Dasgupta, *A Masterful Spirit: Homi J Bhabha (1909–1966)* (New Delhi: Penguin Books, 2010), 35.

38. Anderson, *Nucleus and Nation*, 178.

39. Ibid., 190.

40. Ibid.

41. C. V. Sundaram, L. V. Krishnan, and T. S. Iyengar, *Atomic Energy in India: 50 Years* (Mumbai: Department of Atomic Energy, 1998), 7–8.

42. Former Chairman and Managing Director of Electronics Corporation of India Limited A. S. Rao, interview with S. P. K. Gupta, 1973, transcript, personal collection.

43. Raja Ramanna, *Years of Pilgrimage* (New Delhi: Viking, 1991), 56.

44. Appendix-2, "Technology Proposal for a Real-Time Computer for Space Science and Technology," prepared by ECIL, February 1969, D-2004-01050, TIFR Archives.

45. R. Narasimhan, "Men, Machines and Ideas: An Autobiographical Essay," *Current Science* 76, no. 3 (February 1999): 447–454, 448.

46. R. K. Shyamasundar and M. A. Pai, eds., *Homi Bhabha and the Computer Revolution* (Oxford University Press: New Delhi, 2011), 5.

47. "Note on Import Content of TIFRAC," September 1959, D-2004-01343, TIFR Archives.

48. R. Narasimhan, oral history interview by Indira Chowdhury, May 4–17, 2005, Bangalore, transcript, TIFR Archives.

49. Ibid.

50. "Note on Auxiliary Equipment for TIFRAC," from Dr. D. Y. Phadke to Dr. H. J. Bhabha, September 17, 1959, D-2004-01340, TIFR Archives.

51. H. J. Bhabha, "Electronic Computers," July 2, 1959, D-2004-01340, TIFR Archives.

52. Rudra, *Prasanta Chandra Mahalanobis*, 277–278.

53. Bhabha, "Electronic Computers."

54. Letter from R. L. Garwin, IBM and Columbia University professor of physics, to Dr. H. J. Bhabha, July 2, 1960, D-2004-01340, TIFR Archives.

55. M. G. K. Menon, "Notes on Computer Facilities at TIFR," August 19, 1961, D-2004-01343, TIFR Archives.

56. "Minutes of TIFR Council Meeting held on September 11, 1961," D-2004-01340, TIFR Archives.

57. Letter from K. T. Irani, IBM, Bombay, to M. G. K. Menon, May 17, 1963, D-2004-01340, TIFR Archives.

58. Letter from Bhabha to Khosla, August 22, 1961.

59. Letter from K. R. Nair, Additional Secretary to the Cabinet to Director, TIFR, February 3, 1962, D-2004-01344, TIFR Archives.

60. Letter from D. Y. Phadke to Director, Central Statistical Organization, July 2, 1962, D-2004-01340, TIFR Archives.

61. Letter from D. Y. Phadke to Director, Central Statistical Organization, February 23, 1962, D-2004-01344, TIFR Archives.

62. Letter from H. J. Bhabha to P. C. Mahalanobis, August 22, 1961, D-2004-01340, TIFR Archives.

63. Letter from Bhabha to Khosla, August 22, 1961.

64. Letter from P. C. Mahalanobis to H. J. Bhabha, August 25, 1961, D-2004-01344, TIFR Archives.

65. "Recommendations for the Organization of a Computer Centre and the Installation of a Large-scale Digital Computing System at TIFR, Bombay"; submitted by Computer Committee, August 1962, D-2004-01340, TIFR Archives.

66. "The National Computation Centre," in *TIFR: 1945–1970* (Mumbai: TIFR, 1970), 426.

67. Ibid., 427.

68. N. Seshagiri "Completely Self-Diagnosable Digital Systems," *International Journal of Systems Sciences* 1, no. 3 (1971): 235–246; N. Seshagiri and P. Sadanandan, "A General Algorithm for the Optimal Coordination of a Space-borne Computer-Transmitter Coupling," paper presented at the Symposium on Computer Processing in Communications, Polytechnic Institute of Brooklyn, April 1969.

69. Letter from Captain K. R. Ramnath, Director of Weapons Equipment, to M. G. K. Menon, October 26, 1964, D-2004-01350, TIFR Archives.

70. "Work in Computer Sciences and Technology: A Summary and a Projection," D-2004-01355, 30–31, TIFR Archives.

71. *An Interim Report of the Committee Appointed to Consider the Development of Higher Technical Institutions in India* (New Delhi: Government of India, 1946), 1.

72. Ibid., 4.

73. Stuart W. Leslie, "Exporting MIT: Science, Technology and Nation-Building in India and Iran," *OSIRIS* 21 (2006): 110–130, 115.

74. *Kanpur Indo-American Program: Final Report* (Newton, MA: Education Development Center, 1972), 4.

75. Ibid., E1.

76. H. N. Mahabala, "Early Computer Education in India—A Reminiscence," in *Computer Education in India: Past, Present and Future*, ed. Utpal Banerjee (New Delhi: Concept Publishing Company, 1996), 41–46.

77. Former professor at IIT Kanpur V. Rajaraman, interview with the author, Bangalore, July 2006.

78. Former professor at IIT Bombay J. R. Isaac, interview with the author, Bangalore, October 2006.

79. Former Director of NCSDCT S. Ramani, interview with the author, Bangalore, October 2006.

80. Ross Bassett, "Aligning India in the Cold War Era: Indian Technical Elites, the Indian Institute of Technology at Kanpur, and Computing in India and the United States," *Technology and Culture* 50, no. 4 (October 2009): 783–810.

81. P. V. Indiresan and N. C. Nigam, "The Indian Institutes of Technology—An Experience in Excellence."

82. Leslie, "Exporting MIT," 117.

83. Ibid., 118.

84. Annalee Saxenian, "The Bangalore Boom: From Brain Drain to Brain Circulation," in *IT Experience in India: Bridging the Digital Divide*, ed. Kenneth Keniston and Deepak Kumar (New Delhi: Sage Publications, 2004), 169–181, 169.

85. Robert S. Anderson, *Bhabha-Saha: A Study in Contrast* (Montreal: Centre for Developing Area Studies, 1975), 35.

86. Narasimhan, "Men, Machines and Ideas," 449.

87. "Work in Computer Sciences and Technology: A Summary and a Projection," 1972, D-2004-01355-28, TIFR Archives.

88. Bassett, "Aligning India in the Cold War Era."

89. "Preliminary Project Report on R and D Facilities and Production Capabilities for Microelectronics Devices System," sent by D. Y. Phadke to R. D. Choksi, Tata Sons, April 17, 1967, D-2004, 01046, TIFR Archives.

2   The Beginning of State Involvement

1. "Electronics in India: Report of the Electronics Committee" (Bombay: Government of India, 1966), 4–6.

2. Robert S. Anderson, *Nucleus and Nation: Scientists, International Networks and Power in India* (Chicago: University of Chicago, 2011), 265.

3. B. V. Srikantan, "Sixty Years of the Tata Institute of Fundamental Research 1945–2005: The Role of Young Men in Creation and Development of This Institute," *Current Science* 90, no. 5 (March 10, 2006): 1022–1025.

4. A. S. Rao, interview with S. P. K. Gupta, New Delhi and Hyderabad, 1972–1973.

5. Ibid.

6. *Electronics in India*, 4.

7. Ibid., 237.

8. Ibid., 238–239.

9. Rao, interview with Gupta.

10. C. R. Subramanian, *India and the Computer* (New Delhi: Oxford University Press, 1997), 5.

11. *Proceedings of National Conference on Electronics Organized by the Electronics Committee*, Bombay, March 24–28, 1970 (Bombay: Electronics Commission, 1971), 39–40.

12. *Selected Speeches and Writings of M. G. K. Menon* (New Delhi: Council of Scientific and Industrial Research, 1988), 9.

13. A. S. Rao, "Sarabhai and Electronics," *Electronics Today* 5, no. 2 (1972): 124–128.

14. Appendix-2 of "Technology Proposal for a Real-time Computer for Space Science and Technology," ECIL, February 1969, D-2004-01050, TIFR Archives.

15. Electronics Corporation of India Limited, Case Study BP 236 (Ahmedabad: Indian Institute of Management, 1996).

16. A. S. Rao, "A Survey of Development of Computer Field" (1978), in *Computer Education in India: Past, Present and Future*, ed. Dr. Utpal K. Banerjee (New Delhi: Concept Publishing Company, 1996), 27–35.

17. S. Manikutty, "Barriers to Strategic Changes in Organizations: A Case Study," *Vikalpa* 15, no. 1 (January–March 1990): 37–46.

18. Ashok Parthasarathi, *Technology at the Core: Science and Technology with Indira Gandhi* (New Delhi: Pearson Longman, 2007), 52.

19. *Perspective Report on Electronics in India* (Bombay: Electronics Commission, 1975), 24–27.

20. Former DoE Secretary M. G. K. Menon, interview with the author, New Delhi, April 4, 2007.

21. *Report of the Committee on Automation* (New Delhi: Ministry of Labour and Rehabilitation, 1972), 30.

22. Ibid., 85–85.

23. *Perspective Report on Electronics in India*, 51.

24. Department of Electronics, *Annual Report* (New Delhi: Department of Electronics, 1972).

25. Perspective Report on Electronics in India, 88–89.

26. Ibid.

27. *Perspective Report on Electronics in Indi*a, 210.

28. Ibid.

29. Manikutty "Barriers to Strategic Changes in Organizations."

30. *Annual Report 1975–76* (New Delhi: Department of Electronics, 1976), 46.

31. Ibid., 46–48.

32. *Report of the Review Committee on Electronics* (New Delhi: Department of Electronics, 1979), 68.

33. F. C. Kohli, *The IT Revolution in India—Selected Speeches and Writings* (New Delhi: Rupa & Co, 2006), xvii.

34. *121st Report of Public Accounts Committee (1975–76) on Computerisation in Government Departments* (New Delhi: Lok Sabha Secretariat, 1976), 276.

35. A statement on "Minicomputer Policy" tabled in the Indian parliament on March 9, 1978; quoted in Subramanian, *India and the Computer* (see note 10).

36. Ibid.

37. Ibid.

38. *Report of Committee on Mini Computers* (Bombay: Electronics Commission, 1974).

39. Subramanian, *India and the Compute*r, 9.

40. "Computers: Cautious Growth," *India Today*, December 1–15, 1977.

41. Menon, interview with the author.

42. *Report of the Review Committee on Electronics*, 13.

43. Ibid.

3   The Rise, Fall, and Rise of IBM

1. Former manager at IBM India O. P. Mehra, interview with the author, New Delhi, December 2006.

2. "To Them August Is Particularly Significant," *IBM Report* (New Delhi: IBM World Trade Corporation, July–August 1972), 7.

3. "Card Plant Is Back at Bombay," *IBM Report* (New Delhi: IBM World Trade Corporation, September 1971), 11.

4. Gordon R. Williamson, *Memoirs of My Years with IBM: 1951–1986* (Bloomington, IN: Xlibris Corporation, 2009), 377.

5. This information is based on a timeline supplied by IBM India to the author.

6. "PRL Installs IBM System/360," *IBM Report*, September 1972, 3.

7. "Indian Institute of Science Does It Again," *IBM Report*, June 1972, 4.

8. "Launching India into Space," *IBM Report*, September 1972, 26–27.

9. Vinod Pal, "Railways and Computerization," *IBM Report*, September 1971, 4.

10. Former IBM India and DCM DP engineer Joe Cleetus, e-mail interview with the author, April 2007.

11. Former IBM India engineer K. R. Trilokekar, e-mail interview and phone discussion with the author, November 2006.

12. Mehra, interview with the author.

13. "Computerization in Bombay-Poona Region," *Electronics Information & Planning* (September 1975): 1143.

14. *121st Report of Public Accounts Committee (1975–76) on Computerisation in Government Departments* (New Delhi: Lok Sabha Secretariat, 1976), 50.

15. Former IBM India engineer Shashi Ullal, interview with the author, Mumbai, June 7, 2006.

16. *Report of the Expert Committee on Utilization of EDP Systems in Government* (Bombay: Electronics Commission, 1979).

17. "IBM Language," *Economic and Political Weekly*, April 9, 1977, 584–585.

18. Former DoE Secretary M. G. K. Menon, interview with the author, New Delhi, April 2007.

19. Manohar Prabhakar, *Dimensions: An Intimate Portrait of Mr. K. R. Singh* (Jaipur: Public Relations Society of India, 1994), 13–14.

20. Former PR executive at IBM India K. R. Singh, interview with the author, New Delhi, June 2007.

21. Ullal, interview with the author.

22. *121st Report of Public Accounts Committee (1975–76)*, 6–7.

23. Note on IBM Proposal, December 27, 1968, Electronics Committee, D-2004–01356, TIFR Archives.

24. *Report of Committee on Automation* (New Delhi: Ministry of Labour and Rehabilitation, 1972), 34.

25. *121st Report of Public Accounts Committee (1975–76)*, 243.

26. Ibid., 9.

27. Ibid., 242–255.

28. Former senior executive at IBM India Dan Gupta, telephone interview with the author, April 2007.

29. Former DoE official Dr. N. Seshagiri, interview with the author, Bangalore, July 2006.

30. Ibid.

31. An anonymous IBM executive (1967–1977) in discussion with the author.

32. Williamson, *Memoirs of My Years with IBM*, 375–377.

33. "IBM Problems in India," cable sent by the Department of State to U.S. missions in India on April 6, 1976, WikiLeaks, accessed January 5, 2014, http://www.wikileaks.org/plusd/cables/1976STATE081933_b.html.

34. Ibid.

35. Baldev Raj Nayar, *India's Quest for Technological Independence: Policy Foundations and Policy Change*, vol. 1 (New Delhi: Lancers Publishers, 1983), 391.

36. Joseph M. Grieco, *Between Dependence and Autonomy: India's Experience with the International Computer Industry* (Berkeley: University of California Press, 1984), 19.

37. Former Industry Minister George Fernandes, interview with the author, New Delhi, July 2006.

38. "IBM May Quit India," *Times of India*, October 3, 1977.

39. "IBM to Sell Rented Gear to Customers," *Times of India*, November 16, 1977.

40. "IBM Withdraws from India," *Time*, November 28, 1977.

41. "No N-arms Even if We Perish," *Times of India*, June 16, 1978.

42. Menon, interview with the author.

43. Former IBM executive and IIF founder Saurabh Srivastava, interview with the author, New Delhi, May 2006.

44. Grieco, *Between Dependence and Autonomy*, 48–49.

45. Mehra, interview with the author.

46. "Explorers of a Rare Kind," *IBM Report* (July–September 1977), 9–10.

47. Peter Hall, "How British Computer Industry Muddled Through," *Resurrection* 35 (Summer 2005): 8–16.

48. Subramanian, *India and the Computer*, 322.

49. Paul Gannon, "Trojan Horses and National Champions," *Resurrection* 34 (Spring 2005): 22–28.

50. Paulo Bastos Tigre, "Technology and Competition in the Brazilian Computer Industry," cited in Subramanian, *India and the Computer*, 317–333.

51. Menon, interview with the author.

52. Grieco, *Between Dependence and Autonomy*, 48–49.

53. Ibid.

54. "Rationale of the New Computer Policy," *Dataquest*, December 1984, 39–57.

55. "Hungry Tiger, Dancing Elephant: How India Is Changing IBM's World," *The Economist*, April 4, 2007, 67–69.

56. "IBM Chairman and CEO Announces Plans to Triple Investment in India over Next Three Years," IBM Press Release, June 6, 2006.

4   The Dawn of the Computer Age in India

1. Pyramid Research report on the Indian Telecom Industry, quoted in G. B. Meemansi, *The C-DOT Story* (New Delhi: Kedar Publications, 1993), 35.

2. Nicholas Nugent, *Rajiv Gandhi: Son of a Dynasty* (London: BBC Books, 1990), 40–41.

3. Minhaz Merchant, *Rajiv Gandhi: The End of a Dream* (New Delhi/New York: Viking, 1991), 61.

4. Sonia Gandhi, *Rajiv* (New Delhi: Viking Penguin Books, 1992), 4.

5. Prabhakar Shankar Deodhar, interview with author, Mumbai, November 2006.

6. Ibid.

7. Merchant, *Rajiv Gandhi*, 86–87.

8. "Sondhi Committee and Menon Committee Reports: Government's Decisions," *Electronics Information & Planning* 8, no. 8 (May 1981): 595–618.

9. Manishankar Aiyar, ed., *Rajiv Gandhi's India. Vol. 2: Economics* (New Delhi: UBS Publishers, 1998), 118.

10. Seshagiri, interview with the author.

11. T. N. Ninan, "Computers: Opening the Doors," *India Today*, December 1985, 132.

12. Nugent, *Rajiv Gandhi*, 67.

13. Ibid., 40–41.

14. "Rationale of the New Computer Policy," *Dataquest*, December 1984, 41–52.

15. "Policy on Software Export, Software Development and Training" (New Delhi: Department of Electronics, 1986).

16. Former Director of NCSDCT S. Ramani, interview with the author, Bangalore, July 2006.

17. Rekha Jain and G. Raghuram, "Management of Large IT Projects: The Passenger Reservation System of Indian Railways" (Ahmedabad: Indian Institute of Management, 1992).

18. Former IR official N. C. Gupta, interview with the author, New Delhi, May 2006.

19. Ibid.

20. Former CMC R&D engineer at CMC Arvind Sharma, interview with the author, Hyderabad, December 2006.

21. Gupta, interview with the author.

22. Jain and Raghuram, "Management of Large IT Projects."

23. Ibid.

24. "Report of the Committee on Computerisation in Banks" (Bombay: Reserve Bank of India, 1989), 18–22.

25. "Professional Contributions and Publications of Prof. P. V. S. Rao (head, speech and digital systems group, TIFR)," 1980, D-2004-01366, TIFR Archives.

26. Mayank Chaya, *Sam Pitroda: A Biography* (New Delhi: Konark Publishers, 1992), 50.

27. Ibid., 54.

28. M. V. Pitke, "C-DOT DSS: A New Family of Digital Switching Systems," in *TENCON'89, Fourth IEEE Region 10 International Conference* (New York: IEEE, 1989), 727–730.

29. Sam Pitroda, "Development, Democracy, and the Village Telephone," *Harvard Business Review* 71, no. 6 (1993): 66–68.

30. B. Bowonder, "Development of Digital Switching Systems Technology: An Analysis of C-DOT," *Electronics Information & Planning* 18, no. 5 (February 1991): 223–239.

31. *Rajiv Gandhi: Selected Speeches and Writings (Science and Technology)* (New Delhi: Publications Division, 1987), 258–260.

32. Ibid.

33. *Rajiv Gandhi*, 174–175.

34. Aiyar, *Rajiv Gandhi's India. Vol. 2: Economics*, 90.

5 Discovering a New Continent

1. HCL cofounder Arjun Malhotra, interview with the author, Noida, May 2006.

2. DCMDP founder Dr Vinay Bharat Ram, interview with the author, May 2006.

3. Ramchandra Guha, *India after Gandhi* (New Delhi: Picador, 2007), 434–435.

4. Fairchild Oral History Panel, "The Legacy of Fairchild," Computer History Museum, 2007, catalog no. 102658284.

5. T. N. Ninan, "Electronics: Fast Forward," *India Today*, September 15, 1983, 106–109.

6. Leslie Berlin, *The Man Behind the Microchip: Robert Noyce and the Invention of Silicon Valley* (New York: Oxford University Press, 2005), 132.

7. M. J. Zarabi, "Electronic Calculator Industry in India: An Analysis," *Electronics Information & Planning* 4, no. 1 (October 1976): 33–41.

8. HCL cofounder Ajai Chowdhry, interview with the author, Noida, January 2007.

9. "The Making of a Giant," *DataQuest*, March 11, 2002, accessed December 15, 2007, http://www.dqindia.com/dataquest/news/154138/the-making-giant.

10. Order for Micro 2200, Indian Institute of Technology, Kharagpur, HCL.

11. Chowdhry, interview with the author.

12. Malhotra, interview with the author.

13. Former design engineer at DCM DP N. C. Maheshwari, interview with the author, New Delhi, May 2006.

14. J. M. Grieco, "Between Dependency and Autonomy: India's Experience with the International Computer Industry," in *United Nations Library on Transnational Corporations: Governments and Transnational Corporations*, ed. John H. Dunning (London: Routledge, 1993), 110–136, 115.

15. Ibid., 127.

16. Ibid., 129.

17. Former engineer at IBM and DCM DP Joe Cleetus, e-mail interview with the author, April 4, 2007.

18. "HCL Launches a Full-fledged Microprocessor-based Machine," *Economic Times* (May 20, 1978).

19. Former HCL President S. Raman, interview with the author, New Delhi, February 2007.

20. Chowdhry, interview with the author.

21. Owen W. Linzmayer, *Apple Confidential 2.0: The Definitive History of the World's Most Colorful Company* (San Francisco: No Starch Press, 2004), 13–14.

22. Om Vikas, "Indigenous Development of Computer Systems, Peripherals and Communication Facilities," *Electronics Information and Planning* 5, no. 11 (August 1978): 773–842, 820.

23. Malhotra, interview with the author.

24. "DCM Data Products Slips to Second Place," *Economic Times*, June 21, 1980, HCL Archives.

25. Malhotra, interview with the author.

26. Chowdhry, interview with the author.

27. Gary W Loveman and Jamie O'Connell, "HCL America" (Cambridge, MA: Harvard Business School, 1995), 9–10.

28. Ibid., 4.

29. Former professor at the Indian Institute of Science N. J. Rao, interview with the author, Bangalore, July 7, 2007.

30. Steve Hamm, *Bangalore Tiger* (New Delhi: Tata McGraw-Hill, 2006), 36.

31. Dr. Sridhar Mitta, interview with the author, Bangalore, March 2006.

32. Ibid.

33. K. Ramachandran, K. P. Devarajan, and Sougata Ray, "Corporate Entrepreneurship: How?," *Vikalpa* 31, no. 1 (January–March 2006): 85–97.

34. "Product Engineering Solutions," accessed May 6, 2007, www.wipro.com.

35. Dipa Jaywant, "Computers: Filling the Vacuum," *India Today*, May 1–15, 1979, 76.

36. R. Rastogi, "Electronics Production and Export Profile: 1991," *Electronics Information and Planning* 19, no. 9 (June 1992): 490–508.

6 Software Dreams Take Flight

1. A. K. Bahn, "Software Manufacture: Its Feasibility and Possible Problems," in *Electronics: Proceedings of National Conference on Electronics, March 24–28, 1970* (Bombay: Electronics Commission, 1971), 399–401, 400.

2. Edward B. Roberts and Charles E. Easley, *Entrepreneurial Impact: The Role of MIT-An Updated Report* (Netherlands: now Publishers, 2011), 20.

3. PCS founder Narendra K. Patni, interview with the author, Mumbai, November 2006.

4. Ibid.

5. Ibid.

6. Suzanne Rivard and Benoit A. Aubert, eds., *Information Technology Outsourcing, Volume 8 of Advances in Management Information Systems Series* (Armonk, NY: M. E. Sharpe, 2008), 310.

7. Elizabeth U. Harding, "After IBM's Exit an Industry Arose," *Software Magazine* 9, no 14 (November 15, 1989): 48–54.

8. "Murthy, Patni aur Woe," *Economic Times* (October 4, 2002).

9. Infosys founder N. R. Narayana Murthy, interview with the author, Bangalore, April 2007.

10. "Murthy to Patni, with Love," *Economic Times* (October 18, 2002).

11. Hari C. Polavarapu, "Infosys in a Controversial CAMP," *Dataquest*, January 1989, 40.

12. "Values First: Interview with N. R. Narayana Murthy," *Seminar*, no. 485 (January 2000): 82–86.

13. Jitendra V. Singh, "Infosys Technologies: Case Study" (Philadelphia: The Wharton School: University of Pennsylvania), 4.

14. *A Report on the Evolution of IT Industry in India* (New Delhi: Manufacturers Association for Information Technology, 1992), 91.

15. Chidanand Rajghatta, "Some Facts and a Little Masala," *Times of India* (December 14, 2003).

16. Infosys cofounder Nandan Nilekani, interview with the author, Bangalore, July 2007.

17. Ibid.

18. Lalit S. Kanodia, founder of TCS and Datamatics, interview with the author, Mumbai, February 2007.

19. S. Ramadorai, *The TCS Story and Beyond* (New Delhi: Penguin Books India, 2011), 27.

20. Former TCS President Yash Pal Sahani, interview with the author, Mumbai, March 2007.

21. Former TCS Vice Chairman F. C. Kohli, interview with the author, Mumbai, November 2006.

22. Ramadorai, *The TCS Story and Beyond*, 40.

23. Joseph M. Grieco, *Between Dependence and Autonomy: India's Experience with the International Computer Industry* (Berkeley: University of California Press, 1984), 85.

24. Robert E. Kennedy, "Tata Consultancy Services: High Technology in a Low-Income Country" (Cambridge, MA: Harvard Business School, 2000), 17.

25. Richard Heeks, *India's Software Industry: State Policy, Liberalization and Industrial Development* (New Delhi: Sage Publications, 1996), 88.

26. "India's Software Patriarch Still A Pace-setter," *The Business Times*, November 5, 2001, 21.

27. In 1986, Tata Burroughs became Tata Unisys when Sperry and Burroughs merged to form Unisys. After Unisys pulled out of the joint venture in 1996, the company was renamed Tata Infotech and finally merged with TCS in July 2005.

28. Softek founder Diwakar Nigam, interview with the author, New Delhi, December 2006.

29. Softek was sold to the Dalmia group in 1990, and in 1992, Nigam founded another software product company, Newgen Software, focused in the niche segment of business process management.

30. Mastek founder Ashank Desai, interview with the author, Mumbai, November 2006.

31. Future Software founder K. V. Ramani, interview with the author, January 2007.

32. Flextronics International Limited bought 55 percent of shares of HSS for $226 million in 2004, besides Ramani's stake in HSS as well as the entire stock of Future Software. Flextronics then integrated HSS, Future, and three other software firms it had bought in India into one company called Flextronics Software Systems. After two years, Flextronics sold off 85 percent of this entity to Kohlberg Kravis Roberts for $900 million. The new entity was called Aricent.

33. Srivastava, interview with the author.

34. NIIT cofounder Rajendra S. Pawar, interview with the author, New Delhi and Gurgaon, February 2007.

35. Kohli, interview with the author.

36. Patni, interview with the author.

37. K. R. Trilokekar, email interview with the author, November 2006.

38. Nagy Hanna, *Exploiting Information Technology for Development: A Case Study of India* (Washington, DC: World Bank, 1994), 32.

39. Ibid., 31.

7 The Transition to Offshore

1. "Building on Brainware," *India Today*, May 31, 1994, 115–12, 115.

2. Both media reports are quoted in Francis Assisi, "Government to Promote Software through Series of Conferences," *India West*, October 9, 1987, 17.

3. Richard Heeks, *India's Software Industry: State Policy, Liberalization and Industrial Development* (New Delhi: Sage Publications, 1996), 245.

4. "Citibank to Set up Unit at SEEPZ," *Dataquest*, August 1985, 32.

5. *A Report on the Evolution of IT Industry in India* (New Delhi: Manufacturers Association for Information Technology, 1992), 75–79.

6. "COSL—The 1989 Ace Performer at SEEPZ," *Dataquest*, June 1989, 27.

7. In 2000, CITIL was renamed i-flex, dropping the Citi prefix as its flagship product, Flexcube, had become a widely accepted banking product globally. Oracle acquired Citi Venture's 41 percent stake for $650 million. In August 2006, Oracle increased its ownership to 55.1 percent from 52.5 percent by paying another $125 million. The parent company, COSL, which had continued to serve the needs of Citibank and its subsidiaries, too was sold to the Chennai-based software firm Polaris in 2002.

8. Founder of GDA Prabhu Goel, interview with the author, Meerut, January 2007.

9. Sharad Marathe, interview with the author, New Delhi, January 2, 2007.

10. Josh Martin, "India's Search for New Technology," *Multinational Monitor* 4, no. 9 (September 1983), accessed August 9, 2014, http://www.multinationalmonitor.org/hyper/issues/1983/09/martin.htm.

11. Ibid.

12. N. Seshagiri, "Information Plus Communication in NIEO," *Yojana* 24, nos. 1–2 (January 26, 1980): 79–82.

13. Ibid.

14. *Consultant's Report on Project RINSCA* (Paris: UNESCO, 1981), 42.

15. *The Role of Transnational Corporations in Transborder Data Flows: Report of the Secretariat* (Geneva/New Delhi: United Nations Center on Transnational Corporations, 1984).

16. "Terms and Conditions for Establishment of Technology Parks for Software Export through Dedicated Satellite Earth Station" (New Delhi: Department of Electronics, June 1985).

17. Eric N. Berg, "Big Layoff at Texas Instruments," *New York Times*, December 8, 1984.

18. David E. Sanger, "Texas Instruments' Net Slides," *New York Times*, April 19, 1985; and David E. Sanger, "Texas Instruments," *New York Times*, October 26, 1985.

19. Former DoE Secretary M. G. K. Menon, interview with the author, New Delhi, April 2007.

20. Former Managing Director of TI India Srini Rajam, interview with the author, Bangalore, March 2007.

an Adbul Latif, "TI Exports First Lot of Software Through Satellite," *Dataquest*, August 1987, 49.

22. S. S. Oberoi, "Software India—1987 (Indo-US Conference)," *Electronics-Information & Planning* 15 (March 1988): 414–418, 417.

23. "Technology Parks to Boost Software Exports," *Dataquest*, June 1989, 23.

24. Srivastava, interview with the author.

25. S. S. Oberoi, "Indian Software Scenario," *Electronics Information & Planning* 18 (August 1991): 603–606.

26. N. Vittal, "My Years with the Department of Electronics," *Electronics Information and Planning* 21 (August 1993): 547–553, 549.

27. Pronab Sen, "Software Exports from India: A Systemic Analysis," *Electronics Information & Planning*, October 1994, 55–66, 62.

28. Mark Halper, "Deere's Faraway IS Solution," *Computerworld*, February 15, 1993, 76.

29. Alok Tiwari, "Software Exports: No Easy Way," *India Today*, October 15, 1991, 109–111.

30. Sen, "Software Exports from India," 58.

31. Ibid., 62.

32. Deepti Ahmad Kharod, "Silicon Valley: Logging on to India's Potential," *India Today*, June 30, 1991, 80–83.

33. "Indian Software & Services: Export Potential & Strategies" (Washington, DC/New Delhi: World Bank, 1992), 33–34.

34. Nagy Hanna, *Exploiting Information Technology for Development: A Case Study of India* (Washington, DC: World Bank, 1994), 246.

35. Dewang Mehta, "Nasscom's Success Reflects Buoyant Industry," *Business and Political Observer*, December 22, 1992.

36. Watts S. Humphrey, "Three Process Perspectives: Organizations, Teams, and People," *Annals of Software Engineering* 14, nos. 1–4 (December 2002): 39–72.

37. Raghav S. Nandyal, *Constellations of CMMI* (New Delhi: Tata McGraw Hill, 2011), 102.

38. Michael A. Cusumano, *The Business of Software: What Every Manager, Programmer, and Entrepreneur Must Know to Thrive and Survive in Good Times and Bad* (New York: Free Press, 2004), 187.

39. Otis Port, "Will Bugs Eat Up the US Lead in Software?," *Business Week*, December 6, 1999, 118.

40. Former programmer at Mafatlal Consultancy Services Sharad Godbole, interview with the author, Mumbai, June 2006.

41. "Annual Report 1999" (Bangalore: Infosys, 1999), 10.

42. "Satyam Expects 50 PC Growth," *Indian Express*, June 12, 1999.

43. Ashok Kumar, "TCS Factory to Avert Millennium Crisis," *Indian Express*, February 23, 1998.

44. *Indian IT Software and Service Directory* (New Delhi: National Association for Software and Service Companies, 1999), 18.

45. Kumar, "TCS Factory to Avert Millennium Crisis."

46. *Strategic Review* (New Delhi: National Association for Software and Service Companies, 1999): 32.

47. Vittal, "My Years with the Department of Electronics," 550.

8   Turning Geography into History

1. The data on IT revenues and employment generation is released by the industry body, NASSCOM, and generally accepted by government agencies. Hardware and domestic sales figures are also included in IT-ITeS revenue data of NASSCOM. The Planning Commission estimates put the size of IT-ITeS exports at $69 billion for 2011–2012 ($39.2 IT services, $16.5 BPO, and $13.3 software products and engineering). See "Report of the Working Group on Information Technology Sector Twelfth Five Year Plan (2012–17)" (New Delhi: Planning Commission, 2012), 165.

2. Hormuz P. Mama, "Net-Enabled Services—The New El Dorado," *Indian Express*, December 7, 1999, accessed August 11, 2014. http://expressindia.indianexpress.com/fe/daily/19991207/fed07039.html.

3. Former General Manager of World Network Services Roy Marshall, personal communication with the author, June 2007.

4. Seetha, *The Backroom Brigade: How a Few Intrepid Entrepreneurs Brought the World to India* (New Delhi: Penguin Portfolio, 2006): 26

5. "Back Office Processing Case Studies in IT Enabled Services" in *The ET Knowledge Series* (New Delhi: ET Intelligence Group, 2002), 93.

6. Michael F. Corbett, *The Outsourcing Revolution: Why It Makes Sense and How to Do It Right* (Chicago: Dearborn Trade Publishing, 2004), 42.

7. "Back Office Processing Case Studies," 93.

8. Robert Watts, "Indian Takeaway," *Telegraph,* December 16, 2003, accessed August 11, 2014, http://www.telegraph.co.uk/finance/2871146/Indian-takeaway.html.

9. Ravi Aron, "The Little Start-Up That Could: A Conversation with Raman Roy, Father of Indian BPO," *Knowledge@Wharton,* June 4, 2003, accessed August 11, 2014, http://knowledge.wharton.upenn.edu/article/the-little-start-up-that-could-a-conversation-with-raman-roy-father-of-indian-bpo/.

10. Ibid.

11. Ibid.

12. Seetha, *The Backroom Brigade*, 34.

13. Jack Welch and John Byrne, *Jack: Straight from the Gut* (New York: Warner Books, 2001), 314.

14. "Genpact Reports Results for 2013 Full Year," company press release, February 6, 2014.

15. Prasada Reddy, *The Globalization of Corporate R & D: Implications for Innovation Systems in Host Countries* (London: Routledge, 2000), 111.

16. Ibid., 117.

17. Ibid., 108.

18. "IBM to Establish Solutions Research Center in India," company press release, July 22, 1997.

19. Welch and Byrne, *Jack: Straight from the Gut*, 308–309.

20. "The New Face of Global R&D and Innovation: Deciphering the Indian Advantage" (Gurgaon, India: Evalueserve, 2004), 21.

21. "FDI in the R&D Sector: Study for the Pattern 1998–2003" (New Delhi: Technology Information, Forecasting and Assessment Council, 2006), 14–23.

22. N. Mrinalini, Pradosh Nath, and G. D. Sandhya, "Foreign Direct Investment in R&D in India," *Current Science* 105, no. 6 (2013): 767–773, 770.

23. *New Face of Global R&D and Innovation*, 22.

24. Rakesh Basant and Sunil Mani, "Foreign R&D Centres in India: An Analysis of Their Size, Structure and Implications" (Ahmedabad, India: Indian Institute of Management, 2012), 55.

25. "Cisco Systems Makes Major Strategic Investments in India," company press release, October 19, 2005.

26. Basant and Mani, "Foreign R&D Centres in India," 19–22.

27. "Global Reach from India," *Bechtel Briefs*, December 1998.

28. "Wipro Reaffirms Position as World's Top Third Party R&D Service Provider," company press release, May 18, 2011.

29. Mukesh Dialani, "R&D/Product Engineering Services—How Is HCL Technologies Thinking Out of the Box and Providing Value to Technology Product Customers?" (Framingham, MA: IDC, 2012).

30. "Demand for Engineering Services Outsourcing Is Increasing, Particularly for Offshore Vendors" (Hampton, NH: Technology Business Research Inc., 2012).

31. "Mastering Engineering Service Outsourcing in the Automotive Industry" (Munich: Roland Berger Strategy Consultants, 2010).

32. Manjeet Kripalani, "India: The GE and McKinsey Club," *Business Week Online*, February 23, 2006, http://archive.today/D0fxz.

33. Evalueserve CEO Marc Vollenweider, interview with the author, June 2007.

34. Evalueserve cofounder Alok Aggarwal, interview with the author, June 2007.

35. Ibid.

36. Evalueserve COO Ashish Gupta, interview with the author, February 2007.

37. "The Future of Knowledge Process Outsourcing—Make or Buy in KPO" (Gurgaon, India: Evalueserve, 2007).

38. Ibid.

39. Most of the examples given in the following paragraphs in this section have been drawn from "Global Integration through Knowledge Process Outsourcing," a report prepared by PricewaterhouseCoopers and the Confederation of Indian Industry, 2005.

40. "Global Integration through Knowledge Process Outsourcing" (New Delhi: PricewaterhouseCoopers and CII, 2005).

41. Ravi Datar and Sujoy Chohan, "Business Process Outsourcing in India: A Fact Book" (New Delhi: Gartner Research, 2002).

42. *Strategic Review 2005: The IT Industry in India* (New Delhi: NASSCOM, 2005), 167.

43. Gupta, interview with the author.

44. Shelly Singh, "At Mysore, We Are Running a US Law Firm," *Economic Times*, June 13, 2007.

45. "FDI in the R&D Sector", 2006.

46. "Globalization of Engineering Services," 2006.

47. Based on the author's discussions with officials of HCL Technologies, Noida, June12, 2007.

9 Conclusions

1. Rahul Mukherjee, "India's Aborted Liberalization—1966," *Pacific Affairs* 73, no. 8 (Fall 2000): 375–392.

2. Aradhana Aggarwal, "Export Processing Zones in India: Analysis of the Export Performance," working paper, Indian Council for Research on International Economic Relations, New Delhi, November 2004.

3. Atul Kohli, "Politics of Economic Growth in India: 1980–2005, Part I: 1980s," *Economic and Political Weekly* 41, April 1, 2006, 1251–1259.

4. Harsimran Singh, "IT Cos. Can Earn More Only By Employing More Hands," *Economic Times*, July 31, 2007.

5. Remarks by Ambassador Nirupama Rao at the Asia Society, July 26, 2012, accessed July 30, 2012, http://www.indianembassy.org.

6. "Report of the Working Group on Engineering Education" (New Delhi: National Knowledge Commission, 2008), 4.

7. P. Balaram, "Indian Institutes of Technology," *Current Science* 84, no. 5 (March 10, 2003): 613–614.

8. Sugata Srinivasaraju, "Coaching Factories Are Dumbing Down the IITs," *Outlook* (April 30, 2007), accessed August 11, 2014, http://www.outlookindia.com/article/ Coaching-Factories-Are-Dumbing-Down-The-IITs/234521.

9. "Less than 15% of Technology Engineers Can Apply Their Computer Programming Skills," company press release (Gurgaon, India: Aspiring Minds, November 2013).

10. "The English Gap Measured: English Learning Levels Engineers Graduates Report," company press release (Gurgaon, India: Aspiring Minds, July 2012).

Index

Offshoring (cont.)
Japan and, 164, 175, 179
joint ventures and, 160, 167, 173–174,
179, 183
liberalization and, 157, 160, 168–169,
172–176, 180, 183–184, 199
licensing and, 163–165, 169–170, 173,
176
Madras-Chicago link and, 171
mainframe computers and, 158, 171,
178–180
market issues and, 157–184
New Information Order and, 161
Patni and, 133
private and state-supported enclaves
for, 159–163
quality issues and, 176–178
regulation and, 166, 175, 183
research and development (R&D) and,
167, 191–195, 214, 216
satellite communications and, 157,
161–172, 180–183
software and, 157–184
"Software India" conferences and,
166–168
Software Technology Parks (STPs) and,
4–5, 140, 157, 160–165, 168–172,
179–183, 211
Tata Institute of Fundamental Research (TIFR) and, 161
telecoms and, 162, 165, 171–172, 174–
175, 179–181
United States and, 158–160, 164–167,
171–175, 177, 179–180, 183, 211
Vittal and, 169–172, 183
Y2K issue and, 178–180, 184
Ohio State University, 30
Oklahoma State University, 124
Omron, 112
Online Data Processor (OLDAP), 45
Open General License (OGL), 87,
154
Open Systems Interconnect, 89

Operations Research Group (ORG), 146–
147, 152–153
Oppenheimer, Robert, 18
Oracle, 147, 159, 173, 201, 235n7
Ordnance Discrete Variable Automatic
Computer (ORDVAC), 20
Original equipment manufacturer
(OEM), 123
Overseas Communication Service
(OCS), 163
Overseas Private Investment Corpora-
tion (OPIC), 160, 164

P1024 protocol, 153
Pakistan, 46, 79
Palace Grounds, Bangalore, 1
Palmisano, Samuel J., 1, 75
PanAm, 162
Paper tapes, 26, 33, 116, 132–134
Patel, C. K. N., 174
Patel, Nitin, 142
Patents, 42, 65, 96, 185–186, 195, 199–
200, 203
Patil, Shivraj, 84
Patil, Suhas, 174
Patni, Narendra
data conversion and, 132–136, 141,
153, 210
Murthy and, 136
offshoring and, 133
Patni, Poonam, 133
Patni Computer Systems (PCS), 134–
137, 146, 152–154, 210, 232n3
Paul, K. Roy, 169
Pauli, Wolfgang, 18
Pawar, Rajendra, 151
PC World (magazine), 157
PDP 11 computer, 115
PDP-8 computer, 44
Pentium, 173
Permits, 47, 170
Personal computers (PCs), 80f, 158, 210,
213